Books by Robert Coles

CHILDREN OF CRISIS, I:
A STUDY OF COURAGE AND FEAR

STILL HUNGRY IN AMERICA

THE IMAGE IS YOU

UPROOTED CHILDREN

TEACHERS AND THE CHILDREN OF POVERTY

WAGES OF NEGLECT
(with Maria Piers)

DRUGS AND YOUTH
(with Joseph Brenner and Dermot Meagher)

ERIK H. ERIKSON:
THE GROWTH OF HIS WORK

THE MIDDLE AMERICANS
(with Jon Erikson)

THE GEOGRAPHY OF FAITH
(with Daniel Berrigan)

MIGRANTS, SHARECROPPERS, MOUNTAINEERS
(*VOLUME II OF* CHILDREN OF CRISIS)

THE SOUTH GOES NORTH
(*VOLUME III OF* CHILDREN OF CRISIS)

FAREWELL TO THE SOUTH

TWELVE TO SIXTEEN: EARLY ADOLESCENCE
(with Jerome Kagan)

A SPECTACLE UNTO THE WORLD:
THE CATHOLIC WORKER MOVEMENT
(with Jon Erikson)

THE OLD ONES OF NEW MEXICO
(with Alex Harris)

THE BUSES ROLL
(with Carol Baldwin)

THE DARKNESS AND THE LIGHT
(with Doris Ulmann)

IRONY IN THE MIND'S LIFE:
ESSAYS ON NOVELS BY JAMES AGEE,
ELIZABETH BOWEN, AND GEORGE ELIOT

ANNA FREUD:
THE DREAM OF PSYCHOANALYSIS

RUMORS OF SEPARATE WORLDS
(poems)

THE SPIRITUAL LIFE OF CHILDREN

THE CALL OF STORIES:
TEACHING AND THE MORAL IMAGINATION

THEIR EYES MEETING THE WORLD:
THE DRAWINGS AND PAINTINGS OF CHILDREN
(with Margaret Sartor)

THE CALL OF SERVICE:
A WITNESS TO IDEALISM

For Children

DEAD END SCHOOL

THE GRASS PIPE

SAVING FACE

RIDING FREE

HEADSPARKS

THE MORAL
INTELLIGENCE
OF CHILDREN

THE MORAL
INTELLIGENCE
OF CHILDREN

ROBERT COLES

RANDOM HOUSE NEW YORK

Grateful acknowledgment is made to Howard Axelrod for permission to print his story
"Starry Time." Reprinted by permission of Howard Axelrod.

ISBN 0-679-44811-X

Printed in the United States of America

Book design by Lilly Langotsky

To Ruby Bridges Hall,

Arnold Hiatt, Cheryl Pickrell, Larry Ronan:

living examples

The mind now thinks, now acts, and each fit reproduces the other. When the artist has exhausted his materials, when the fancy no longer paints, when thoughts are no longer apprehended and books are a weariness—he has the resources to *live*. Character is higher than intellect. Thinking is the function. Living is the functionary. The stream retreats to its source. A great soul will be strong to live, as well as strong to think.

RALPH WALDO EMERSON

Let us sing a new song not with our lips but with our lives.

SAINT AUGUSTINE

PREFACE

For over thirty years I have been trying to understand how children of various backgrounds acquire their particular assumptions, beliefs, and values. Much of that work was done in homes and schools, as well as hospital wards and clinics, and has been described in books such as *The Moral Life of Children* (1986) and *The Spiritual Life of Children* (1990). Additionally, in early 1990 I worked with the Girl Scouts of America to implement a survey, done by Louis Harris and Associates, called "The Beliefs and Moral Values of America's Children." After the quantitative research was done (thousands of questionnaires were answered by young people across the nation) I began to meet with children who had answered the questionnaire in order to obtain from them, individually and in group settings, something that multiple-choice answers don't quite provide: access to the complex range of attitude, conviction, feeling, and sentiment that may inform any of the values we uphold—the ambiguities and even inconsistencies or outright contradictions that inform our opinions as we try to think of them, express them. I also began meetings with groups of those children's parents and teachers, men and women who had brought them up, had struggled to do right and well by them, or had been teaching them. I myself am the father of three sons, and I have taught in elementary schools and high schools as a volunteer, as well as at several universities, where I have worked with undergraduates and with medical students.

In the writing just mentioned I tried to describe how various children *think* about moral issues, ethical and religious and spiritual questions. Here I am addressing another matter: how we as adults, as mothers and fathers and schoolteachers and friends, give shape to the values of children as expressed in their behavior, their conduct; how we encourage and instruct them to uphold in daily life one or another set of beliefs. We have heard much in recent years about literacy, about I.Q., about mental health. Books such as *Cultural Literacy* and *The Bell Curve* have reminded us that the mind's cognitive activity continues to be very much a subject of interest and argument, even as Howard Gardner has tried to help us broaden the discussion by emphasizing the different aspects of that life, in *Multiple Intelligences: The Theory in Practice*. Moreover, for decades psychologists and psychiatrists have emphasized that cognition doesn't take place in a vacuum, that the mind is where we harbor anxieties, affections, fears, and worries as well as facts and figures; and so a book such as Daniel Goleman's *Emotional Intelligence* has correctly struck a chord in many of us. Here, I hope to amplify further this continuing consideration of the cognitive, the psychological or emotional, by taking up the moral side of our children's life—a third realm, as it were, of the mind's activity: character as it develops from the very start of life right through adolescence.

The idea for this book began as a consequence of an article I wrote for *The Chronicle of Higher Education* (September 18, 1995), titled "The Disparity Between Character and Intellect." I was flooded with responses to that essay (which is worked into the third part of this book). Soon enough, prodded by some of those letters, I was trying to address at greater length the issues raised in the essay, and to do so with the parents and teachers in mind whom I have met in the course of the research I've done these past years. I thank those men and women for all I've learned from them, and from the children they've brought up and taught. I thank, too, Kate Medina, whose editorial assistance and guidance have been crucial to this attempt to speak directly to my fellow parents and teachers, and Amanda Urban for her constant encouragement. I thank, as well, Ed Gerwig for his knowing help with this manuscript. I also thank, not least, the four individuals to whom I dedicate this book: Ruby Bridges Hall, for everything she taught all Americans when she pioneered school desegregation in Louisiana in the early 1960s, and for all she has continued to teach us as a mother and as her very own kind of teacher now working in the New Orleans schools; Arnold Hiatt, an extraordinarily sensitive and thoughtful Massachusetts businessman; Cheryl Pickrell, an Arizona teacher of great moral energy; Larry Ronan, a Boston physician "out there" with the hurt, the vulnerable, the needy. Bless these four and the many like them across the nation for all they do to make this life a better one for their fellow citizens of the United States and for all their fellow human beings.

CONTENTS

Preface   xiii

I Moral Intelligence   1

  1. THE MORAL IMAGINATION: WITNESSES   3

  2. THE GOOD PERSON   13

  3. A NOT-SO-GOOD PERSON: MORAL UNDERTOW   21

  4. MORAL CROSSROADS—BAD BEHAVIOR, BAD "WITNESSES"   31

II The Moral Archaeology of Childhood   61

  1. THE EARLY YEARS   63

  2. THE ELEMENTARY SCHOOL YEARS: THE AGE OF CONSCIENCE   98

  3. ADOLESCENCE   135

III Letter to Parents and Teachers   167

Appendix   197

Index   201

I

MORAL
INTELLIGENCE

I

THE MORAL IMAGINATION:

WITNESSES

This book is about moral intelligence, about how it is enabled through the moral imagination, our gradually developed capacity to reflect upon what is right and wrong with all the emotional and intellectual resources of the human mind. This book is about what it means to be a "good person," as opposed to a "not-so-good person" or a "bad person." This book is meant to offer some thoughts on how "character" develops in children, how their moral imagination grows at different moments of their lives; it is meant for those who are bringing up children, teaching them. In *The Moral Life of Children*, I examined moral *thinking*, as it gets shaped by influences outside the home: by class and race, by social events, by cultural forces—school desegregation, the presence of nuclear bombs in our midst, the particular neighborhood where a boy or girl lives, the assumptions it fosters. In this book, by contrast, I take up the issue of moral *conduct*, of the child's lived life, as it develops in response to the way he or she is treated at home and in school. The book aims to show how moral *behavior* develops, a response to moral *experiences* as they take place, day after day, in a family, a classroom.

I first heard the term "moral intelligence" many years ago, from Rustin McIntosh, a distinguished pediatrician who was teaching a group of us how to work with young patients who were quite ill. When we asked him to explain what he had in mind by that phrase, "moral intelligence," he did not respond with an elegantly precise definition. Rather, he told us about boys and girls he'd known and treated who had it—who were "good," who were kind, who thought about others, who extended themselves toward those others, who were "smart" that way. Some children even at six or seven had an evident desire to be tactful, courteous, generous in their willingness to see the world as others saw it, to experience the world through someone else's eyes, and to act on that knowledge with kindness. He told us stories of clinical moments he found unforgettable: a girl dying of leukemia who worried about the "burden" she'd put upon her terribly saddened mother; a boy who lost the effective use of his right arm due to an automobile injury, and who felt sorry less for himself than for his dad, who loved baseball, loved coaching his son and others in a neighborhood Little League team.

But I remember wanting more than a doctor's tales. I wanted Dr. McIntosh to be precise, to give me a formulation, a categorical description that I could summon conveniently as I went about my life, went about the business of learning to be a pediatrician, a child psychiatrist, a parent, a schoolteacher—four ways I eventually ended up being involved with young people. Eventually I got from this beloved medical school professor only this folksy summation: "You know 'moral intelligence' when you see it, when you hear it at work—a child who is smart *that* way, smart not with facts and figures, but with the way he's behaving, the way he talks about others, takes them into consideration."

He could see that I still hungered for more. He looked at his bookshelf—all the volumes there, telling of the illnesses that afflict children, and telling, too, of their cognitive and their emotional development. Then, he looked back at me, an anxiously precise young doctor sitting opposite him: "All the time we comment about 'smart' children or 'emotionally troubled' children, but we're not so quick to speak of good-hearted children, or the ones who upset us because we think they're *not* very good at all—they may, in fact, have traveled, already, a long way toward badness."

I could tell I wasn't going to get what I then nervously wanted, a satisfying generalization that would enable me to be "smart" about a particular aspect of human behavior, goodness in children. Instead, a physician was teaching me by his own example—the way we teach children ourselves: we make them witnesses to our own behavior. Moreover, he did something else we can do, too: he resorted to stories, memories of moments observed in particular young lives. Stories from real life as well as stories from the movies, from literature, can stir and provoke the moral imagination. Didactic or theoretical arguments don't work well; narratives, images, observed behavior all do.

"Moral intelligence" isn't acquired only by memorization of rules and regulations, by dint of abstract classroom discussion or kitchen compliance. We grow morally as a consequence of learning how to be with others, how to behave in this world, a learning prompted by taking to heart what we have seen and heard. The child is a witness; the child is an ever-attentive witness of grown-up morality—or lack thereof; the child looks and looks for cues as to how one ought to behave, and finds them galore as we parents and teachers go about our lives, making choices, addressing people, showing in action our rock-bottom assumptions, desires, and values, and thereby telling those young observers much more than we may realize.

When I think of what I mean for this book to offer you, I remember myself as a young doctor, and as a witness to that elder doctor; I remember *his* "moral intelligence"—his respect for other people as well as himself, the deep awareness he acknowledged of our human connectedness. I was a witness to how he approached his patients, hurt and ailing children, but also their parents, and us interns, residents, nurses, and as well, the orderlies and nurse's aides and volunteers and janitors, all of whom make a hospital run smoothly and all of whom he took pains to acknowledge with consideration, respect. In fact, I remember that doctor, a father to a generation of pediatricians who trained under him, going out of his way to thank an orderly for taking such good care of a child's toys, a child's room; complimenting a nurse on the way she spoke with a four-year-old girl who was dying; taking time to sit on the floor with a boy in order to look at a train set and help fix one of the tracks that had come loose. Here was a big-shot doctor who was also a psychologically solid and even-tempered doctor, and who was something else, too—a man of high character, of great humanity. He was respectful of others, no matter their station in life; he was "a good person"—courteous, compassionate, caring, warm-hearted, unpretentious, gracefully willing to stop himself in his tracks, his big and important tracks, in order to link arms with various others, to acknowledge them as his companions in a shared, daily effort to make a pediatric ward run well, so that some exceedingly vulnerable children might get a bit more out of life than otherwise would have been possible.

He didn't give lectures and sermons as to how we interns and residents ought to behave with one another, with the hospital staff, with the children we were treating. Nor were we handed articles to read, guides to good behavior on those hospital wards, "self-help" books meant to boost our "moral intelligence" (our M.I. as opposed to our I.Q.!). "Not the letter, but the spirit," this kindly old doc seemed to be saying to us. In fact, he *said* very little to us; he lived out his moral principles, and soon enough, we were witnesses to his behavior, to his ways of being with others, which we were challenged to absorb, as all young people are inclined to do, when they have learned to admire and trust someone older: try to follow suit.

On the other hand, he *had* mentioned directly the idea of moral intelligence, the specific notion, surprising and perplexing to us at first, that we ought to keep in mind a person's moral actions as well as his or her intellectual caliber, emotional balance, or state. At first we got carried away with the idea, tried to make a list, with subdivisions: cognitive intelligence, psychiatric well-being, moral life or character. But he laughed when he entered our staff meeting room and saw these lists on a blackboard. To paraphrase from memory: "You folks—I just wanted to suggest that you stop and think about these kids we're treating in such a way that you don't always tell me how smart they are (or how they're not too smart) or how calm they are (or how emotionally disturbed, troubled). Give me an idea about—well, to use an old-fashioned word, their *conduct*: Are they generous or are they selfish? Have they got an eye out for others, *their* situation, or are they all wrapped up inside their own world? Even among our sickest children, we get the whole range—kids who give thought to those around them, and kids who don't have the time of day for others, including people in their own families."

In that spirit I try here to offer what a book makes possible: stories and thoughts meant to inspire the shaping of the moral imagination; lots of words, but with the repeated reminder, learned from that doctor and others (my own parents, my wife, certain others who have in my life stood *in loco parentis*) that these words are not to be memorized for a test, graded by yet another teacher, but are meant to help trigger a lifetime of honorable human activity. Put differently, this book is meant to provide nourishment to the reader's moral imagination, that "place" in our heads, our thinking and daydreaming, our wandering and worrying lives, where we ponder the meaning of our lives and, too, the world's ethical challenges; and where we try to decide what we ought or ought not to do, and why, and how we ought to get on with people, and for what overall moral, religious, spiritual, practical reasons.

A reflecting and self-reflecting mind at some point gives way to a "performing self": the moral imagination affirmed, realized, developed, trained to grow stronger by daily decisions, small and large, deeds enacted, then considered and reconsidered. Character is ultimately who we are expressed in action, in how we live, in what we do, and so the children around us know: they absorb and take stock of what they observe, namely, us—we adults living and doing things in a certain spirit, getting on with one another in our various ways. Our children add up, imitate, file away what they've observed and so very often later fall in line with the particular moral counsel we wittingly or quite unself-consciously have offered them.

Of course, some children don't explicitly tell us what they have witnessed, the sense they've made of us, of our moral ways of being. It can be hard for our sons and daughters, who want to love us (who do indeed look to us, love us), to stand up to us, their parents and teachers, and point things out that trouble them. I once realized this all too memorably when I was driving my nine-year-old son to the hospital. He had injured himself in an accident; he had disobeyed his mother and me by "playing" with some carpentry tools we had set aside in our garage. I was upset because he'd sustained a deep cut that obviously would require surgical attention and because he'd ignored our "rule," our household instructions. I raced with him to the hospital on a rainy morning, careless that my car was splashing pedestrians crossing the street; at one point I ignored a yellow light, then immediately a red light—at which point my son intervened. Amid this headlong rush to an emergency ward, he said, "Dad, if we're not careful, we'll make more trouble on our way to getting out of trouble."

I could feel that he was biting his lip, that he wanted to say more. I had earlier used the word "trouble," had said that "we're in trouble" as I rushed us both toward that car. Now, a boy was pointing out, tactfully, respectfully, and, yes, a bit fearfully, a major irony: that this effort to get us out of "trouble" could lead to more trouble, and he was also giving me a reproving as well as an anxious look: be careful, lest you hurt people on your all-too-hurried journey, one in danger of becoming disastrous and wrongheaded. A son's character on display, so to speak: his worry on behalf of others put to word, no matter his own vulnerability. He was able to think of imagined others who might be hit, hurt by a car defying traffic lights and speeding along with its own, quite narrow moral momentum: what matters for us is all-important, and to the devil with those others. I realized the ethical implications of my son's admonitory if not admonishing remark: there's something important at stake here—the lives of others. A boy had reached outside himself, thought of those others, no matter his own ordeal, with its justification of a heightened self-regard.

The Mutuality of Moral Guidance

That is what our children can offer us, and what we can offer them: a chance to learn from them, even as we try to teach them. Too often this matter of "character," of "values clarification," of "moral development," gets presented as a one-way street: a boy or girl finally getting the point. Yet within a family or in a classroom, children and their parents and teachers are having conversations, responding to one another, learning from one another. On that speedy trip to the hospital my son was helping shape my character—prompting me to slow down not only literally but symbolically, asking me to stop and think about right and wrong, good and bad. When we got to the hospital I was tempted to pull rank a bit, as a physician whose friends, fellow physicians, were there and surely ready to attend to us pronto, with no extended wait. Yet this was an emergency room, and others were there waiting, others who had their share of pain and anxiety and fear to bear. I remember thinking that my son had become my moral instructor that day, and that I would not dare claim some special status. Moreover, he surely was strengthened morally by having me to watch, to challenge, to teach.

This book, then, is about the way character develops in the young; about the way they obtain their values; about what makes a good person; and about how we might help shape a child's moral intelligence. This book contains stories that tell of the ways our children struggle to find moral direction. This book is about questions as well as answers; about moral problems and possible solutions to them; about developing workable answers to those questions of right and wrong that come up continually over a lifetime. This book is about the moral conversations we can and might and do have with our children as well as with ourselves and with one another as adults. To bring up children with some moral success we have to bring up matters of conscience, of ethical concern, again and again. In this book we look at how people keep trying to figure out what they're doing and how it affects those around them. For all I know, my son's warning to me, delivered in an offhand yet pointed manner, might have spared us an accident, even saved a life or two. To this day I thank God that the boy spoke up and that somehow, amid my self-preoccupied, self-important time of it, I was able to take in the import of what he was trying to convey: a situation in which his character was being tested, and mine put to its own trial as well.

That is how we become the people we are, morally—through experiences and our response to them and to one another as we go through them. Soon enough our children begin to be considered (by us and others) as reasonably "good" or as "not so good," as "headed for trouble," or as one child psychiatrist I knew during my hospital residency years put it, as "going on bad."

What Makes a Good Person

"There are the good of heart," a teacher observed, and she continued, "there are also the ones with hearts of stone." A group of classroom teachers and I were chilled by the latter thought, of the child who develops into a not very good person. And of course we wondered together what might be done in the classroom (or at home) to make for more good-hearted souls and fewer stony-hearted ones. I had no magic wand to wave, nor did any of them. They asked me what I do (or would do) in the face of some of the dilemmas or troubled moments they described to me—that is, how to make the Golden Rule, the matter of empathy, so crucial to any discussion of morality and of being a "good person," come alive for students in such a way that their lives (their behavior), and not only their minds (their thoughts), are affected. As I sat there wondering what to say, I thought of a brief but powerful story by Leo Tolstoy, one that can be read together or taught to anyone at almost any level, from elementary school through high school and college to the various postgraduate schools. The story is called "The Old Grandfather and the Grandson":

> The grandfather had become very old. His legs wouldn't go, his eyes didn't see, his ears didn't hear, he had no teeth. And when he ate, the food dripped from his mouth.
>
> The son and daughter-in-law stopped setting a place for him at the table and gave him supper in back of the stove. Once they brought din-

ner down to him in a cup. The old man wanted to move the cup and dropped and broke it. The daughter-in-law began to grumble at the old man for spoiling everything in the house and breaking the cups and said that she would now give him dinner in a dishpan. The old man only sighed and said nothing.

Once the husband and wife were staying at home and watching their small son playing on the floor with some wooden planks: he was building something. The father asked: "What is that you are doing, Misha?" And Misha said: "Dear Father, I am making a dishpan. So that when you and dear Mother become old, you may be fed from this dishpan."

The husband and wife looked at one another and began to weep. They became ashamed of so offending the old man, and from then on seated him at the table and waited on him.

When I had finished reading, we all sat there, silent, under Tolstoy's spell. Finally a teacher turned to me and said, "Powerful." But another teacher wondered whether soon enough even the magical words of the story wouldn't lose their hold on at least some young people, who for various reasons have become all too cynical, callous, self-absorbed: the "stony-hearted." I had more to tell, though—how I've used that Tolstoy story with various kinds of students. I've read it aloud. I've asked for interpretations of it, comments about it, thoughts about what it has to say to us. I've told the class how I got to know the story, from my mother's love of Tolstoy; I told of her reading his various stories and novels over and over again, of her habit of reading them aloud to my father. I've told the class of certain events in my life, times when I've failed to respond to that story, failed to respond to this or that person, so preoccupied was I with my own responsibilities and interests. The point of such personal stories, I say, is not self-accusation, nor am I ironically intent on getting myself off a hook by publicly putting myself on it, in the hope that the students will soothe my soul. The point is to summon one's frail side so as to enable a more forthright sharing of experiences on the part of all of us: that guy has stumbled, and he's not making too much of it, but he *is* putting it on the table, and thereby I'm enabled to put some of myself, my remembrances, my story, on the table, whether explicitly, by speaking up or, in the way many of us do, by also remembering—another's memories trigger our own. In time, after we've talked, I've asked the students to write an essay about the Tolstoy story, about its meaning to them, about what they imagine themselves doing with the story if they were parents or teachers. Soon enough, of course, I am reading introspective memoirs or suggestions for this or that course of action—all of us become witnesses, with Tolstoy's help, to the moral imagination at work.

2

THE GOOD PERSON

For many years I have been asking children to tell me their ideas about what makes for a good person. Rather obviously, those children have varied in their responsive definitions, some emphasizing a person's interest in reaching out to and assisting others, some putting stress on a person's religious beliefs, some pointing out the importance of certain secular values such as independence of mind, civic responsibility, commitment to work, to a solid family life.

In an elementary school class I taught, twenty-eight children sat before me, their desks lined up row upon row; I remember how they reacted when we had a discussion of "goodness." We exchanged moral scenarios. At one point I told the children a story; it had been written by a college student of mine, Howie Axelrod, a young man of great intelligence and heart, both. The story, a moral fable, if you will, was called "Starry Time," and it went like this:

Once upon a time, there were no stars in the sky.

Only the lonely moon shone at night. And since it was sad and alone, it gave off very little light.

One person had all the stars. He was not a powerful king. And she was not an evil witch. But a little girl named Stella. When Stella's mother turned off her lights at night, Stella's ceiling turned into sparkles brighter than any Christmas tree.

Sometimes she felt as though she was looking down from an airplane over a city of lights.

Stella loved falling asleep under her starry ceiling. She always had bright and wonderful dreams. One day in school, she overheard some boys and girls talking. One boy said, "I can't sleep at night. My room is very dark and I get scared."

A girl agreed, "Me too. That sad old moon doesn't do any good. My room is as dark as a closet."

Stella felt bad. She hadn't known that she was the only one with stars in her room.

That night, when her mother turned off the lights, her ceiling lit up like the lights of a city. But Stella could not sleep. She thought about all of the boys and girls who were lying awake in the dark, and she felt sad.

She climbed out of bed, and opened her window. The moon hung sadly in the sky.

"Moon, why don't you give off more light?" Stella asked.

"Because I am lonely. I have to spend the whole night out here by myself. Sometimes I get scared."

"I'm sorry," Stella said. She was surprised that something as big and beautiful as the moon could get scared just like little boys and girls.

"Plus, I get tired," said the moon. "It's a big job to light the whole sky."

Stella thought for a while.

"Moon," she said, "Would my stars help to keep you company?"

"Yes," said the moon.

"And would they make the sky brighter?"

"Yes, and they would make me happy."

Stella stood back from her window. She looked up at her stars.

"You should go and help the moon," she said. "I will miss you, but every night I will look out my window and see you in the sky." She wiped a tear from her eye. "Now, go."

With that, the stars burst from her ceiling and whirled around with a dazzling glow until they gained enough speed to shoot towards the moon. They streamed out of her window, and fanned out across the sky. It was the most beautiful sight Stella had ever seen.

From then on, the nights were brighter. The moon had many friends, and he beamed with happiness.

And with the light of the new night sky, grandmothers and grandfathers sat outside on their porches telling stories about the old days. And young couples strolled hand in hand along the streets.

And best of all, Stella could sit outside with a friend, and they could watch the stars together.

The children were enchanted. They wanted to hear the story again. They wanted me to make copies of the story, so that they could take it home, read it to their parents, or ask their parents to read it aloud to them. They were anxious to discuss the story, glean from it a message, a line of thinking. Most of all, they were touched by Stella's gesture, and by her capacity, her willingness, to think of others, and more than that, to give of her world so that the world of others would be brighter. Stella's generosity prompted them to marvel at their own humanity. A girl said, "She was being—she was being good. It was natural—it's what you'd want to do, if you could." Another girl took immediate issue, wondered whether "natural" is quite the word to use, since, she observed, "Lots of people wouldn't want to share those stars with anyone else, probably." In no time, these ten-year-olds were having a spirited discussion of the extent and limits of generosity, an aspect of the subject of "goodness" that we had been exploring with some considerable and (for all of us, I thought) quite instructive determination.

Moreover, I soon learned, "Starry Time," starring Stella, had a stirring life in home after home for several weeks. Parents read it, read it to their children, and talked of it, so that when we addressed it once more (I asked several children to divide it up and read aloud to us their chosen segments), their exchanges were even more lively, knowing, at times passionate. These children began to think of what *they* had in their closets (in their lives, really), that they might want to share with others—and, also very important, of what the consequences would be of so doing.

Words into Action

That last word, "consequences," needless to say, was quite important: it is one thing to make a list of qualities that in their sum make for a good person or child; it is something else to try to picture oneself enacting this or that virtue, to live it out in daily life—to turn nouns such as generosity, kindness, thoughtfulness, sensitivity, compassion into verbs, words of action.

When that class was over, I thought I'd finally stumbled into some old-fashioned "advice" that I could offer to the parents of children I teach or work with as a doctor—and all of us parents have our moments of hungry eagerness for such advice. Take those nouns that denote good moral traits, and with the help of your sons and daughters try to convert them into verbs: tasks to accomplish, plans for action, to be followed by the actual work of doing. An imagined plan or plot is a mere prelude to a life's day-to-day behavior, yet over the long run of things, the sum of imagined plans turned into action becomes one's "character." With imagined scenarios we are quite possibly setting the stage for later actions, whereas lists of good qualities, of values and virtues, can be rather quickly forgotten, as quickly as they are memorized.

At one point in the discussion of "Starry Time," a boy wondered whether the story might help us figure out how to describe a "good child"—as I've mentioned, I'd been pressing those children and others for some time to help me come up with some useful specifications. "If you read the story," the boy declared, "and you go give something to someone, and it's a good thing you've done—you've given the world a star, and that means you're better than you were before. But you could fall back and forget about the next guy, so you have to keep sharing with others, or you'll be good for one day, and then the next, you're not doing what's good, and that's a missed chance, my mom said." As I listened I thought of the myth of Sisyphus in Greek mythology—with its image of a man condemned to rolling a heavy rock up a hill, only to have it fall down each time, just as he nears the top, and its reminder of the constant struggle to lift up ourselves, as it were, with backsliding an ever-present possibility. And I thought of Emerson's notion of each day as a god, his way of emphasizing the enormous moral possibilities a given span of time can offer. All of that worked into a child's worried, yet vigorously demanding ethical speculation.

A Good Person

Good children are boys and girls who in the first place have learned to take seriously the very notion, the desirability, of goodness—a living up to the Golden Rule, a respect for others, a commitment of mind, heart, soul to one's family, neighborhood, nation—and have also learned that the issue of goodness is not an abstract one, but rather a concrete, expressive one: how to turn the rhetoric of goodness into action, moments that affirm the presence of goodness in a particular lived life.

Another child's testimony—he was thirteen, in middle school, when he told me this: "My dad says a lot of people talk and talk a good line—but their scorecard isn't so good, because talk is cheap. If you just try to remember to be polite, and help someone, if you can; if you try to be friendly to folks, and not be a wise guy, always knocking them down in what you think of them, and what you say, then you're off to a start, because it's on your mind (you see?), it's on your mind that you should be out there doing something about it, what you believe is right, is good, and not just talking it up, the subject [of goodness], and to tell you what I believe: if you do a lot of that [talking it up], you're really talking yourself up, I mean, if you don't match your words with what you end up doing." A silence, a few seconds long, and then a brief, pointed—stunning, even—afterthought: "You know, a guy who's out there, being a good guy, that guy (even him!) could ruin everything; he could keep on calling attention to himself, and all he's doing, all the good, and he comes off as a big ego, someone looking for everyone's applause."

An accomplished righteousness that has turned self-righteous, self-serving is a risk, surely, for many of us, who can be tempted to wag our fingers at others, and not so subtly point at ourselves with a good deal of self-satisfaction. In further remarks, that boy worried out loud and at some length about becoming a "goody-goody" person, his cautionary spin on the subject of "goodness," as we were pursuing it. I still remember that moment, that expressed concern, that time of moral alarm: wait a minute, buddy, give this subject another round of consideration, lest you become smug, priggish, all too full of yourself, drunk on your self-congratulatory goodness, even your enacted goodness, all of which can, Sisyphus-like, come tumbling down morally. Yet another of life's ironies that can await any of us around any corner, even an apparently promising one.

A Film as a Moral Moment: *A Bronx Tale*

That youth's brother, older by three years, had taken him to the movie *A Bronx Tale*, directed by Robert De Niro, who also acts in it. I will always remember what that movie got going in the two brothers, even as I have seen that other young people who had watched it were moved to considerable thought. The film takes the viewer to the streets of a working-class Italian neighborhood in the Bronx, where a bus driver, Lorenzo Anello, lives with his wife and his son, Calogero, known as C. The father is a hardworking, honorable, humble man who has no intention of succumbing to the authority of a local mobster, whose iron hand strikes fear into just about everyone. The boy, C, witnesses a murder committed by the mobster, but won't tell the police anything, and so earns the murderer's gratitude. A complex friendship now develops, so that C soon enough has two fathers: his honest, ethically demanding biological one, and the man whose work, whose business, is obviously outside the law. The mobster can be kind, generous, even wise, hence the moral power of the film: we link arms in our hearts, our guts, with this youth, who is torn by various attachments, loyalties, desires, and yearnings, and who lives in a world where good and evil can't be utterly, neatly, conveniently distinguished, in individuals and in social situations. Race enters the narrative, too—the youth is attracted to a black schoolmate—even as it is so much a presence in the lives of those who live in similar working-class communities of the Bronx, Brooklyn, Queens, and across the nation.

"We got lost in that movie," the older of the two brothers told me, and then gave a personal statement as to why: "You can feel the pull— you can agree with the father, that once you give in and get connected to those people, the Mafia, you're through. I mean, you may make more money than you'd ever make otherwise, but you've given up something that's more important: you're not free. You're a prisoner— they own you. The bus driver, he owns himself. That's the difference. You let people buy you off, and you lose all respect for yourself. You stand up for what you believe—that way, you can look yourself in the mirror, and you don't need to run and hide.

"That Mafia guy, though—the picture was great, because you begin to realize how lonely he is. He didn't have a family. C became his son. You go back and forth, you agree with his father, but you think this Mafia guy, he's got a lot of good things to say to the kid. It's not black and white, all good and all bad—and the same with the black and white people, there's plenty of fear to go around, and hate. I was going back and forth, back and forth, all during the movie. When it was over, I kept thinking of the father and what he said, and the gang-guy, the Mafia guy, and how he had a good side to him—but he was no good."

The boy went on to say, "I thought there was a whole lot in that movie to ask yourself. What do you believe? Could someone 'buy' you? Why do people get mean and nasty, and the result is they're in trouble—they don't have anyone they can trust? Why can't people 'live and let live,' like our priest says we should, and not be looking for fights, the black people and us, like in the flick? You see what can happen—you leave a show like that, a movie, and your head is all turned on!"

I *could* see, that he had been prompted by a film to become a moral witness of sorts, quite stirred to contemplate this life's rights and wrongs, not always so distinctly, conveniently, categorically differentiated, the one from the other. While watching the movie he had begun to look inward and, thereafter, to pay close attention to the world around him. The film and the contemplation it prompted became for him a moral moment in his life. In his own philosophical words, "You get to wondering, about how you're going to live, how you should [live]." I suppose it can be argued that a boy of sixteen who can use a film such as *A Bronx Tale* that way—become wholeheartedly engaged with its moral energy, so that it becomes his own—is already well on his way to becoming a good person. Still, as that same boy was savvy enough (and, yes, modest enough) to remind me, "You can lose your balance sometimes, and you say something or do something, and you know you're making a mistake, and you feel bad—so, you have to keep reminding yourself, keep telling yourself what's the right thing to do, and what's wrong, or you'll make more and more of those mistakes, and pretty soon, you're in deep, deep water, you're over your head."

This boy had let me know that he, a moral witness to his own growing struggle to learn how to live a reasonably good life, had figured out how continually we are challenged morally. We don't conquer this world's mischief and wrongdoing and malice once and for all, and then forever after enjoy the moral harvest of that victory. Rather, we struggle along, even stumble along, from day to day, in need of taking stock yet again, with the help of a story, a movie, not to mention the experiences that, inevitably and not so rarely, come into our daily lives. The good person is the alert witness not only of others, but to his or her own ethical tensions as they flash their various signals, warn of conflicts ahead or of ambiguities not so easy to resolve, or of mixed feelings and temptations and the rationalizations that justify them. This is the stuff of *A Bronx Tale*, the stuff of your life and mine.

3

A NOT-SO-GOOD PERSON: MORAL UNDERTOW

T he task for each of us, I suspect, is to try to learn not only what we want for our children morally, but also what we *don't* want. No question, some of our young are most certainly caught in a moral undertow, headed nowhere, fast. George Eliot would surely agree, were she by some miracle to be among us now and thus to confront certain quite harmful children, children who are already not so good, going on bad, children who are impulsive, demanding, insensitive, wrapped up in themselves to the point that others mean very little. Yet, for many of our children, for many of us, their elders, the issue is one of tension: we know enough where we want to go, but we recognize in ourselves and in others the obstacle, "the unreflecting egoism" (George Eliot's phrase, used in *Middlemarch*), that surely fuels much of what a lot of us would call the behavior of a "not-so-good person."

Best, then, as we approach the subject of values—what we want to offer our children—for us to think of what we *don't* want them to be like, as well as what we do want them to embrace. What values do we want to contest, do we even abhor, as we deliberate on raising morally literate children?

Generally speaking, what characterizes a not-so-good person is a heightened, destructive self-absorption, in all its melancholy variations. Even as we all have known the tension between natural self-regard and the occasional lapse into an isolating self-preoccupation wherein we lose sight of our obligation to others (indeed, lose sight of those others), some of us unfortunately fall utterly victim to a moral undertow, lose our bearings, get entirely swept into a life that responds to the mind's wishes and moods, with scant attention to the rights of others, not to mention one's own ethical obligations within a family, a classroom, or a community.

Misery Likes Company

A fourth-grade teacher says, "I tell my children [on the first day of class] that we've got our *lessons* to learn, and our *behaving* to learn." This bright, alert, middle-aged woman makes a frank distinction: "I prepare each day's lesson very carefully, even though I've been teaching here for fifteen years. If the kids give me trouble—that's when I'm sometimes unprepared! The other day a boy started talking with another boy. That's happened a million times, but each time is different for me. This boy was pushing his gift of gab on the kid sitting across the aisle, and the other kid clearly did not want to reciprocate. He knew it was wrong, and I saw him nervously looking my way. I felt a surge of anger rise in me! Then I wondered what that [first] boy wanted, and I saw that he was looking at the other boy's paper on his desk—they were all writing an 'in-class' composition for me. I knew he wasn't actually cheating, but in a way, he *was*: he was distracting his neighbor, probably because he himself was having a hard time writing. What to do? What should I have done? What was the best thing to do?"

This fourth-grade teacher is one of seven teachers with whom I'm sitting in a school conference room. We are discussing the kinds of questions this book is meant to address: How does one do a good job of helping children become good—and how does one stop them from becoming bad? As this teacher said, "That boy was actually very smart.

He's too smart for his own good. He loves distracting other people, getting them to slow down, getting them in trouble—then he can slip away, and come up roses. He can write wonderful papers. He's the brightest boy in the class, and there he is, not a very nice person. I appreciate his mind—and I can't stand his heart or his soul! My husband says they're a dime a dozen like that in the fancy universities [where *he* teaches], so that's how it all begins, and if only we could nip it in the bud [this early tendency of some students to be insensitive, manipulative, all too self-regarding, self-serving], but I don't know how you do it—[how you] intervene in a class as a moral agent, I guess you could call me, in a way that really makes a difference. I mean, I can shout, I can punish, I can say this is wrong or bad—but my words sure go in one ear and out the other, I sometimes think."

She stops, then continues. "I know what I should have done. A day later, while I was driving home, I thought of it. I was listening to something by Vivaldi on the radio, and the music was moving along faster and faster, and as I listened—I love Vivaldi—I saw that class of mine, and I saw that smart boy, that smart-aleck boy bothering his neighbor, being an idle troublemaker, and then I heard myself: 'Well, young man, misery certainly does like company!' I think he's bright enough—he would have gotten my point. I think he would have been stopped in his tracks, made to think. But I could have gone further. I could have told the class that we had to put aside everything, because nothing mattered more than how we behave, how we act toward one another. I could have explained what I meant by that cryptic remark, 'Misery likes company'—how we like, sometimes, to draw others into our trouble: if I'm bored, I'll get the person across the aisle to be bored. If I feel lousy, I'll make someone else feel lousy! I could have challenged the whole class: How do we do *better*, how do we avoid the trap? I could have put it to them: What should a teacher do when she sees one of her students trying to get someone else into trouble, or trying to cheat, or whispering, and in that way bothering others? Let's talk about it! Let's write a composition about it! Let's read some of those compositions aloud! Let's—let me, or better, let that boy who got us into all this, let him write on the blackboard: 'Misery likes company.' A psychological lesson! A moral lesson! A warning to us all! You see, I'm really cooking with gas—now, too late! Too bad it's too late—too bad that happens so often: we let go of our best teaching moments, we lose them. The big question is *why*? How could we learn to prepare for those moments, to be on guard, so that when certain children 'strike,' we're ready to 'strike back'—that's what was running across my mind as Vivaldi ran through my mind!"

From Awareness to Action

We had all been moved by her; she got us going with further sugges-tions, meant to highlight a particular moment, turn it into a very hard-to-forget (maybe unforgettable) moment, a moral experience for the entire class that had a substantial life and import. Nor need the class have been diverted from its intellectual activity, its valuable and sched-uled task: the writing of an impromptu composition. Those children would have written their essays, all right—and, maybe, remembered long and hard the messages they contained, or so we dared hope. To be sure, "There are no guarantees," as another teacher, putting a break on our collective enthusiasm, reminded us. Still, we had come up with our "curriculum plan"—one way of turning a morally connected episode into an experience for everybody in that class: write an essay about it.

The teacher told us that she had this final afterthought: "Maybe I should have shared something of myself with the class, told them of a time, an event, in my life—an incident that resembled this one we'd been discussing. It can really 'get to the kids,' I've noticed, when you stop being 'holier than thou' and join in with them. Oh, you've got to be *very* careful. You have, and you need to have, your moral authority. They don't need you, and they don't want you (even if for a minute they think they do) to 'sink,' to be a constantly confessing wrongdoer! They should look up to you. But there comes a time, every once in a while, when you can let them know that what they're struggling with— well, it's their humanity. When you remember your own mistakes, and let them know that you have thought about them, and you understand what you did and why it was wrong, and you regret it, you're sorry, and you've tried not to let something like that happen again: that's what you want them to do, so you're teaching them by using yourself as a 'case study,' and you're really putting yourself on the line!"

In a little over a half hour we had covered much territory, had begun to consider the question of questions: how to move from knowledge or awareness to action, how to connect one's moral concerns, and objectives to one's obligation as a parent and teacher, how to impart values to the young in such a way that those values mean something to them, mean enough so that they help shape children's daily lives. We continued this discussion for another hour and a half, each of us, interestingly, talking about our personal experiences. I held back in that regard, because the others wanted so very much to connect moments in their classroom life to what we had all heard from the first teacher to speak that evening. Toward the end, though, we took up the matter of empathy, and the lack of it: the way some children really try to figure out how others are feeling and respond to them, whereas other children do not.

Again and again, the Golden Rule, the biblical ideal, came up: empathy as practiced in each day's encounters with those "others" whose role is to help us define our own moral life, our values as they are put to the test of another's needs and vulnerabilities. So, what about a child who seems to have little or no understanding of that Rule, a child who has, by deed, adopted another kind of rule, a penny-ante rule whose essence is "Think of yourself all the time, and let others worry about themselves."

The Bully, the Con Artist

There are times when both parents and teachers have good reason to be concerned about a particular child's behavior—for example, when a child shows signs of having a flabby conscience, even a willful meanness of heart, to the point that other children, never mind adults, begin to take notice and to marshal descriptive words such as "meanie," "toughie." Here is how one eight-year-old boy describes another: "He sits across the aisle from me, and he doesn't give me any trouble, because I'm able to defend myself, and he knows it, but he's a bully, that's what he is, a real meanie. He tries to get his way by picking on kids who he's decided are weaker than him. They help him with his home-work—they give him answers. They give him candy from their lunches. They take orders from him. He cheats—I see him. I think the teacher knows, but the kid's father is a lawyer, and my dad says the teacher is probably afraid—she's got to be careful, or he'll sue her."

Another boy bragged and strutted and pushed others around and showed himself capable of deception, callousness, brutishness. He was also a forceful, shrewd, even charismatic person, able to direct and command and persuade some, while putting others decidedly off. The school's teachers were not entirely critical of him; some regarded him as a leader, with all the possible downside qualities of such a person: a cold canniness, an egoism in constant need of replenishment from others, a manipulative inclination to take what is obtainable and ig-nore those who don't come eagerly (or fearfully) to one's side. That boy's critic, my informant, pointedly wondered out loud about *himself,* never mind the one he'd been reproving, roasting with the blunt, un-sparing language of the street: "He's a slime-bag sometimes, and he thinks he can get away with anything—he's a con artist. But he sure can get his way. I'll never be able to get people to follow me around, like he does. I just don't have it."

When I met this boy I was not sure what to think, let alone say. Per-haps because I was an adult and a doctor, he had his guard up—so high up that there was little for me to see, other than his polite intelligence, his eagerness to engage me in a pleasant conversation. Certainly he es-poused a philosophy of sorts that could be seen as a justification for the kind of behavior I'd heard described as his: "You have to watch out for yourself, or else you'll get in trouble. If there's someone who's un-friendly, you should ignore him. The best way to win, is to have people on your side, and you should think of what could happen, if there's some trouble you could get into." I asked him to describe his view of what makes for a good person. "A good person? He's someone who does his job, I mean, is successful, and he doesn't loaf, and do nothing—he keeps busy. And he goes to church, and he can give the best to his kids, a nice home, and what they need, you know. And he pays his bills, and he doesn't blame other people just because he's got into trouble. That's bad—the worst: to start crying and saying it's all *their* fault. You have to do what you need to do, and not be afraid, and if you get criticized, then you have to stand up and fight, just keep on fighting, or else you'll end up being controlled by a lot of others, and that's no good, that means you've lost your independence."

A combative assertion meant to convey the importance of one's own sovereignty. I struggled hard as I listened to this boy, kept reminding myself, as a person must in a discussion such as this, that one has to distinguish between what one dislikes and what is "bad." "Bad" by whose standards? I kept wondering. All right, the boy is reported to have cheated in class—a clear-cut wrong. But suppose he hadn't done so; suppose the real issue is his vigorous insistence on his survival, on his relative indifference to others—am I in the presence of a not-so-good child, or of one who proclaims values that are not necessarily mine, but that don't therefore deserve outright condemnation? This question won't elude us when we consider moral matters, when we assert our particular values and in so doing inevitably omit affirmations that others very much claim to be desirable. Obviously, the law governs us all (though laws, too, can be challenged, can be terribly unjust), and a child cheating or stealing or setting a fire or lying is most definitely "not-so-good," is bad, bad, bad. Yet one hopes and prays that most of our children are not in that kind of relationship to the world around them, so that teachers or doctors or the police are being summoned who use that phrase "antisocial." Rather, you and I as parents or neighbors or relatives are sometimes challenged by certain children whose words and actions, whose very manner of being, provokes us not only to try to describe or explain them, to be frankly critical of them, but to take notice of ourselves, of what we hold high and dear, what we most certainly regard as "not-so-good," as thoroughly undesirable, as reprehensible, even if legal.

The Stony-Hearted Ones

Of course, lawless, violent, destructive youths pose no challenge in that regard; for the sake of all of us they require judgment from all of us and, when necessary, the law's action. Indeed, I have taught in classrooms where I have had to intervene, where I have had to get the police to help me intervene, and as I have already noted, I once worked with, tried to understand, youths called by judges delinquent (that is, law breakers) in the hope that I might help *them*, also, understand themselves, in the further hope that they would gradually become more upstanding members of their own families, neighborhoods, and ultimately, our nation. The hardest challenge, though, is the boy or girl who hasn't violated any laws, is doing well in school, and maybe is quite "successful" or popular outside of school as well, and yet strikes one as all too self-absorbed, as unsympathetic to others different in various ways, as selfish or stony-hearted. You note the moral judgments in those words; we use them with respect to our adult friends, even relatives, and certain children will tempt us to think of those same words, and the values that prompt us to use them.

Sometimes as I think of such matters I ask for the help of my young informants. I ask them to talk about children they like and dislike and why, and ask them to spell out their notions of who "isn't so good," and for what reasons. It's a very good way to get a lively discussion going in a classroom or a living room. Why do we (you) like certain people, and disapprove of others? Who is good and who is "not so good," and for what reasons? In one sixth-grade classroom I heard selfishness roundly condemned but also justified as necessary and valuable: "If I don't look out for myself, who will? A lot of the time you have to think of your own problems, even if others will call you selfish. They should be doing the same, trying to help themselves. If you keep worrying a lot about others, then you can become weak, you lose your independence."

Some of that girl's friends were taken aback by her bold embrace of her own "best interests," a phrase she used. As I heard her I realized yet again that "character" to some extent is in the eye of the beholder—all the more reason for each of us to think long and hard about what it is *we* want to uphold for our children, for our students, and, as citizens, for our country. So often, the real crux of the matter is in the phrasing we summon, the interpretations we make of those various "virtues" or "good things to be, to do," as so many teachers discover when they suggest a particular quality of mind or heart to a class. In that sixth-grade class, for example, I once wrote the word "goodness" on the board, and another time the word "compassion," and another time the phrase "not-so-good behavior" and was stunned at the variations, the differences of thought and feeling and expression in those twenty-three boys and girls sitting before me. To be sure, there were certain shared assumptions. One ought to help others in need, though certain children wanted to qualify, and then came their reservations. One ought to heed the law—but there, too, some children worried about unjust laws: segregationist laws, Nazi laws, even laws that obtain in many states today. "It's not right to kill someone, the Bible says so—if it's an unborn baby, or a murderer. The baby should be born, and the murderer should be locked up for life, and he can't be let out."

I am saying here that it can help us all to figure out what we want *for* our children and for ourselves if we stop to consider what we find objectionable, what we deem a most undesirable aspect of human behavior. Even as the Golden Rule requires our constant loyalty if it is to be more than a mere slogan, a principle given lip service only, so also those negatives that we have been taught require a lifetime of consideration. They especially need to be conveyed to our children and examined with respect to their essence: What it is about a particular kind of thought or action that we find undesirable, and as a consequence of which principles or values on our part?

Again, I worry about the temptation to reach an easy, a glib conviction as to anyone's future. I have in mind George Eliot's extraordinary wisdom at the end of *Middlemarch*:

> Every limit is a beginning as well as an ending. Who can quit young lives after being long in company with them and not desire to know what befell them in their after-years? For the fragment of life, however typical, is

not the sample of an even web; promises may not be kept, and an ardent outset may be followed by declension; latent powers may find their long-awaited opportunity; a past error may urge a grand retrieval.

Who can quit such a thoughtful and balanced observation, so mindful of life's unpredictability, its plentiful ironies and paradoxes and ambiguities and uncertainties, the luck, good and bad, that can befall any of us — and thereby, shape how we behave, who we become — and make the sort of generalizations about our children that some of us, alas, in the name of modern knowledge (psychology, sociology) are not loath to offer. Still, lives do vary, and lives are often put to the test, sometimes so decisively that their moral outcome hangs in the balance in moments of moral crisis, of moral choice.

4

MORAL CROSSROADS—
BAD BEHAVIOR, BAD "WITNESSES"

The aim of this book is to emphasize and document the moral seriousness, the moral curiosity, of children, and therefore the importance of moral education. It is something for which the young hunger and thirst and seek hard to find on their own, as well as with the aid of us adults. This book also aims to emphasize that the most persuasive moral teaching we adults do is by example: the witness of our lives, our ways of being with others and speaking to them and getting on with them—all of that taken in slowly, cumulatively, by our sons and daughters, our students. To be sure, other sources can count a great deal: formal lectures or explicit talks, reading and more reading and discussions of what has been read, reprimands and reminders with punishment of various kinds, churchgoing or synagogue attendance, the experience of hearing sermons and being told about biblical messages, and the moral lessons and the wisdom of our secular novelists, poets, and playwrights—all of that can count a great deal. But in the long run of a child's life, the unself-conscious moments that are what we think of simply as the unfolding events of the day and the week turn out to be the really powerful and persuasive times, morally.

Headed for Trouble

"My dad says one thing, he's a great talker, but he does another thing." The words of a cynical teenager. A school psychologist and a district court judge had declared this boy a "juvenile delinquent" in 1958, and I was learning to talk with such a person, one of the psychoanalyst August Aicchorn's "wayward youth." Anna Freud often spoke of Aicchorn and his uncanny knack for working with extremely troubled, "antisocial" adolescents. "He knew," Miss Freud wryly remembered, "that the waywardness of those young men [mostly] was in direct proportion to the peculiarities of their 'moral education.' "

I asked her what she meant by that word "peculiarities." She answered, "Oh, I think that [Aicchorn] figured out early in his work that some young people who seem headed in the wrong direction have been headed there for a long time. He once told us, 'I've been noticing that many of these boys headed for trouble and more trouble have parents who seem so upright. They are very good talkers—but their children have found them out, that is the sad truth. The family secret is being revealed by the child, who is telling the world, 'See, they may strike everyone as "straight and narrow," but I know something else, and what I found out has become a big part of my life!' We were all quite impressed with that work; he was a good detective—that is what we [in psychoanalysis] have to be, sometimes."

In this chapter I would like to try to show you how children learn moral lessons, at home and in school and in the neighborhood, lessons that can sometimes get them into a good deal of difficulty—or out of it. In our country at this time we tend to stress the psychological, the emotional, for understandable reasons: we have learned a lot about what happens in families between parents and children, about the anxieties young people experience, about their fears and worries and the general way their minds work. And adolescents, too, are now the focus of a whole clinical specialty, "adolescent medicine," for internists, pediatricians, and psychiatrists.

When I talk with parents, and teachers, they are at pains to tell me about "cases," about so-and-so who had or has this or that "emotional problem." Sometimes the trouble is cognitive: a child is in intellectual difficulty, in need of "testing." Indeed, a psychologist I know who works for a suburban school has wondered with me about past decades, when individuals like him weren't available for parents and teachers. What did people do? He is constantly called to help family members and school authorities make decisions regarding children who are in one or another crisis, and he evaluates them either intellectually or psychologically or both, through tests he asks them to take and through interviews. Again and again the questions are put to him at conferences: Is this child in the right classroom, studying the right subjects for his age? A cognitive or intellectual decision has to be made. Alternatively, is this child in the midst of a psychiatric emergency, or less seriously, going through a time of tension, nervousness, or apprehension, for whatever set of reasons?

I have myself been in those conferences and acted as a consultant to schools, sat in rooms where children are presented to us experts—in the expectation that we will, of course, make our various recommendations: pronounce a medical judgment, a psychiatric judgment, a psychological and cognitive judgment, with a suggested course of action as the ultimate payoff. Yet, often, I have thought to myself, then said to colleagues, that the issue at hand is very much moral: a child has gotten into trouble, all right—done something wrong, hurt someone, or violated a school regulation, a community's customs, or even laws. Often under such circumstances we explain the matter through resort to psychology or, yes, sociology—the child's "psychodynamics," home life, background, medical history, "cognitive functioning" as shown in various tests. Nor is all that to be ignored or downplayed. Still, Erik H. Erikson once commented, "These days, we sometimes spend a lot of time avoiding the obvious, and sometimes, psychology helps us do so!" He too was talking about some of the "wayward youth" early child psychoanalysts such as Aicchorn and Miss Freud and he saw in the 1920s and 1930s, youths in moral trouble, even legal trouble. At what point do we face squarely *that* side of a child's life and conclude that a moral crisis is at hand, one requiring a candid assessment of *character*, an assessment of what a boy's or girl's moral assumptions, attitudes, and values have turned out to be, and with what likely outcome in terms of behavior—law-abiding or "antisocial"?

Before we, in later chapters, take on the general subject of moral development in children, from their earliest days, months, and years to adolescence, I would like to offer three stories out of my clinical life. I did meet these individuals because I'm a child psychiatrist who works with and teaches in schools. But the stories of these children aren't only clinical; essentially, they are also moral. In each instance, a child was at a point of crisis, in accordance with the word's derivation, a time of choice, of decision to go one way or the other. These children were at a moral crossroads with respect to what confronted them, to where they stood in their lives.

Elaine: Cheating

At nine, Elaine seemed a solid, sound girl to her parents, her friends and relatives, her teachers. She was the oldest child of prosperous parents, both lawyers. She had a younger sister, seven, and brother, five. She was going to an idyllic suburban private school, where she was doing very well. She excelled at her studies, loved athletics, and was already a promising tennis player. She was pretty, outgoing, had many friends, and was popular: a poised, spirited girl with an open smile and an easy laugh. She had already been to Europe and Latin America and loved to show friends slides of her travels in her room at home, where she had her own slide projector, which she knew how to operate quite well. The house was casually elegant, boasting its own tennis court and some well-kept gardens, which Elaine already knew how to keep in good condition. In her mother's affectionate description, "She's a good, willing weeder."

Elaine was other things, too: she had learned to ride horses, keep her room tidy, help her mother or father pack when they were to go on business trips. She wasn't a "perfect child," her mother pointed out, but if she were one, that would of course itself be a sign of trouble, as the psychologically knowing father wryly pointed out at a family conference: someone would call her a perfectionist! She had a "stubborn side"; she could be as sloppy in her barn responsibilities (feeding and watering a host of animals—horses, bunnies, chickens, a duck) as she was precisely, meticulously attentive to her room's appearance. When she was told that she wasn't riding her horse, Susie, correctly, she "dug in," resisted correction, became flushed with anger, and several times dismounted and ran off, pouting. But even the "best child" can be "temperamental," so her parents averred.

In school Elaine was a first-rate student. She paid close attention to her teacher, followed directions accurately; though not universally popular had several good, loyal friends, did well on tests, and was therefore among the top performers in all subjects. She was especially able at arithmetic, which was welcome news to her teacher, Mrs. Knowlton, who worried that boys constantly did better than girls in that subject and had written an article on the subject for an educational magazine, citing Elaine as a stunning exception: "Here is a girl who leads the class in science and arithmetic, and I wish there were more like her." Elaine had already told her teacher that she hoped one day to be a stockbroker, like her grandfather: "He is a whiz at numbers"—a remark she'd heard her grandmother make all the time. She was very much their favorite grandchild, the oldest and the one who wanted most to spend time with them. They lived in an adjoining town, and loved taking her with them on their golfing expeditions. The three of them moved in a cart from hole to hole, and Elaine pronounced those days "the best fun."

Here was a sunny, bright child, from a solid, hardworking, able, prosperous family—who one day was caught cheating on a test. She had tucked the answers to some arithmetic questions under the paper she was using to answer the teacher's questions. A boy sitting beside her reported her, and he told the teacher this was not the first time; he'd even discussed the matter with his parents, who had urged him to talk with Elaine rather than go to the teacher. He had talked to Elaine twice, and on each occasion she had become irate, had denied the allegation, had told the boy that he was a liar, that he was "jealous" of her because she was doing so well academically. This time she had been erasing an answer while checking with her crib sheet and had inadvertently shoved the sheet off her desk. As soon as it hit the floor the boy grabbed it, took it up to the teacher, and told her what had been happening.

A surprised, unbelieving teacher, initially irritated at the boy, did nothing. The class, Elaine included, continued to work at the test, but the boy became upset and tearful. The teacher had given him a reproving glare, so he thought, and consequently he couldn't finish his test. He knew he'd done poorly and he felt he was in trouble. Nothing was said that day to him or to Elaine, who flashed more glances at him and who by the end of the day cast his way what he regarded as a triumphant look. On the school bus the next morning she handed him a one-word note: "See!"

He told his parents what had occurred. They were very upset. The mother had been a schoolteacher herself before she started having children; the father was an oncologist who attended young patients with leukemia, lymphomas, and Hodgkin's disease. Both these parents were honorable and self-effacing in manner, I concluded when I met them, and they deliberated a long time about what to do. They decided to suggest to their son that he let the matter drop. Perhaps the teacher, in her own time and manner, would speak to Elaine and punish her.

The trouble was that several days later this boy was still being snubbed and teased by Elaine, who had emerged a boastfully unblemished survivor, so it seemed, of her accuser's action. The boy became increasingly upset. He felt the teacher, too, was less friendly to him— and he had flunked that test. The more his parents heard about this, the more inclined they were, however reluctantly, to involve themselves. A week to the day after the incident, the boy's mother, to everyone's surprise—his included—showed up in her son's classroom to talk with the teacher.

The result was a stormy confrontation. The teacher felt put upon, insisting that she intended to handle the matter in her "own way." The boy's parents ultimately charged that she was protecting Elaine, whereupon the teacher summoned psychology: the girl was going through a "stressful time"—her beloved grandfather had been diagnosed as having cancer, and her mother had lost a law case that had meant a lot to her and had preoccupied her for many months. *Before* the cheating episode, Elaine had told all that to the teacher, and now she, in turn, was telling the girl's doubters, Be more understanding and let me go about my work as I think best.

At first and for a week or so, the boy's parents, who felt properly rebuked and had apologized to the teacher, worked at reassuring the boy that all would turn out well. The boy tried to forget the incident, which was the advice given him by his parents. The only problem: days later his alert, observant eyes caught a glimpse of another crib sheet, this one used as an aid in a spelling test. This boy was a crack speller himself, and he really took to heart what he saw: someone secretively checking the spelling of words as she wrote them. He wanted to march up to the teacher again and report Elaine. His right hand almost flung itself high in the air—but he checked his impulse and waited until he got home. His parents were almost incredulous: How could it be that this very nice girl, so well liked, and from a well-liked family, could behave in such a manner! They told their son about the strains in Elaine's life, even as they worried about what they were doing, by more than implication: condoning a girl's cheating and lying, too. But the boy had become extremely upset, and now *his* behavior, feelings, and state of mind became the primary interest of his parents—and soon enough of the school's principal, to whom they would eventually present this sticky dilemma.

That is how I became involved. I'd been doing interviews with boys and girls in the school as part of my study of so-called privileged children, and so knew both these children, and their parents. The principal viewed this as a psychological crisis: Elaine was obviously behaving out of character, and the boy who had caught her cheating and to whom she lied was now upset, fearful out of an exaggerated sense (so the principal believed) of his own jeopardy.

I immediately wanted to know if anyone at the school other than the boy had talked to Elaine about her cheating. No one had; would I want to do so? I said that I thought instead that it was very important for

Elaine's teacher to be brought into this matter quickly. When she came to talk with the principal and me, I heard once more about the family's good standing, about the family's medical and psychological "crisis," and I heard of the child's academic achievement, her overall and long-term achievements. As for the boy, *he* seemed "distressed" too: his work wasn't up to par, and he seemed noticeably "timid" in class, meaning he kept a careful distance from his teacher.

What did I make of all this? I asked the teacher what *she* made of it, though I knew she'd already told us, *demonstrated*, her views to everyone by her actions—in fact, her unwillingness to act. Did she believe the girl? Was she intimidated by the parents, their affluence, influence? Was she afraid to intervene directly under such circumstances? I got no direct answer. I referred to the cheating in spelling, and she observed that it was "one child's word against another's." I said we had yet to find out whether Elaine might admit to wrongdoing, make an out-and-out confession. The teacher doubted that would happen, whereupon the principal allowed that "we'd best find out."

The teacher was right; Elaine denied ever having cheated. She insisted that her alleged crib sheets were study guides. Her problem, however, turned out to be more than a familial or a psychological one. The boy who witnessed her cheating had asked others if they had seen what he had seen and had found another witness, a girl, who said she knew of "it" for weeks—"ever since school started." The boy's parents reported this promptly to the principal, and we rather quickly had quite a "scene" going. I found all this sad, and also instructive. I was not surprised by the way Elaine's parents rallied around her. I was a little surprised—frankly, worried—by this girl's self-possessed cool. She seemed imperturbable and gave not an inch to any critic or judge: all of this was someone else's dishonesty and lying, not hers. Her accuser was, again, "jealous," envied her her high performance in arithmetic and spelling as well. What *was* his problem! He should go talk to, yes, "a doctor"! When told that two fellow students told similar stories about her cheating, she quietly observed that they were his "friends," and so one rallied to the other's "side," and then we heard a well-modulated account, with no evident paranoia, of her trials and tribulations as an academic leader, a sports leader, a popular figure: again, "People get jealous, they say things."

Weeks later, after I'd talked with everyone—each of the children, each of their parents, the teacher, five other children chosen at random in the class—I had what I believed to be a sense of things: the girl had been cheating for some time, before her grandfather had taken ill, before her mother had lost the law case. The teacher was not, it turned out, "completely surprised," because she had seen Elaine "fudge a little" as an athlete; the girl's parents had known that she "occasionally exaggerated things" and "told white lies" because she was "very ambitious" and she "hated to lose—ever."

What to do? Meaning, ought this child to start psychotherapy? Everyone asked that question; I certainly did, as did her parents, the parents of other children, her teacher, the principal. It was my wife, also a schoolteacher, who kept pressing another line of reasoning: this is primarily a moral matter, and we ought to consider it as such and talk with the girl and her parents in that vein, rather than keep emphasizing so exclusively the psychiatric nature of the difficulty, the "emotional problem" of this child, as her teacher kept calling it.

To do so, however, was easier to urge than accomplish. I sat with Elaine's parents several times and heard her defined as if she were in a courtroom and I was a mistaken prosecuting attorney. I was asked to remember who *I* was—a child psychiatrist, not "a moralistic person who doesn't want to understand why children gossip and turn on one another." Here was a family rallying around one of its own, I came to realize, a family at a moral crossroads: the parents weren't able to deny completely that "maybe something did take place," the father's eventual and reluctant concession. Yes, Elaine "might have peeked at something." Why? Well, she's "so conscientious," she could "get herself into a trap." This evasive, protective talk, grounded in psychology, told me a lot. A *family*'s moral life was really at stake here: a mother and father had signaled to a child how she ought to behave, what she ought to accomplish. When I finally asked Elaine's parents whether they wanted to regard this entire series of incidents as "a moral question," as an occasion for some meetings with them and their daughter that would concentrate on that issue rather than the "emotional stress" I kept hearing mentioned, I got demurrers and requests for "time," during which the family would "think about it." The decision, unsurprisingly, was never made in a clear-cut manner. The answer to those conferences was neither yes nor no but rather a request that the matter be dropped; that Elaine be "given the benefit of the doubt"; that the teacher be watchful, of course; that the two material witnesses of sorts be taken out of the case, since, as the mother put it, "The teacher, who is impartial, will be on her toes."

I had no more to do with it, but I certainly felt I had been educated by what I'd seen and heard. I'd learned a lot about others, but also a lot about myself, not to mention the use—the abuse?—to which my profession can occasionally be put in the more advantaged segments of late-twentieth-century, secular America. Ironically, for a while I worried about Elaine in a manner trained into my head for years—what was her "problem," and how might all of us be of "help" to her? For that matter, when I shifted my opinion—began to be more than a little skeptical of her, suspicious of her talk, her claims, and those of her very well-spoken parents—I did so on psychiatric grounds: I wondered if she didn't have even more serious "problems" than her parents and her teacher claimed for her! I gradually realized that a girl's cheating and lying had become a school's and a family's major moral challenge. Yet this event had become immersed in psychological jargon, a revealing reminder that on occasion parents and teachers can be too clever by half, and a child with them: a kind of moral evasion. Elaine got her reprieve—rather, her clean slate—and her parents, I learned, got their time with a "family therapist" who talked with Elaine, and her grandmother as well, about a tragedy that was taking place, a husband's, a father's, a grandfather's, slow, painful dying. Well, of course they should all "work" on that "issue," I had to agree. Yet I couldn't help but wonder whether in so doing, another "lie" of sorts wasn't being enacted—even as Elaine's teacher insisted (whistling in the dark?) that "the whole thing will blow over," convinced that a gifted, able child would go on to be a similarly outstanding, accomplished adult.

A year later that teacher's prediction was to some extent being fulfilled: Elaine was an outstanding student intellectually and even, it
seemed, psychologically: a leader in the classroom and in sports. Still,
she put off some of her classmates, and not only because they may have
been envious of her. She also confounded her fifth-grade teacher, who
admired her yet found her "a bit manipulative."

I thereafter lost track of this child and her progress in school, so I
have no report on the nature of her eventual character. She may have
become an utterly decent and trustworthy person, or she may have become yet another student whose moral intelligence lags behind her intellectual accomplishments. For the sake of that entire fourth-grade
classroom, however, I hope that had I been its teacher I would have
been willing and able to take immediate notice of what was happening,
moved quickly to talk with Elaine and her observers, her skeptics, and
her accusers, individually and together. I would have made clear to all
of them that this was a serious matter, that the integrity of the entire
class was at stake, that cheating was impermissible, and that hence-
forth, cheating noticed by others would become an issue for the entire
class to consider. In that way, I'd be sparing Elaine and those who alleged wrongdoing on her part an immediate public confrontation —
unless there was a next time. I would also hope to have learned from
this experience, so that at some point the whole class would indeed be
asked to engage with the issues of cheating through discussions and
written compositions.

Marie, Charlie, and The Crowd: Drinking and Drugs

One town over from Elaine's, I got to know a group of high-schoolers
who called themselves, proudly and with deadpan irony, "The Crowd."
(These young men and women, when younger, had taken part in the
Girl Scouts' survey of moral attitudes mentioned earlier.) The Crowd
was actually a very small number of youths who kept resolutely to themselves: seven eleventh- and twelfth-graders, four boys and three girls six-

teen, seventeen, and eighteen years old. The ringleaders (as they called themselves, in jest) were Marie and Charlie, each one a strong, even charismatic person. They hung out together, moved from home to home, or drove into the city, there to take in rock concerts and find themselves "smokes"—a word that then applied to both ordinary cigarettes and pot. They also got themselves plenty of beer illegally, and both Charlie and Marie tried snorting lines of cocaine. Each member of The Crowd claimed sanction for all of the above—cousins in Ivy League colleges who did likewise and, in Charlie's case, an older brother who was a senior in one of those colleges and who was an occasional supplier to The Crowd of "high-powered" grass, not to mention a bottle, now and then, of 106-proof Wild Turkey. "No mean stuff," said Charlie.

I met these youths doing my research at the well-known private school they attended. I was not the only one to know of their drug habits; several teachers suspected as much but had no proof. As with Elaine, there were other students who had heard things, had seen with their eyes the stuff: hey, cool, man—and besides, lets try it! And why not! Studying and those all-too-regimented athletic games and the rules handed down by the teachers who lived in the dorm—what kind of life is *that*, and what kind of person would choose it!

"So *what*?" they'd say to me as we talked. Charlie: "You must see this all the time, or if you don't, then you've missed a lot!" Marie: "We're keeping ourselves out of trouble this way! This weed—it keeps you 'sweet and low'; no hot-under-the-collar business. That's what they [the school authorities] really want: no waves! They booze it up, but we're under twenty-one, so nothing doing! Fakes, a lot of them—they talk a big line, but man, we're here, and we know more than they'd dream we do! There's the guy who's cheating on his wife with the new teacher. There's the teacher who goes to AA meetings every night in this town or some other ones—she can't miss one day! There's the one who goes away on weekends, and when he comes back, his hands are shaking and his face is flushed, 'red as a beet,' as they say. I saw that old movie *Lost Weekend* on TV, and I was going to go try renting it, and I'd leave it in his [mail] box. Trouble is, I'd never get it back, so I'd have to pay for it, buy it. No way."

There was more, she assured me, as if I was a naïf and she a worldly-wise, world-weary veteran of a million moral wars, and here was the result: a convinced awareness of adult hypocrisy, which for her and the rest of The Crowd translated into an equally convenient justification for sneaking out of the school to go for a smoke, or doing likewise (or "snorting") while on weekend passes. They crash in the college dorms of relatives, older friends, get "zonked," and come back, as Marie put it wryly, "too tired to be bored by this place."

I am glad this Crowd will come to my college office, sit there and tell me more—this way I learn a lot. But I begin to worry (talk about a "moral crossroads"!) as to my obligations and responsibilities: to keep mum; to talk with school officials; to talk with The Crowd itself about my desire to talk with others; to become less the research chronicler, more the clinician—or some, or all, of the above? The more they tell me, the more I learn, but the more I become a part of what is happening—so I fairly soon come to think, and I worry. Matters get more troubling when I try to have a candid discussion and remind these youths that they are violating school regulations and state and federal laws, buying booze, even cigarettes, and those so-called "illegal substances" while underage. They reassure me: "Don't worry about us, man—we're fine." I dare suggest that I'm also worried about myself, to which I hear, "No sweat, man, you're clean, so far as we're concerned—no sweat!" By then, I'm more than sweating. I'm feeling a headache stir over my forehead and wish for aspirin, though if it were there, I wonder if I'd use it in front of them: an admission that they were more than getting to me, and that I also call upon "drugs" for assistance.

We go on, my head throbbing. I find my irritation, my anger, at these youths taking this form: they are self-centered, self-indulgent, snotty, spoiled, smug—and on and on. Who is looking after them? The boarding school, supposedly, but they are successfully (flagrantly, I conclude) pulling the wool over the school's collective eyes. Actually, they tell me that they are sure there are some teachers who know "everything," yet look the other way. That's how it is—why should *they* get into trouble! I register surprise, become ironic: get into trouble by clamping down on trouble? Poor dumb me—they let me know that it's "no bonus" for the school if their parents end up angry at the place. Why (how) would *that* happen? See, stupid, their parents are busy—boy, are they busy, and so they have sent those youths in The Crowd to boarding school to get them off their parental backs. If they had to be hauled into "some conference" they'd be "jumping mad." They'd say: What kind of place is this? We entrust our kids to you, and you go and drop the ball! Bad news! Then, five of The Crowd turn in a silent pointing chorus of sorts to Charlie and Marie and together say, "Trustees!" Charlie's dad and Marie's mom are trustees! I smile—they take that as evidence that I'm following their advice, chilling out. But I am getting ready to end this meeting, the eighth I've had with them, so that I can get myself some aspirin, and some much-needed advice from a colleague or two, not to mention, again, my wife.

What to make of this Crowd, and myself with them, and their observations about the school they attend, and their influential, well-educated parents, any number of whom, so their sons and daughters have told me, are "seeing shrinks," indeed, "don't move without consulting them"? Two aspirin don't help me in that regard. I begin to realize that the nub of this matter is that this school's "adults," its teachers, don't have the moral authority they need to deal with these youths. I contemplate making a visit to the school's headmaster. I contemplate an end to my meetings with them—hey, I've learned what I need to learn, and their revealed, narrated escapades are not my business, anyway. I contemplate one final meeting with them, during which I will tell them what is on my mind. Meanwhile, I remind myself that the meetings were approved by the school, the parents of the students, and the students themselves and that I promised all of them, unsurprisingly, routinely, "confidentiality," the sine qua non of an investigator's life—including the confidentiality that comes with thorough concealment of individual identities in any writing I should do.

All that runs through my head. All things considered, I decide to meet with them again. Now we have a lot to say, because I clearly am troubled and let them know it. What's gotten to me, they evenhandedly wonder? What's my *problem*? I tell them. I talk about rules and laws, and finally, closer to their turf, their homes, psychiatry, drugs as a form of self-medication to take away pain. (Those aspirins cross my mind as this part of the oration comes up.) They listen, nod—no argument, really: they tell me I may know a lot, but I don't know "the half of it"—about them and their generation's habits, values. I smile, then get annoyed, enough so to tell them that I "may know a little more" than they are giving me credit for. A silly impasse, this—their vanity and arrogance, against my bald egoism, a threatened narcissism that can go with a profession's perch, not to mention the usual awe and deference and gullibility people like me can take for granted and not rarely come to depend on and ultimately exploit. I try to break free, in several senses. I mention that my "work," these "research interviews," are coming to an end. I thank them for their patience and for the cooperative interest they have given me. *All right*, all right then, they tell me—"We can go." But I say no, not yet. There's a conflict that I feel—and that word elicits apparent sympathy from them, expressed in their wide-eyed looks, the tilt toward me of their heads, their bodies, even, and the hush, the diminution of that low-level noise we all make as we shift positions, scratch our heads, jingle our keys with our hands in our pockets. Then I play this hand: "moral conflict."

I try not to emphasize that first word, just toss off the phrase quickly. Cool, man, cool, they respond, indifferent at first. But they pick up fast—and we're into it, a long talk, an exchange of views, a big, big, heated argument. The gist of theirs: You're making a scene, when there isn't one. The gist of mine: I can't just walk away from this, not by saying a simple good-bye and thank you, and not by the equivalent, wishing them future luck with doctors, and of course, letting them know I can always (right then and there, even) recommend some. The gist of theirs: What are you going to do? The gist of mine: tell you, as I have been doing this afternoon, what is at stake here, what is going on—the truth, the law, the right and wrong of things, the self-deception, the lies told to ourselves. I tell them explicitly that they are violating the law; that they are taking stuff that hurts their minds and their bodies; that morally and psychologically they are running fast down a blind alley. They do listen, but not with the eager attentiveness I would have wished. They feel sorry for me, I realize. They are disappointed in me,

I come to understand. They are disappointed in themselves; they thought their cocky, self-assured, boastful, cosmopolitan "cool" had won me over, the me who is anxious to be "with it," not to mention eager to learn, to get the score, to be savvy.

Finally, I say to myself, we've got to strike some deal here—an interesting word to cross my head, as it struggles with what it's just called a *moral* matter. Another irony: I worry about the ethics of our agreed-upon "relationship," defined, carried on, and now a source of my anxiety. I acknowledge their trust. I tell them I'm not interested in being an informer. I repeat my refrain, that drugs are a kind of killer, a killer of pain—so, let's face it, face *that*. I ask whether they think that anyone can avoid pain in this life. I ask whether the cost to them of killing pain won't be even more and worse pain down the line. I insist that if I don't say what I'm now saying, if I don't come clean with them morally as well as psychologically, I'm actually an ally of those drugs. You go against the law here, then there, you chip away like that, and you're choosing, man, you're going down a road, and all of us who know that—the best we can do to be their friend is to say this, to put it on the line, to say what we see in the works for them, out there coming at them: a lot of trouble for themselves, sure, but also with the police, with schoolteachers, with a society that has said no to things that they, with some defiance and canniness, insist upon doing.

Toward the end of this three-hour spell of anxiety and mixed feelings and anger on my part, and annoyance, mixed feelings, anger, and more than a touch of derisive disappointment on their part, I am pushed to the wall: "O.K., O.K., are you going to say something?" I blurt this out before I can even mull over, as they would put it, "the whole enchilada": "I'm not talking about turning you folks *in*." A second's pause, and my mind tries to turn clever, maybe facilely so: "I'm interested in turning you folks *around*. I have to say it; even though I know you'll laugh, you'll think, 'This guy, who the hell is he—*presumptuous*, man!'" I am hoping against hope, playing every card I know, or rather, my last one, a mix of ingratiation and sternness, even desperation: I'm with you, I talk your lingo, but let's leave this scene and go for a much better one. But they don't buy it, or me, or whatever. Well, what *will* I do? We part with more reserve than ever before—an ironic reversal of the usual piety that is supposed to characterize fieldwork: the more time you spend with people, the better things go, based, obviously, on increased acquaintance.

A week later, after prolonged talks with my wife and a couple of good friends and colleagues, I go to the boarding school where those youths are students for a routine visit to have a chat with the headmaster about my general impressions. I feel ill at ease, worried that I'll be spotted by some of The Crowd; hence, I speculate, I must feel a bit ashamed of myself, as if I'm doing something wrong, or am tempted in that direction. I catch myself: I should be worried, all right—about those young men and women, who at times are behaving like spoiled preteen children. What *am* I going to say to the headmaster? In no time I'm sitting in his office, evasively saying little, politely and circumspectly offering gratitude on behalf of my research project.

Suddenly, I feel a surge inside of me—I have to say something, and I do. I start by beating around the bush, but that *is* a start, and I begin to realize that I am not only being understood as to my intent, but the specific content I have in mind to relay. I'm concerned about these youths in The Crowd, I aver. Yes, of course, he replies—and he looks directly at me, our eyes locked knowingly for long seconds. He adds this: "I can understand why." I want him to go on, tell me why he "can understand." But he clearly won't do so. I mention the ringleaders, Charlie and Marie—ask if they're doing all right in school, wonder if they'll graduate with good records. Again, he looks directly at me and tells me that they are both quite bright, that both could handily be way at the top of their class, but that they have their "problems" and so they lag in the middle and below.

Their "problems"—we are on my territory. Yes, indeed, they certainly do, I say, saying nothing really. He surprises me: What do I think their problems *are*? I am looking right at him: I decide to talk, as in spill the beans. When push comes to shove, though, my voice is hesitant, my words equivocal: "I worry about them and their close friends. I think they could get themselves into a lot of trouble." Silence on both our parts, another surge within me; I come closer: "They may well already be in a lot of trouble." He answers: "We think they are." Who is this new "we"? Teachers who do indeed know and have told the headmaster? I want to pose questions but don't: it's none of my business. Or is that true? Isn't all of what we're circling around very much my business, and everyone's? These youths are not only plagued by "problems," they're in moral and legal trouble. They're buying illegal substances, and even bringing some of what they buy back with them to school for some of their friends, who pay them some money—not a lot, and I know that making dough is not the major motivation in all of this, but still, this is drug-dealing, as well as the personal use of drugs.

As all of the immediately above charges cross my cortex, I feel newly tense but more talkative, less cagey: "I think those folks, they could very well be in trouble with the law one of these days." He nods emphatically. What does he know? I wonder. If he knows what I know, then for heaven's sake, why doesn't he take action—and fast? I try to say as much, with a respectful but pointed comment: "I worry that they'll get themselves in some terrible hole before we get to them." He nods again—and now begins to level with me: "We're fairly sure they're into drugs, but we have no actual evidence. We've kept a close eye on them, but they are pretty shrewd, and more careful than some of our students have been."

He stops only momentarily, then crosses onto my "psychology" turf with confidence and thoughtfulness: "I suppose that's a good sign for them. If they were in very bad shape, they'd stumble and fall. They'd get picked up by the police on the outside, or by our teachers here at the school. They'd do something wrong, and the jig would be up—*is* up, we'd all be telling them. The fact is that we only have our suspicions—hell, more than suspicions, we've heard plenty from other kids, reliable and honest and well-intentioned ones, with no axes to grind. This is a serious matter, *very* serious. But I've learned that with such students—well, I hate to put it this way: you have to give them rope. Things have to get worse, I mean, something has to *happen*, and then their families will rally; they will, I mean, recognize that there's trouble, real trouble, and so will they, the kids. Before that, they'll deny everything. They already have; we've tactfully tried to let them know that we know! And their parents are perfectly capable of—outrage: How *dare* you say this, on *what basis*, exactly?"

Lord, I think to myself, we've come to the end of this discussion, for all practical purposes. I think of Elaine, this business of the law, not in the sense of its mandates, such as "no drugs," or "no cheating in class," but in the sense of "innocent until proven guilty." I am not disputing the great importance in a democracy of such a principle. Still, here are youths headed for legal trouble—but also *already* in trouble, deep trouble, *moral* trouble. I'm supposed to think as a doctor, and I do think as one—I think that the headmaster of their school, and some of their teachers, and we (the adult world), are in our *own* trouble: What to say, what to do, and under which set of circumstances? As I get up to leave, the headmaster walks with me toward the door, abruptly stops, looks squarely at me, and asks this: "What would you do if you were in my shoes?" I have no ready response. I hem and haw within myself, grasp for words and await their arrival for an embarrassingly long time. Thoughts scramble in me: Insist on some kind of medical surveillance, even urine tests. Bring in a group of doctors or psychiatrists to talk with the students in general, aiming at The Crowd, of course, and others influenced by them. Call them in, confront them, insist on a closer scrutiny of them. Invite their departure.

I want to say some of that. I want to tell the headmaster that I'd probably be tempted to call them into this very office, holler bloody murder, do likewise with their parents, insist that these youths are in grave moral danger, never mind the psychological kind, that we've all got to declare an emergency, not only a psychiatric one, but again, a moral one. But this is easy bombast on my part, I unfortunately conclude. So, I say no such thing; rather, I become mournful: "It's so sad—there's no language that enables us to have this all out, try to deal with it *before* there's some legal incident, or whatever." Yes, yes, he says. I want to go on, talk about young people adrift morally—without any real guiding beliefs, convictions, other than to be "cool," to get "zonked," to feel pleasantly (so they say it is) "wasted."

I leave. There it is, and there we are. I think not only of Charlie and
Marie and the rest of *their* Crowd but maybe of me and my kind, *our*
crowd: a secular society that calls itself enlightened and in many ways
is just that and yet lacks the means, it seems, to take on its children
when they cheat or tell lies, when they drug themselves up and sell
drugs so that others can do likewise. We wait until the child, the youth,
is caught red-handed, and then offer only "therapeutic" recommendations! Miss Freud, again: "I find talking with certain adolescents, that
they know everything wrong about everyone, but they're not quite clear
for themselves what wrong is, and when it is and why that one goes
wrong oneself." That remark, stunning in its breadth and depth
morally and sociologically as well as psychologically, rings in my ears as
I drive away from the school. A daydream comes to mind as I press the
gas pedal. Miss Freud is driving a van, and in it are the members of The
Crowd, and she lets them know in that delightfully firm Viennese ac-
cent of hers that she's taking them down *this* road, one of her choosing,
not the alternative road, where they thought they were headed, where
they seemingly wanted to go. "Nothing doing," she says when they
want her to go their way—a phrase of the 1930s, I realize, so very suit-
able for her.

The daydream over, I think of practical suggestions I might have offered that headmaster, guidance for him and all of us who are bringing
up and teaching children. He ought to have called in those students
and told them what he knew, what he suspected, and what he would
not condone, not tolerate. He ought to have called in their teachers,
rallied them around his decision, a school's decision to challenge
wrongdoing whenever and wherever it is discovered. He ought to have
called in the parents of those youths, let them know where he and his
school stood—moral leadership in action. He ought to have indicated
clearly that he intended to stand firm, thereby making it clear that he
would have to be fired or would resign if a test of wills were to take
place. He ought to have asked that moral questions be discussed in
classes, through stories in literature classes, through discussions in history and civics classes, thereby connecting a school's curriculum to
those questions. He ought to have brought in speakers to discuss the

matter—doctors, naturally, but also athletes, people with some moral credibility for the students. All of that would be a start toward, in W. H. Auden's phrase, the creation of "a whole climate of opinion" that would give a school's entire community, teachers and students alike, a clear sense of what will and will not be tolerated, and why.

Danger and More Danger: Early Sexual Activity in Adolescents

I am sitting with three youths, all fourteen years old. One of them is pregnant, two are her envious admirers on that count—they tell me that they want to become mothers soon. I have been talking with these youths and others, young women and their boyfriends, or occasional boyfriends, for five years. I was asked to do so by the Kaiser Foundation with a clear purpose in mind: how to understand relatively early sexual activity in adolescents. I have accumulated dozens of personal narratives, to the point that when I meet a teenager of, say, sixteen who has had no sexual experience, I scratch my head in near disbelief and find myself hearing Handel's "Hallelujah" chorus. Actually these three young women knew sex long before adolescence. Each of them remembers episodes of molestation at the hands of relatives (by blood or marriage) or visitors. Sex is something they have apparently accepted— a casual acceptance, I conclude for a while, but I am wrong. In fact, when several such young women sit together (they seem to gain strength and confidence that way, become much more talkative that way as well) stories of fear and hurt, of terror, pour out: awful stories of children treated as no decent, halfway-balanced person would ever think of treating anyone. Now, the awful irony: they are glad to have men come "visit" them, glad to be on the road to maternity, or headed there, even as they know they'll be as alone and vulnerable as they once were when younger. How is all this to end, I wonder. I dare broach the matter with these three youths, because I have known them for a long time, and they talk easily and are intuitive, bright, and sensitive.

Delia and Her Friends

Delia, a mother of a six-month-old girl, has more distance on herself and her situation than one might expect. She attributes it to having a child, but I saw that thoughtful side of her before she became pregnant and was told of it by her middle school teacher, who mourned what she called "the waste" and told me once, tersely, "She's very smart, but she doesn't know it, and no one has given her any means to find out about it."

In one monologue Delia tells of a life of sex and violence that goes back to her earliest remembered years. "I can see two men. I'm not sure who they were. I mean, I can't see their faces, only—well, below: their arms and legs, you know, coming toward me, at me. Mama's friends, I suppose. One of them might have been my daddy—I don't know. Mama never has told me [who he is]. I look for him in my mind. When I meet a nice man, in a store—like the teacher I liked best, he taught us sixth grade—I think, if only he was my daddy! Silly, I know! I saw on *Oprah* a program, they were all like me; they never knew their daddies, and their mamas had to work, or they got welfare, but then they got sick, you know, with drugs, like that, or some disease, and they couldn't be good mamas. My grandma, she tried, she would have saved us all [her and her two sisters and a brother], but she caught a bullet. She was walking home with the groceries, and she got 'in between,' you know. [This is a common expression, meant to summarize so very much: a gang confrontation, often over turf or drugs, that culminates in shooting—and innocent victims.] That was the end of the world for me. I don't think there'll ever be a beginning—you just try to find a little peace and quiet here, and it can be hard, even that. I look at my Sally, and I say, I'll try to get a better ticket for you in the lottery, but you know, it's chance, a small chance that I'll win—for her or myself, either of us.

"You ask how I try. Well, I don't know, maybe it's just by hoping. That's all I know to do, hope a little. They say, get yourself more schooling, that teacher said. But I see kids here, they've stayed in school, right through, and it's been no big blessing to them. I have to be honest, though: I can't concentrate, like I should. If my granny—we used to call her 'honey-granny'—if she'd stayed around, if she hadn't been taken, she would have helped us all a lot, I know that for a fact. I do. Now, my brother is in that gang; he tried to stay out, but it was join or else, you gotta know, and my sisters, they're in trouble, using stuff. It's been bad for so long, I just laugh it off, especially when I tickle my kid and she laughs back: that'll get me through it all."

I then ask her if there is anything else that might help her "get through it all." Surely, I think, her baby is a mixed blessing at her age and in her situation, and besides, I've noticed how low she can get, even with the baby and, actually, because of the baby: Sally has her own substantial requirements and demands, and Delia can feel quite inadequate in the face of them. She gives me a quick, knowing stare and begins a soliloquy on the joys of motherhood, which her two friends vastly enjoy—and then she stops. We have circled this subject before, and besides, she needs no help from me in doing so, only the right frame of mind, no easy acquisition, as she lets us know: "I know the baby won't save me! She'll help—but first I've got to save *her*. If I don't, we'll both end up in bad trouble; we could get killed, just like that." She snaps her fingers. "There's crazy men around; there's guns and drugs around, and gangs; there's trouble around every corner. You have to keep your mind *up*, or you'll go *down*, that's what we say! If I could have something to believe, then it could be better—I don't know what, though. The [welfare] worker says I should take classes on how to take the right care of my baby, and they'd be good for me. I guess that's the way. I guess if I could learn about the baby, I'd be discovering something for myself, you know."

She did indeed go to those classes, and she enjoyed them. She learned a lot—how to feed her baby healthier food, how to dress her more comfortably, clean her more often and more effectively. There were times while she sat in the classroom that hope descended on her, a kind of hope she'd never known before, a hope that provoked daydreams, in which she and her baby were on a bus, their destination uncertain—but at least they were headed away from the life they were living. This fantasy took over her mind, to the point that in spite of the pleasant side of such a phenomenon, she got worried. "Seems my head is trying to escape from me! I told me, I told it: go, go. But that's stupid—you can't go from a place that's only in your head! I know why I'd like to catch that bus; here, it's danger and more danger. You have people my age, I grew up with them, and they're shooting each other like crazy, over those bills [drug money], and they're shooting [up] themselves, and that's worse than a gun's bullet to them, if you ask me. Besides, a lot of guys here, they're bad, real bad, even before they got to drugs. They're copying the men they saw, growing up—trying to be big, big, big shots. Knock up the girls, one after the other! Play nice with them, give to them, until they give in, then walk away, and when you hear they're carrying, carve another one on your big belt: yo, look at me, you guys, I'm taller than anyone, 'the fastest guy around,' they brag to each other, in-out, in-out—that's what you hear.

"I said to the [welfare] lady: Now how you going to stop that? You think you can get those Joes to those [baby-care] classes! I laugh—they'd think you was crazy, if you came and suggested it. Long as those guys are [behaving] like they do, there's no end to this coming, the trouble. You live through your teens here, you've got Lady Luck looking out for you. The boys don't know how to get out of here any more than us girls. The boys catch their kind of trouble; we catch ours, the girls. It's all you can do, to stay out of it, the trouble—it's a full-time job. You have to watch your every step on the street, and when you be with someone, a guy, you have to watch your every step there, too, so it never ends."

She stops, looks down at the floor, and I'm sure she has had her full say for a while, so I prepare to respond—but she suddenly has more to tell: "I know it's good to learn to help my baby better, but you know, when she's bigger, the important thing she'll have to learn—they don't teach you in that course, or in school: how to take care of yourself *here*, where we live. That's another kind of 'taking care' than they teach you about in that course!"

After I left that meeting, I thought about what she'd been trying to let me know—the world of impulsive sex and violence that she and thousands of other children inhabit, that is their particular inheritance.

Why wouldn't that welfare worker and people like her, like me, offer courses in "child care," in "human development," to Delia and to her friends? Why not, of course, try to help such youths stay in school, graduate from high school? Yet this bright, thoughtful young lady kept indicating, I thought, a need for something else besides school courses or extracurricular psychological instruction. Naturally she wanted to escape to another world, yet, very important, she had trouble imagining what that world might be like. Her fantasies put her on a bus headed, alas, nowhere. Hence her agitated despair as she tried at the very least to extend the range of the fantasy, picture a few of the details of a better, safer life. When I asked her where she hoped that bus would take her, she defined her destination in terms of her origins, her place of departure: out of here. Where is the "there," though? "Oh, someplace." What *kind* of place? I ask, to get us away from the literalism of geography and nearer to the subjective, a region all its own. "The kind of place—where it's different from here, safer." Around and around we go, until at last I understand what may well be keeping that bus scene so obsessively constricted: a moral imagination that has never been nourished, at least since Delia's grandmother died. The girl was only seven, but she remembers the stories her granny shared with them, her grandchildren grouped around her. "She'd tell us about the Bible, and all the adventures in it, and she'd say we can have our own adventures. She said God was waiting on us, to help us have them. Then she died, and we never did hear of God anymore, that's for sure!"

How to bring back to her her grandmother's moral energy, biblically connected? How to help her imagine those "adventures" her granny wanted to give her sisters and brother, those moral narratives that Delia might have made her own, had she heard them enough, had the one who aimed to teach them stayed alive? How to give her a hand at dreaming an alternative to her present situation, a place where the bus could take her and where she'd feel able to disembark with some confidence in her ability to manage *there*. After all, as she reminds me repeatedly, she has indeed learned how to manage *here*. The ultimate issue, I begin to think, is not cognitive (of course, more education of various kinds will help), or even psychological (Delia is already astute about the psychology of survival, the kind that really matters for her in her present circumstances), but rather one of direction: a "place" she might be able to construct for herself within her mind that would shelter her as she took those steps of exit, of leaving for an "elsewhere" that she would at last imagine to be possible for herself. She knew all of that, knew it in her blunt, earthy, tough-minded way, her hurt, vulnerable, scared, melancholy way: "I could take my child and leave here and not come back, if I had a place where I believe I could manage. Here I manage, I guess. If I could get some inspiration, maybe I could find me a place and manage there. That's what I think on the days I'm feeling strong."

I dwelled in my mind afterward on her choice of two words, "manage," and "inspiration." She didn't say a place to which she would *go*, but a place where she could *manage*, and what she needed to stay successfully in such a place was the breath of someone's faith, values, and convictions become her own: inspiration. She could stay right where she is physically and still be elsewhere morally; it would be hard, very hard, but still it might be possible, so she sometimes speculates. Put differently, she is looking at moments for a destination within as well as without, a destination built not only on the intellect or on a growing psychological awareness, valuable as they both are, but on "inspiration," a moral direction that will serve her in such a way that she can manage. Manage what? Not only the external world: a change of address, a street that is safer, important as such a breakthrough, such a breakout, would be. She must manage her memories, her stray and fearful impulses, the undertow of her life that pulls at her so constantly and with a power and a success that she knows deep within herself—a consequence of her inability to swim for any length of time with any lasting measure of confidence. To master the instincts, one has to have found a reason to do so, a source of moral energy that enables one to do so. Her granny and her granny's one book (the only book she ever saw at home in her childhood, and, yes, it was literally buried with her granny, put in her coffin, as Delia remembers!) were unfortunately a mere start in that direction.

What Ought to Be Done?

As I think of Elaine, and of Charlie and Marie and their Crowd, and of Delia and her friends and the predator boys who link with them and leave them (and thereby leave themselves so little, turn themselves into their own victims), I ask myself what these young people require that would give them a good chance to be good or, indeed, better in the moral sense than now seems possible for them. Those boys and girls are obviously different in background—rich and poor and in-between, black and white, urban and suburban, publicly and privately educated, or dropouts from schooling. Yet I find that while I distinguish among them by resort to those characteristics, important though they be, I find myself seeing them as together, on common ground. They are all in jeopardy on that ground; all are struggling with mistakes of moral judgment, of moral perspective: lying and cheating; drug abuse and cynical meanness toward others; an early sexuality that eventuates in a persistent loneliness, in being, as Delia once described it, "alone, with nothing to hold on to, no one you'd ever want to hold on to." This aloneness is not only emotional; it is moral, too. We isolate ourselves from a community, its values, by what we do, then we pay the price within ourselves.

To cheat and lie is to be alone; to knock oneself out with drugs is to be alone; to sleep with men because they want to knock you up, you and a million others on a sexual assembly line that passes for a life, is to be alone, even as to behave like that to women is to be alone; and finally, to shoot to kill in order to survive and prevail (just barely, and so often only for a short time) is to be murderously alone. These boys and girls, these teenagers, the ones mentioned in the foregoing pages and all whose lives resemble theirs in certain important respects, crave a moral strength that is within them, that would enable for them a kind of survival that so far threatens to elude them: a survival of goodness, of respect for both themselves and others, as against the variations of moral thoughtlessness and heedlessness each of them, in ways, demonstrates.

What ought to be, might be done on their behalf? I'm all in favor of trying to be of emotional help, cognitive help: let us try to teach our children right and wrong in schools, through reading; and let us try to help those children who have been psychologically wounded in one or another way to be healed. But after the courses are over, and the therapeutic sessions end, there are those endless hours that await our children—and their questions ought to be ours: Where are the grown-ups in our life upon whom we can really rely, whom we can trust, whose values are believable, desirable, because they have been given us out of the shared experience, moment to moment, of a life together? Where is a moral companionship that has been experienced—a daily context for the expressed shoulds and should-nots, the injunctions that have been pressed on us? Perhaps the common heritage of all this chapter's children, it took me some time to realize, has to do with that loss in their lives: Elaine's parents struggle with the misdeeds of others, and there she is with her misdeeds—a cry for a moral as well as an emotional time with them, a cry as well for moral guidance and leadership from teachers willing to make clear exactly what they will and will not tolerate, and for what ethical reasons; Charlie and Marie and their buddies talk of parents in Barcelona and Rio de Janeiro, speak of brief vacations north of Nice, but have trouble being nice to themselves and others; and Delia lost her granny and saw the Bible being put in the casket. There is no question that absent parents, detached parents, haunt these narratives and the lives they portray—and the result is not only psychological pain but moral loss.

The conscience does not descend upon us from on high. We learn a convincing sense of right and wrong from parents who are themselves convinced as to what ought to be said and done and under what circumstances, as to what is intolerable, not at all permissible; parents who are more than convinced, actually—parents who are persuasively at the ready to impart to their children through words and daily example what they hope to hand on to them; mothers and fathers who eagerly embrace such a duty. Without such parents, a conscience is not likely to grow up strong and certain. When parents indicate to children their own feeble, contradictory, compromised moral life, no wonder their children find their own often truculent way to follow suit. I say "truculent" because a child can be quite angry at being denied the protection of a strong guiding conscience, at being left morally rudderless.

Had Elaine's parents wanted to sit down with her, to sit down, too, with her accusers, and take serious, saddened notice of what had happened as it connected with *their* lives, never mind the life of their daughter, they might well have started themselves and their daughter down a road different from the one all three of them took, that of hunkering down, circling the wagons. They even went on the offensive, criticized *them*, called their charges false, waved aside their bothersome accusations as a meddlesome annoyance to parents and child who believe themselves to be beyond the reach, properly, of such allegations. As for the rich ones at a private school and the poor ones on a ghetto street, in both places moral abandonment has a high cost: the anxiety that goes with a sense of purposelessness; sex and a pregnancy that try to conceal such an anxiety. Who will connect with those youths, so similar despite huge differences of class and race, connect with them in such a way as to offer them values to uphold and believe in, values that will give them control over impulse, over the woebegone bitterness, dejection, and futility that plague people who cannot rely on a deep-down guiding ethical compass? Can teachers in a fancy school, can welfare workers, all of them in loco parentis, offer this to the youths with whom they work? Maybe sometimes, somehow, but not easily, and against great odds. Meanwhile, all of us—morally imperiled youngsters, their kin and neighbors, their nation, its citizens, its judges and police—wonder worriedly and with good reason fear the worst. Meanwhile, too, many of us wonder how we might do better and spare ourselves and our children the kinds of moral impasse this chapter presents. Such times of moral jeopardy, of moral crisis, obviously don't come out of nowhere. They are in fact an aspect of a particular life's history, an aspect that begins with the very start of that life. And so we turn to a moral archaeology of childhood: how values are born and get shaped moment by moment over the all-important first two decades of life.

II

THE MORAL
ARCHAEOLOGY OF
CHILDHOOD

I

THE EARLY YEARS

A child is shaped at the very start of life by the values of certain adults. Even before a boy or girl is born, his or her parents are already giving expression to their values in a way that will matter for their son or daughter. A woman tries to think of others, not only of herself—and so she watches what she eats and drinks, stays away from cigarettes, establishes regular contact with an obstetrician, not only out of concern for herself but with her future child in mind. A man takes an interest in the woman who is carrying his child as well as hers, visits the doctor with her, offers her comfort, reassurance, affection as someone himself deeply involved in an important event: a pregnancy as two people thinking about, concerned for a third person soon to arrive. This attitude of caring, lived out daily, has direct consequences for that growing fetus: the earliest time in its life when the Golden Rule will decisively affect its life. To be sure, many women and men who are soon to become parents don't give explicit or continuing thought to the moral significance of their attentive concern for their future child and for one another as that child's much-needed parents. Rather, they are simply being sensible, natural; they are trying to do what is medically right, what everyone does or would do. Yet all too many women and men who are responsible for a pregnancy don't act responsibly, don't take what's best for the other, the child, into account and act accordingly. The result is an unborn child already at risk—there is a distinct possibility of physical harm from the mother's use of alcohol, drugs, or cigarettes or from disease, and a likelihood of psychological vulnerability that can arise when parents show from the start that they are unlikely to value the child enough to behave in a way that will make a difference down the line.

That word "value," the verb, not the noun—to repeat: It is one thing to lay claim to values, to espouse them, and quite another to try to live them out, enact them over time in connection with others. A soon-to-be mother who is giving careful thought to her pregnancy, who is trying to do the "right thing" is, of course, prompted by medical knowledge, but is also acting out of moral conviction: I value this child I am carrying, and I value myself as the one who will, soon enough, be its mother, and as a result I will keep a close (medical, physical, but again, by implication, moral) watch on how I live, what I do.

We know that infants who are grossly neglected and ignored turn apathetic and retreat from a world they have already learned to find indifferent, if not threatening. But other children, not so ominously put off, sent into recoil, have their own ways of responding to an environment that somehow, for whatever reasons, fails to reassure them sufficiently. They become irritable; they turn restless; they can be demanding, clinging, as if they have learned that they are in jeopardy and so must hold on for dear life, assert again and again their claim on the adult world, whose beneficence (or lack thereof) rather obviously determines their day-to-day fate.

A Moral Life That Precedes Language

The above-mentioned is the stuff of a psychology observable in nurseries and day-care centers, in the bedrooms and kitchens of apartment houses and private homes—some of us in pediatrics and child psychiatry talk of "infant behavior," of "emotional patterns that precede the development of language." So speaking, we caution ourselves, are careful to remember that a child of, say, six months isn't going to be able to tell what is on his or her mind. We are, therefore, surmising as observers rather than hearing from someone directly what is being thought and felt. Still, I go to day-care centers and on occasion hear certain babies, only a few months old, described as "temperamental," as "hard to please," as "possessive" or "bossy"—words meant to be taken not literally so much as evocatively. "This boy wants and wants [attention], especially when he sees one of the other children fed or played with, even though we've just spent a lot of time with him." A nursery school teacher addresses a doctor with an eight-month-old boy's psychological life as the topic, yet I feel that a moral matter is up for consideration. She clearly is challenged by the child, but not only as a caregiver, or a relatively detached observer (who is on her way to a master's degree in child development). I have been visiting the nursery for over a year, and this young woman had been a college student of mine, so she candidly tells of her thoughts, her concern that she is witness to an early kind of selfishness.

I demur, point out that we would do well to refrain from a rush to judgment here. She nods, understands my obvious assumption: character formation takes years, decades even, in all of us. But she reminds me of her long hours spent with these youngest of children, and insists on making this point: "I don't know how these kids will end up, but I do know that there are differences in them, in their behavior right now, and that we [she and others on the staff] call some of them 'good,' and 'nice,' and 'friendly.' Some are a big help to us, we say that because they don't clutch and scream, and they're pleasant with other kids, and some are (I hate to say it) *terrible*." She stops abruptly, and naturally, I want to hear more, explore the dimensions of that adjective as she has used it: "There are kids who won't let us get away with anything; I know they don't want us to leave them, they don't want to let go of us, and they are already—we call them 'whiners.'" Another pause, and I am again asking for clarification: "If they don't have us at their beck and call, they make life miserable for us and everyone else. I want to go buy earplugs!"

The Spoiled Child

In time I would learn about such children—from her and others in that first-rate nursery. I learned that the particular child she found most irritating and objectionable was not by any means an abandoned or overlooked child (my first guess). Rather, he was a much-adored infant whose mother was frank to say that she "doted" on him. Another word to investigate! I would eventually hear this from my nursery teacher colleague: "She can't stand it when the baby cries—even for a few seconds. They've got the baby sleeping with them [in a nearby crib], and they're at his mercy! He murmurs, and they run!" Whereupon I unwittingly shook my head—and she brought me up short: "So, you're ready to make up your mind, too!" I tried to hold out for more time, reiterated my worry lest we consign this infant, not yet a year old, to some psychological purgatory, if not inferno. Still, I had come to understand what this reasonably experienced nursery worker had to go through as she tried to care for a child who could already be assertively loudmouthed and quite competitive with others his age, whose needs, it seemed, drove him up the wall, hence his reflexive crying in response to the time others got with the adult world of providers. Once, upon leaving the nursery for my car, I found myself remembering a remark made by Milton J. E. Senn, the pediatrician who for many years headed the Yale Child Study Center. He was talking to a room full of doctors and nurses who worked with infants and preschool girls and boys. "Even at six months there are children who make life easy for us and children who make our life hard—and a few who drive us to distraction!"

He was quick, I add quickly, to admonish himself and his audience, lest we all become too hasty scolds of infants, who have yet to master the task of language acquisition. On the other hand, he did allow, upon questioning from experienced pediatricians, that even at an early age a baby can be "spoiled." That word, too, required an explanation or two, and in that regard we got a long disquisition of sorts, from which I wrote down this fragment: "If you give a baby everything, and never resist its demands, you are teaching it never to expect a refusal—and I'm afraid that is not a good preparation for life." He was being wry, understated, but we all laughed—a wave of agreement that expressed, I thought at the time, our nervous awareness that even in the first weeks of life an infant can be on its way to a moral crossroad (and beyond); can be a reasonably obliging, cooperative person or a cranky, petulant one who confronts adults constantly with its requirements (and their limitations).

Parents may have their own way of knowing what some of us who work with children learn only slowly, and sometimes with fearful reluctance. As I have already indicated, I hesitated a long time to sort out infants by recourse to words of obvious moral significance. Let others refer to "good" babies or "difficult" ones, or "impossible" ones (meaning "bad" ones). Let others say that this infant was a "joy" and that one an "awful pain to have around." If I was going to make distinctions, I would render them in the cool, dispassionate (yes, "value-free") language of psychiatry and psychoanalysis: some children are already anxious or fearful, or have been treated well, and so are quite "normal" or unthwarted. Only when I started talking weekly with a group of young mothers and heard them talk about their babies, express their sense of what they hoped for them, speak about how they took care of them, and with what purposes and expectations in mind, did I begin to realize (pure common sense!) that already these infants were experiencing quite distinct and, often, quite different worlds.

In pediatrics and child psychiatry, we often refer to the "mother-infant symbiosis" of those early months, the utter intimacy or connectedness that takes place, of a kind that has enormous medical and psychological consequences. Without saying so directly, the seven mothers with whom I met indicated that there is a moral side to their daily intense involvement with their infant sons and daughters—and why wouldn't there be, one eventually begins to realize: here are women bringing so very much of themselves (and, too, of their husbands) to the babies they look after, worry about, try to do justice by, hold continually in their thoughts and prayers as well as their arms.

"I'm trying to give my son everything now," one mother said. Her reason: "Later on, he'll have plenty of frustrations." But another disagreed: "You have to prepare your child, even now, for the world. I talk to her, even though she doesn't understand the words. I say 'Look, you can't have everything all at once; you've got to have patience.' I have to let her know that there are other people—that she's not the only one." A third mother tries to reconcile those two points of view, and in doing so makes clear their dissimilarity: "I try to be everything to my girl, I do. But a lot of the time I just can't be—because I love another daughter, and there's my husband, and I try to have a little life for myself, hard as that is. I feel bad at times. My baby wants me, wants me, and I have to make her wait. Other times, I'm with her in body, but I'll admit, my mind is somewhere else. Maybe she picks it up—she'll be fretful. Or maybe I'm making a mountain out of a molehill, and she's fretful because she's fretful and not because I miss my job [as a lawyer], and am thinking of it while I nurse her! I do know that I try to give her a lot, but I've learned to draw the line, too: you can spoil an infant, even an infant!"

Learning from Mistakes

Already these women have learned to think of their quite young children, none over a year old, as even then on the way to adulthood, and so in need of being strengthened or disciplined, protected or taught to accommodate themselves to the needs of others. The word "spoiled" rather quickly became a topic of discussion, one that edged them all closer to a broader philosophical or moral discourse. I am soon hearing a vigorous, passionate discussion of what, if anything, it means to spoil a baby of six or eight months. Two mothers deny the very possibility, claiming for infants needs that require fulfillment, and that is that. Two others are convinced that infants can indeed be spoiled, and both, as it turns out, speak from personal knowledge. Each claims to have spoiled her first child and learned from her mistakes.

The more forthcoming of the two puts the matter this way: "I gave my son everything. He'd whisper and I'd come running. Now [at four] it's become a part of his personality, I believe—what I did. He's that 'I snap my finger and you better pay attention' type of person. I know it doesn't sound so good, but to tell you the truth, I guess it'll stand him in good stead: that's the kind of world that's out there and you have to be ready for it—you either expect the world to pay attention to you, and make it [do so], or you're left behind. My husband keeps saying so—and I guess he's convinced me; but I'll have to admit something: I don't think like that, and I don't want my baby girl to be like that, so I'm different with her."

She stops, and in a moment's time everyone wants her to spell out the differences in the way she has brought up her two children, so that we can figure out whether the qualities of character she has in mind as already an aspect of her son's life and (she hopes) a future part of her daughter's life can really be attributed, at least in part, to what has happened to those offspring during the first months of life with her. She tells us that she doesn't rush to her baby daughter's side as readily as was the case with her son, that she thereby "gives her credit" for a budding capacity, even in the first year of life, to learn to be patient, to develop a modicum of self-control. A skeptic says no, "It's too early"—because of the extremely limited susceptibility of a preverbal child to the moral and cultural influences a family explicitly or by implication eventually brings to bear on a child. She states her objection in this manner: "I'm sure our children are treated differently by each one of us, and I'm sure it has an effect, but I think all that happens later. The first few months is too early, way too early for infants to know what's going on. So long as they're fed and kept clean and comfortable, cozy—they're in their own world. My husband [a biologist] says the brain is still developing in the first year of life."

Others disagreed, called upon cultural anthropology, the various ways children are held, fed, clothed, and the degrees of leeway allowed them to crawl, to lie in a relatively confined or closed space, to be fed on demand or by schedule, to have full and close access to the mother, or to be kept a substantial bodily distance from her, and of course, to be breast-fed or fed from a bottle.

Signals from Day One

"I think we start sending signals to our kids from day one" was the remark at the end of that somewhat heated conversation from a quiet woman who hadn't hitherto said much to us. We wondered about those signals, and she said she was speaking only for herself—but they are "conscious signals," and by that she meant this: "I'm trying to tell my boy from the start that I want him to feel wanted, and feel free to grow, but I don't want him to think that he's so high and mighty that he can run me and run his father—run us! You let a child go down that road and you're going to have a kid who thinks he's a big deal, a real big deal, and I'd like my kid to be thinking of others, not only himself. I say that, I say that to myself after I've gone back to bed, after feeding him and burping him: O.K., O.K., you've had plenty, all you need, you've got to learn that the world doesn't *totally* revolve around you. You've got to learn that there are others, and they have to live, just as you do, and so you just cry a little and go to sleep. If I come running all the time, that's the start of something: a big ego. When I came home with the baby, I heard my sister say that you build their character right away, from the start.

"You want to hear something, a story? Her son, Don, had a great appetite right from the beginning. She bottle-fed him. She had trouble with breast-feeding—not enough milk. Well, they're going along fine—six months, seven months, and you know what? He'd be sitting in the bassinet or the high chair, and he'd gulp down that milk, and as he got bigger, and had a little more control, he started throwing the bottle away, throwing it on the floor. He knew what he was doing, he heard the 'bang', the 'thump', and he was obviously pleased with himself. A neighbor told my sister: 'He's just flexing his muscles, so let him do it. Be glad he's like that.' But Maisie said no, no. She said she wasn't going to let her kid get the idea that he could behave like that: toss something away when he was through with it and see other people come running to clean up the mess he'd made! You know what she did? She didn't shout or get real tough with him; she just made sure she was *there*, right there, her hand ready, as the baby took his last bit of milk, and she took the bottle from him while talking to him, or cleaning his face. In a while the baby lost interest [in throwing the bottle down]. She tested him a few times by not being so quick to ease the bottle away. Now, to my mind, my sister had started teaching her son right versus wrong—how he should behave, and what he shouldn't do, as early as it was, as young as the boy was."

We were all more than a little silenced by that story—its concreteness, its interesting, low-key, almost palpable drama, its lesson of gentleness yet firmness, its overall canniness got to us and, not least, its success: fewer impulsive acts, and a toehold for the child on a ladder that a future moral child will have to climb. Maisie was no moral propagandist, yet she seemed to know in her bones (rather than abstractly, in accordance with some ideology) that it did neither her nor her son any good for him to be able to keep tossing down that bottle. She also knew that this boy was too young for any kind of conversation. Nor did she wish to call upon fear and intimidation. Casually, yet ever so intentionally, she was able to be *there*—a mother quick to help her baby finish his bottle, but a mother also determined to help both herself and her son avoid what she feared might become a "bad habit." When one of the mothers asked for a clarification of that phrase, we all heard this reply: "Maisie couldn't prove to you what was going on in *his* mind, her son's. She knew that. But she knew what was going on in *hers*: she was being turned into a bit of a fool by the child, an obedient servant who's ready to keep picking up after him. If she got used to that, she'd be more inclined a few years down the line to let him treat her like that again, and again. She thought to herself: 'Maisie, stop this right now, it's never too early to start teaching your child right from wrong.' My mom told Maisie and me that when we were in high school. Maisie said she'd forgotten those words, actually, until they came back to her one morning, suddenly. She heard the *thump* of that bottle, and she swears she thought she saw a gleam in her boy's eyes: he was getting a kick out of calling her over and seeing her bend down and reach for that bottle. All right, she told herself, she'd let this happen a little bit, but it didn't take long for the baby to decide that he had a real deal going, and it was then that she recalled what my mom used to say, and she just told herself: here you are, this is the start of it, my son's education in what's right and what's wrong."

With those words Maisie's sister won over most of her fellow mothers, save one, who worried about why the baby had been so intent on hurling his bottle downward in the first place. I have to admit that I was also curious in that regard. The theories of Melanie Klein, the English child psychoanalyst, kept coming to my mind. She was convinced that infants of four or six or eight months are by no means too young for a wide range of psychological attitudes and feelings: anger, rage, greed, depression, a profound skepticism she dared call paranoia, not to mention, of course, a possessive passion directed at their mothers. The child analysts in this country who supervised my training had not been at all taken with Klein's theories, and Anna Freud had been similarly hesitant to embrace them without serious reservations. I remembered a conversation with her I'd taped in 1970, twenty years before this meeting with young mothers, even as I heard them struggling to learn what takes place in an infant's mind: "How can we ever really be sure what a baby is thinking or feeling? We make surmises—we watch and we watch, and after a while we take a chance! We guess! We say the baby seems cheerful, or the baby seems lethargic, or the baby seems irritable or cranky or very unhappy or upset, quite upset. All those descriptions are our conclusions based on our observations. When a baby gets older and can talk, can draw pictures, we can learn directly from the boy or the girl what is directly on his mind, what she is struggling with. But in those first months the baby's behavior is ours to describe, not its to affirm or confirm. One thing is certain, though—we can learn a lot about what babies cause their mothers to think is going on in them by listening to their mothers, and the same holds for us [child analysts]. We, too, are inspired by babies to stake out [psychological] claims for them!"

Yet the woman whose child had taken to throwing bottles was distinctly more modest than the child analysts whose "claims" Miss Freud had with some bemusement (maybe doubtfulness) been mentioning and examining. This mother had declared that she was less interested in plumbing her son's emotional depths than in responding to his deeds. Moreover, she was thoughtful and self-confident enough to decide that the boy wasn't in any discernible difficulty—wasn't throwing his bottle at her, wasn't in a fit of temper or pique, or so it seemed, at least, as he reached for the object, lifted it, tossed it. For her the question of moral education had arisen. She was smart enough to move in her mind from a boy who teased his mother, so she saw it, to an older child who had a similarly cavalier attitude toward his parents and others in authority. Her use of the word "cavalier," told us by her sister, indicated her willingness to make a judgment, and her use of the phrase "in authority" indicated a willingness to stand at the plate, to make assumptions, assume responsibility. In an interesting, reflective afterthought that prompted all of us to make a connection of sorts between modern technology and child rearing, she offered this speculation, courtesy of her sister: "I wonder how I would have behaved if we didn't have plastic bottles, unbreakable ones! What if the bottle was made of glass, like they used to be, and I heard a crash on the floor, and had to clean up a mess of shards! I might have screamed and shouted *no* instead of being so tactful. After he'd thrown the bottle a few times, I thought that to myself. All these improvements in our quality of life— maybe they help some of us be a little better at mothering."

Language and Moral Introspection: Yes and No

Soon enough, of course, the babies whose actions those women were describing would be starting to talk, entering a whole new life. In a sense language defines us—we are the creature of words, a gift to us of our genes, our neurophysiological capability. Once a child begins to use words, he or she can be reached by the rest of us in an altogether new way, and we by the child. But if the glue of language binds us, it also puts demands upon us: now we can really try to understand what is happening in another's head; now the child throwing the bottle can be told no and can also be asked why. Moreover, a mother can explain her reasons for saying no. With language, then, comes possibilities, opportunities, responsibilities, burdens—comes the life we know as talking, interpreting, conceptualizing creatures, creatures who can also be given to moral introspection.

As parents discover rather quickly, "yes" and "no" certainly figure prominently among the first words their very young children start using at the end of the first year of life and the beginning of the second. Even as babies learn to address their mothers and fathers, brothers and sisters, and grandparents by name, they also learn about the minds of these other people, what they welcome and what they don't much like, or what they won't at all tolerate.

I started meeting with the mothers mentioned above about a month after four of them had given birth, and from two to three months after three of them had done so. A year after we started they were all delighted to hear the growing vocabulary of their offspring, yet also were troubled, each in a different way, by those two words yes and no, especially the latter. The mother who had adroitly thwarted her southpaw bottle-flinging son came to meet with us periodically as a guest so we could talk directly with her. By then she had become nostalgic for the good old days, when a plastic milk bottle was her greatest nemesis: "I am so tired of hearing that word 'no' come out of my mouth," she told us at one of our biweekly Monday evening meetings, held in a lounge at a local hospital. She did not need to go into any explanation, and she knew that to be the case, but she obviously wanted to discuss her effort, as she kept putting it, to be "a thoughtful mother." By then the others, half pleased to hear her ideas and speculations, half taken with her moral energy, but also made nervous by a conscientiousness that prompted in them a troublesome self-consciousness, were quite accustomed to her reflective ways, even anxious to egg her on, despite their often anticipated disagreement.

When that remark about "no" came from her, the mother sitting to her left spoke right up: "Maybe you're overdoing it." Another mother joined in: "It's hard to find the right balance." The mother who had provoked those two reactions lowered her head, seemed lost in thought. One of the four women who had so far said nothing continued to be silent but shook her head rather noticeably several times. Another hitherto silent mother picked up on that signal and said this: "It takes a lot of the fun out of being a mother, having to be so negative with a child who is only a year and some months old." Nods of agreement from everyone, except the mother who had weathered the bottle-throwing crisis and now seemed unusually quiet, even withdrawn. For a few more moments the others shared their frustrations and their exhaustion. Then she came alive: "I'd be worrying, if I didn't have to say no to my child over and over these days! I'd be ignoring him; I'd be too preoccupied with myself to be paying enough attention to him! I hate the word 'no' sometimes, but it's all we've got sometimes! When you say 'no' to your kid you're teaching him the meaning of the word 'yes'!"

She stopped abruptly, as if she herself had to take that comment in, especially the last sentence. The others had begun shaking their heads in obvious exasperation: the visiting philosopher off on another of her tangents! A chorus of no's, finally, to her interestingly put affirmation of "no." She was quick to reply: "What does 'yes' mean if there is no 'no'? I tell my boy: this you mustn't do; you mustn't. He searches my face, my eyes—he knows they're the windows of the soul. That's what my mom told us. He can tell: she means it; I'd better pay attention. I always link 'no' to 'yes,' though. When I tell him he mustn't do this, I present him with an alternative. I invite him to do something else, so he isn't caught there, holding the bag! 'No,' I'll say—and I use 'we.' I say, 'We're not going to do that, we're not, but we'll do *this*, we'll try *this*, it'll be fun,' and then we're off! That's what I mean—'no' leads to 'yes.' If you're left with 'no,' if your child has been taught no, no, no, then that's—that's a no-no in my book!"

Early Cooperation

She smiles. She is obviously pleased with herself. On one mother's face, however, I can see a glower of disapproval, impatience. She is shaking her head—her "no" to that "no-no." She needs no prodding from me, it turns out (I thought for a second I'd have to encourage her, usually taciturn, to speak). She directs her look right at the woman who has given yet another of her self-assured and compelling presentations, then with barely concealed annoyance, lets her have it: "Some of us don't have time to turn each moment with our kids into a seminar! I'm standing at the stove, I'm late with supper, my daughter has worn me down with her activity, her endless activity, and all I want is for her to be still and eat her supper, while I cook ours, my husband's and mine. But no, she's determined to push all the buttons. Oh, I know she doesn't think that way! She's just being a normal kid of a year and a half. Well, I'm just being a normal, exhausted working mother—and I want some *cooperation*! That's what I say. My daughter might not be able to give you the dictionary definition of that word, but she knows what it means: it means, Stop what you're doing! It means, Cut it out! It means, You can't push me one millimeter further! It means, N-O: No! When she hears me say "Cooperate" she stops talking and stops moving. She goes to the table and sits. If I've got time, I give her something to nibble on, or I do like you say: I stop my own life and try to help her with hers. But lots of times, she sits and waits for me, and I get to her when I can, and not before!"

On Spanking

These mothers were struggling at times with their babies, with themselves, and with one another in that room. Often they were about to say something, then pulled back and sat in firm silence. When I occasionally prodded, I once in a while got nowhere, once in a while heard an outpouring, often confessional in nature. Several mothers were frank to talk about the spankings they gave to their children, the final 'no,' as it were, and also frank to express their anger at the notion that spanking is a bad thing to do. What did I think? I hesitate, hem and haw. What did I do? Did I ever spank my children? No. Did my wife? No. I feel more than a bit smug with those terse answers—the big-shot expert who never, ever loses his cool, who knows the right answer and solution and approach for any problem. I hasten to go into a long remembrance, tell of our frustrations and impasses as parents; tell of times when we tried hard to be both firm and understanding with our young children, and when we became confused, upset, angry. Often we did favor diversion: a flat-out no, followed by an explanation of why, followed by an effort to change the subject, "move on," as my wife often put it. Later, while putting the children to bed, reading with them, talking with them, we might briefly (or not so briefly) review the particular troublesome incident that had taken place earlier, find an agreement that distance on a subject can sometimes provide. Several mothers, however, were quick and frank to tell me that they sometimes were overwhelmed by the busy-ness of their lives. A quick spank "dissolved tension," let the baby know that a mother's "no" meant exactly that. What did I think about this way of saying no to a child? I try to steer my way around the question, but finally blurt out the obvious: the issue is manner, context—the way a particular mother gets on most sensibly, effectively with a particular child.

Time—and Plenty of It

But really, I keep thinking to myself, rules and laws and strategies and techniques may be more appealing in a room like this where I sit, or on a book's page, than they are in the midst of a lived life, the child's and the parent's. As I respond to the requests of those women for advice and for the hard facts of my life, my wife's life, as parents (perhaps, thereby, to provide a measure of the worth of my remarks), I find myself realizing that the best moments we had as disciplinarians, Jane and I, were those when we had plenty of time to handle the difficulty, the challenge, plenty of time to give of ourselves to our children, to make clear our reasons, to let them know why we objected to something and why we weren't of two minds on the matter, and so wouldn't budge. (All easy to write, now, but a tough act, sometimes, to uphold, to carry through to satisfactory completion.) Of course, *of course*, I say to myself, a parent needs credibility with a child, even an infant, or maybe especially an infant. The more satisfactory, affectionate, kindly time we can put in with a son or a daughter who is so utterly dependent at, say, a year or two, upon the adult world, for food, for clothing, for protection, and yes, for guidance, the better.

But several women in that room had memories of the long hours they gave to work, the scarce time available for their babies. Phrases such as "quality time" struck them as hollow, even as they reached for some way to give their young children just that—the best they as parents had in the limited amount of minutes and hours available for them all to be together. One mother tells what usually works for her—a firm no, spoken only after she has put her arm around the child, or taken hold of her hand. Another mother apologetically, shamefacedly, lets us know that when she cries, her son stops in his tracks, takes notice, obeys. She feels "like an actress" calling up those tears again, yet they do express the truth of her back-to-the-wall sense of where things stand. Is she a phony? When will her son catch on? A woman sitting beside her says she wishes she could cry—and cry and cry. Instead, she screams, and with enough passion and noise to the scream that the girl of sixteen months "sure takes notice." Another mother, more explicitly of a psychological turn of mind than the others, talks of rewarding her children with praise as a means of disciplining them, selecting their "strong points" for approval, even applause.

But what about lapses, misdemeanors, missteps, willful and harmful disobedience on the part of a son or daughter? Even a child of a year and a half, barely secure as a walker, on the way only then to being a talker, an understanding listener, can become mischievous, can pull at a tablecloth and thereby break a dish; can poke his or her finger into a dog's or cat's eye or nose or ears; can make a mess in a highchair, and laugh and laugh! Is there a best way to respond at such times? A right way?—and, too, a wrong way? Am I being a coward and ignorant, am I whistling Dixie naïvely, with self-serving blandness, when I try to avoid offering unequivocal solutions for such childhood moments? I listen, I nod, I frown and worry, I remember and relate; I recall mistakes and blunders, wish for another chance here, wish I'd done something differently there. I keep coming back, as I speak with these mothers, to the conviction that somehow, in our *various* ways, all parents had best realize that *yes* and *no* really matter to children; that once they have learned the meaning of those two words they have really, quite definitively, begun their moral education, their journey as human beings capable, ever so tentatively and shakily, for starters, of choice—the countless times of either/or that in their accumulation make for our moral life. But as for the specifics of how to say (and implement) a yes, a no, approval and disapproval—I remind them of the range of their responses: different, yet all worthy of consideration.

As I have listened to these well-to-do, well-educated suburban mothers earnestly struggle with what they want for their children, struggle as to how they might best get them to behave (and why), I have often felt my mind, in its thoughts (kept to myself and expressed, both), summoning the contemporary pieties, if not banalities, that so many of us of such a background have learned to accept as truth. None of these women claim any *interest* in spanking their children, though, again, several bravely candid souls admit to doing so—even as we know that the majority of Americans in poll after poll proclaim the virtue of at least some form of corporeal punishment as a helpful means of teaching their young ones (even their preverbal young ones) how to "behave," how to do "right," abstain from "wrong." In contrast, these mothers (and fathers; sometimes three fathers joined us) kept talking about "love" and "care" as instruments of early moral guidance. If only we keep close tabs on our children, many asserted, give them all they need, then they will quickly and eagerly learn to pay attention to our "suggestions," or "recommendations." "I like to think of discipline as a form of education," one mother explained, and she amplified her thoughts on the subject in this way: "If you show your child attention and concern, if you teach her that you're really 'there' for her, and you want the best for her, always, she'll learn to respond—she'll want to take your advice and follow your lead, because she's connected to you real solidly."

Drawing a Line in the Sand

Nods of approval began even as she was talking. Across the room, however, one mother appeared uneasy. She shifted her weight from one side of her chair to the other, and crossed and uncrossed her legs. Finally, frowning, she began to talk, with a tremor in her voice. "I love my daughter and I show it to her all the time—well, as often as I can. But there are times when she really *misbehaves*. I guess some of you might say she doesn't misbehave—she just innocently does something that she hasn't learned, yet, is wrong to do. But I disagree, I've seen my daughter do wrong and know it." She stops for air and, maybe, for courage—and too, I speculate, to test the waters: How far along this line dare I venture? Silence rules: no movement, even of our bodies; there is no reaching for coffee or cookies, and all eyes are concentrated on her. "You see," she resumes—and then a long sigh, followed by an oration of sorts: "Sometimes, I'm trying to say, kids are mischievous— all right, out of ignorance, or because we haven't always given them the right signals, or because they're human beings, even when they're eleven months old, or thirteen months, or sixteen months: they want to peek and push, try this out and see what happens here or there, and if something breaks, or they get hurt, that's just too bad, but how were they to know that would happen, and anyway, you grown-ups are so *nervous* (what's your problem!). Then, there are times when my little girl—I just know it—she's not being 'difficult' and she's not in 'psychological trouble.' She's just letting me know that she's a person too, she's not a pushover for me, and she's ready, even, to stand up to me. I know, you'll say there's something wrong here—I'm doing something wrong. But I don't feel that, believe that. I think there are times my little girl is being *willful*, needs for me to—I guess to understand that, I agree, but sometimes, for her sake and my sake (for my sanity's sake!) I've got to be willful *back*! She's headed in some direction that would get her in trouble, get her in trouble with me, so I've got to say *no*, a big, loud *no*, a *no* that will bring her *to* (all right, scare her plenty), so she'll obey, right away. Isn't that what happens? Don't you have to stand up sometimes, and let your kids know that; know that *no way* is something going to happen, because you could get killed going into the busy street, with all its traffic, or you could hurt someone, sticking that in their face, or spilling that on them, so here I am, your mother, and I'm going to be firm as can be on that score, and if you don't like what I've done (holding you back, or saying *no*, and grabbing you, or taking something away from you), then that's too bad, and you can cry and cry, and I'll be upset, too, but I won't give in, because I believe I'm right, and I sure want you to believe it, too—you've just *got* to, and I'll say it, if worse comes to worse, and the only way you'll 'get it' is by being given a whack or two, then so it goes, because there are times when you have to draw a line in the sand, and the baby has to know that's *it*, that's what you mean!"

Dogs and Cats as Teachers

We had edged toward something important. How to start teaching a quite young child, who hasn't really acquired a conversational capacity with language, how to help that child distinguish between right and wrong, good and bad, and do so in a way that works, is not harmful to the boy or girl in question? In a sense, too, we were discussing not only the origins of a moral sensibility in a child, but the basis of morality. The issue, after all, is not only *behavioral,* how to get children to behave themselves—a fiercely threatening punitiveness can surely accomplish that, at least for a while, and, very important, at a price. The issue is how to persuade a child to adhere to certain behavioral and moral principles, and again, to do so in a way that will convince the child, effectively so, but not in such a way that a victory is a defeat in the long run.

For instance, to protect a puppy being teased by a child by paddling that child hard and long so that he or she is scared badly may secure a reprieve for the animal, but at a high cost, as one of the mothers there surely knew when she confided to me a childhood memory still quite clear in her mind. "We had a next-door neighbor, and he had a dog, and my friend Ricky, he was afraid of the dog, his own father's dog. He told me to be careful because the dog would bite, and once it got going, it would never stop, and you could get 'eaten up alive.' I remember him saying that [using the expression over and over]. The dog was a golden retriever, the 'sweetest thing,' my mother kept telling us. 'That dog wouldn't hurt a flea,' she'd say. I'd tell her what Ricky said, and *she'd* say that he was wrong. But once, she decided to explain it all to me, why Ricky was talking that way. She'd found out from Ricky's mother! The boy had played with the dog, and he must have pulled his hair or something, the way little children sometimes do. The father saw this and went wild. He hit that kid and screamed at him, and the dog got to barking—probably at the father! Anyway, I don't know the whole story, and what Ricky's mother said, and I could tell she was leaving out a lot. She let me know, though, that the husband had given the son 'quite a licking,' and the boy never did bother with that dog again. He stayed clear of it—he got to be scared of it. Ricky's mother was sad about it all. She said her husband has a terrible temper sometimes, and that was one of those times."

A not rare story of rage expressed in the course of a family's life: a father wanting to protect his dog, teach his son control, ended up hitting him and shouting at him in such a way that the little boy, not yet two years old, became frightened thereafter of a thoroughly appealing and unthreatening dog, whose good nature he could no longer appreciate. Now that dog had become something else in the boy's mind, a constant reminder of his father's violent, impulsive behavior. Discipline in the supposed name of good—that a child learn to respect a family's dog, be considerate of it—had turned into an episode with lasting psychological consequences. So often phobias, in any of us, tell of our capacity to express what ails or hurts or worries us by indirection. This boy's fear of his family's dog and, in time, all dogs in the neighborhood spoke of his hesitation to acknowledge his constant terror that his father would lose his temper yet again.

Needless to say, many of us, seeing a child playing with a dog, then getting a bit too frisky or assertive or presumptuous with the animal, taking advantage of it, really, even as the dog tries hard to be patient and forbearing, will want to intervene, as we ought to do—break the entanglement, if not confrontation, rescue both the dog and the young child. After that is done, the matter of moral education remains: how to teach a boy or girl of, say, a year or a year and a few months that there are important limits to uphold; that a dog is a fellow creature, alive and part of the family, and entitled to continuing respect; that there are times when we have to hear the word "no" within ourselves, not only respond to the sound when it's sent one's way by a parent. Again, each of us will have a way to deal with such a situation—though, surely, some ways work better *and* are better than others.

When the mother told us the story about Ricky and the dog and the father, another mother, with some embarrassment, reported a story out of her own family's history. Her sister had a daughter who also for a while became "aggressive" toward a family pet, a cat. The cat knew how to take care of itself, more or less—kept a safe distance from the child, who at times unsuccessfully chased it around the house. The mother eventually tired of this and took her daughter aside: she must stop behaving so threateningly toward the cat. The little girl listened, and laughed, but obviously failed to show the kind of moral awareness and regret that the mother had hoped to witness, whereupon she grabbed her daughter and pinched her and pulled her hair, in imitation of the behavior that the little girl was demonstrating toward the cat. The girl became quite upset, obviously, and cried and cried. The mother tried to find the cat so they all could "make up," but the girl cried even more and became "hysterical" as they searched the house for the hiding animal. When the cat did reappear (cats have a way of being masters and makers of their own fate) the mother realized that she ought not to force this issue anymore. From that time on, the cat was the *mother's* cat, the little girl kept on saying, and she kept her considerable distance from the animal. She was not quite as frightened of that cat as Ricky was of his family's dog and, by extension, of all dogs; but her mother knew and confessed this to her sister: that somehow she had not done the best job resolving this family difficulty.

In no time, as that story's telling ends, I am asked what I'd have done, how I'd handle a child who is making life unpleasant for a family pet— that is, a child who needs to learn self-control and compassion and empathy. I tried to be as honestly forthcoming as I knew how, told them of the ways my wife and I handled such times with our own children; told how we'd taken notice of the situation (as Ricky's father did, as the girl's mother did) and intervened in order to protect the animal, our dog

Grady, and how we'd taken the child aside, my wife, Jane, with our son
Bobby, she and I together with our sons Danny and Mike, in order to
say a firm no but also to give a brief, explanatory speech: this dog is part
of our family, is quite friendly to us, and deserves a similar attitude from
us. We knew at the time that the boy whom we were addressing may
not have grasped our every word or intended meaning, but he did see
quite clearly that we were upset, that we were worried about the dog
and, of course, about him, our son; that we were serious, that we meant
business, as the expression goes, and we were going to make this moment stick fast in the boy's mind, and in our own. A *no* was clearly
stated, after a wrongdoing (the harassment of the animal, however innocent its nature—to give the boy the benefit of the doubt!), and then
a talk was initiated.

I recalled saying that "we don't do this, we *don't*." I recalled speaking
an informal hymn of praise to our dog, his loyalty and friendliness
(many licks of affection given to those children, to us!). I recalled going
to the dog and patting it, gently but warmly. I recalled my wife taking
our son to the dog, encouraging him to follow our lead, to pat the dog
after he'd seen her do so. I recalled a time when one of the boys hadn't
paid heed, when later on he began directing another bout of harassment toward our dog, eliciting a fierce burst of anger from me, my fist
hard upon the kitchen table, a bellowed *no*, and a child's withdrawal to
the next room, and only thereafter, our "make-up" explanatory conversation. When such episodes were over I also recalled realizing that our
dog in his own way was a teacher, one who had helped all of us come
to terms with the meaning of *understanding*: to put oneself in another's
shoes, to see and feel things as he, she, or it does. We need to keep
doing so, again and again over this life.

So it goes all the time, naturally, for us parents; in the first months of
life we have to set limits for our children and, yes, for ourselves. If we
don't demand of ourselves that we say no as well as yes, that we interfere and intervene as well as let things happen or ignore them, then we
are acting as teachers, all right, but we are offering lessons on the nature of indifference, of inattention or unconcern or apathy, and ultimately, lessons that make for moral confusion. Babies require feeding,

but even that most basic of needs ought be offered with regard for the mother's life as well as the infant's, lest the latter learn right off that anything is available on demand. Parents or caregivers need sleep, may have other children to tend, may well have necessary obligations to fulfill, work to do, and so from the start of life babies must learn, even in the hospital, right after birth, before they go home, that some kind of schedule exists, that instant gratification is by no means part of a life's expectable routine. Parents learn to heed the needs and demands of their babies, but they also ought to stand up, sensitively but with growing confidence, for their own limits, their various responsibilities and burdens as they give shape to what they have to offer their children, and when. All of that need not usually turn into a confrontation, a tug-of-war, a trauma visited on a baby and experienced as guilt by a parent—but can be, rather, an informal accommodation of parent to child and also of child to parent. If it be only the former, there may well be consequences, moral as well as psychological, as one of my supervisors who had been a pediatrician and then took training in child psychiatry reminded several of us in a memorable comment: "In those early months of life the mother learns so much, especially if she is a first-time mother, but so does the baby. It's give and take on both sides. If not, if it's all give on the mother's side and all take on the child's, then we doctors may be witnesses to the earliest roots of self-absorption, of selfishness, seeing a baby who is not getting to know "no," that early "no" that takes the form of *some* kind of routine or schedule, *some* kind of structure to life, *some* kind of regulation of how things are to go, to be done: sleep, feeding, dressing, washing, and cleaning."

The Child as Moral Listener

In the second and third years of life, with the arrival of language, with increased muscular control, the possibilities for an explicit moral education grow exponentially. A child now talks, so what he or she hears can take on substantial significance. All the time, often quite unselfconsciously, parents are giving their two-year-old children moral guidance—suggestions, instructions, explanations: here is how we do *this*, *there* is where we go or don't go, now is the time to try *that*, and as for what you just did, let it never happen again, so we hope, we insist. Now the child can comprehend the lessons sent his or her way, has become an increasingly knowing listener. Now parents address their children, and expect the spoken message to sink in, so that gradually the little ones will know how to care for themselves and, not least, how to clean themselves up. All of that is frequently regarded as part of child rearing, is discussed these days as an aspect of child development—and of course books galore are out there to help us become ever so aware of these matters. Yet we pay less attention to the moral implications of those psychological events of early (preschool) childhood than to the practical; less attention to the child as a moral listener. By "we" I mean not only we who are parents, trying to understand our babies and our youngsters not yet off to kindergarten, but we who are the so-called experts, the psychiatrists and pediatricians and psychologists and social workers who work with children and their families.

In psychoanalysis, for instance, there has been talk for over a half a century of the stages through which young children go, to the point that words such as "oral," "anal," and "genital" get connected by many outside hospitals and clinics to the lives of our sons and daughters. We are alert to the intensity of experience that goes with a young child's feeding life, his or her struggle to become free of diapers, and the attachments our offspring make, their passionate interest in us, their mothers and fathers, and in others who figure in their lives. Still, as I began to indicate above, those stages are not characterized only by emotional struggles. A child can be fed in a way that he or she can expect all she wants and needs, but then there is a necessary pause, a respite for both baby and parent. A child can be deprived of what is his or her due. And finally, a child may be offered food whenever the impulse arises—a murmur, let alone a cry, and there it is, a breast, bottle, spoon.

Here, as elsewhere in life, experience shapes character. The character of someone who has been essentially well nurtured but who has also learned that the world isn't going to be *there*, in continual attendance all the livelong day, that there are inevitably moments of frustration, that appetites have to be curbed as well as satisfied, differs from the character of someone who has been denied too much that is needed and wanted, to the point that the child begins to expect less and less, becomes irritable, quite literally unfulfilled, which is a setup for anger, despair, moodiness, suspiciousness—qualities of mind obviously set in motion by chronic disappointment at the hands of others. Then there is the character of someone who has been given and given to, who has never had to deal with the reality of the slightest refusal, and who therefore has been helped to take a giant step toward self-importance, egoism, grandiosity, the swagger of someone not just plentifully given to but on whom the world has doted ceaselessly, so that impulse rules and frustration tolerance has had no chance to develop. These broad descriptions apply in the abstract. Of course we all as parents know moments when we are quite responsibly generous with our children; are for one reason or another quite unwilling or unable to meet their requirements or their wishes; or are generous to a fault, hence the word "spoiled" on the lips of others or whispered self-critically to ourselves. The issue is degree, or general tendency: how we *usually* act with our children.

It is a similar case with children being taught to spring themselves free of that diaper, for a couple of years a baby's constant companion. What nowadays is called "toilet training" is a challenge for both parent and child, as all know who have tried to help a toddler recognize the impulse to urinate or defecate, and then do something, assume a certain authority over its body. Here too we can manage to do reasonably well by our children, so that they can say good-bye with growing confidence to a major aspect of infancy, the helplessness of sorts that goes with the need for a diaper. Or we can veer in one of two directions: hover over the child too early in life, coaxing and urging and, not rarely, insisting, shouting, even slapping around someone who is scarcely if at all practiced at speaking full sentences; or keep too much distance too long, so that the babies in question learn that the world, for whatever reasons, has no concrete interest in enabling them to stand on their own and gain control of themselves. These days we are correctly interested in the psychology of this childhood hurdle, in the child's emotional response to it and the parent's emotional reasons for behaving like *this* or *that*. No question: relaxed, easygoing, yet determined parents are a big help to their children in this early negotiation with the sanitary aspects of civilization, even as uptight parents can all too predictably turn out uptight children, and parents who are neglectful or are indifferent or are loath or unwilling to make demands on their children will visit the consequences on their sons and daughters, producing children who don't really know how to respond appropriately to recurrent, pressing, important bodily functions with no fuss or fear or hesitation.

Anna Freud's Yes and No

Let me draw on a tape-recorded conversation I had with Anna Freud in 1974 on the above matter. "Let us be clear," she said. "The child, the baby, takes its cues every day from the parents. Some parents just seem to know how to do things, to feed a baby to its satisfaction, and then to burp it, then put it down to a good sleep—and if it gets fretful, to hold it and reassure it, but not rush to overwhelm it with nervous attention (and one way *that* gets expressed, we know, is the offer of food at every turn, whenever the slightest whimper is heard). Other parents can't, don't, won't give their babies what they want and need—they are too poor, too distracted or troubled; and still others, let's be clear, overwhelm their children with attention. How does the phrase go? A surfeit of honey!

"The same goes with toilet training. Some parents know in their bones, not from reading someone's book, how to get a child 'with dispatch and ease,' as one of our nurses put it, through the mystery of toilet training, whereas others are made very anxious and even fearful by that responsibility, that requirement. Their own 'problems,' as we are apt to say it, are being given new energy. Those mothers will go after their children without letup, or they'll be so frightened that they'll keep postponing the 'moment of truth.' "

I brought up the subject of paying too little attention to toilet training. "Yes, there are those who have 'utopian fantasies'—if they wait and wait, and don't 'pressure' their children, they'll pick up the skill, become toilet-trained, 'on their own,' 'naturally,' 'without anxiety.' I'm afraid we've been the devil there, we in psychoanalysis. We've given some people the notion—maybe some of *us* had the notion for a while!—that there is a 'correct' way to handle all of this, a way that won't produce anxiety or a moment or two of fear and alarm in children. I've tried to address that 'fantasy' in writing. It is a hard point to make to some of our educated, psychoanalytically sophisticated (or should I say 'interested'?) parents: they want from us more than we can deliver. They want for their children (maybe I should say for themselves as well) more than life can deliver!

"How can we grow without struggle and doubt and a misstep or two? If we spare our children *that—try to*—we'll not be successful anyway; we'll end up prodding them towards other kinds of troubles, the kind we may not have anticipated. Think of the narcissism that will come to a child who has been given everything at all times, and not ever been asked to contain himself, or herself—the appetite, the bodily [excretory] functions!"

I raised the issue of character structure as it gets influenced by these compelling moments and events of childhood. "I agree, there is a moral issue here, in all this, and that is what we could only learn over a long time: we saw in the children we observed, as they grew up, under the influence of modern psychology, the way early-childhood experience influenced their later 'personality.' It is fair to say, I think, that we've *all* learned from this"—from a century's efforts to understand children, do justice to their rearing. "We have learned, I think, that the *yes* that goes with understanding a child's drives has to be balanced by the *no* that goes with understanding something else, the requirements of a reliable conscience."

Miss Freud and I had occasion at that time to discuss that old mainstay of psychoanalytic theory, childhood sexuality. She offered her very own elegantly lean and straightforward way of thinking about an admittedly quite complicated subject. Again we addressed the question of character, how events in the lives of young children persist in their shaping (even at times defining) impact upon those boys and girls become grown-ups: "My father took a beating, as we say in English, for a long time for daring to suggest what I suspect many parents have known 'deep down,' and not so 'deep down,' out of their daily time spent with their children—that they are passionate in their attachment and that [such a] love is no less powerful than the kind of love that we who are adults know in our lives. A child's love, of course, is a response to an adult's love, the parent's, and yet some were so shocked that such [an outcome] should happen! How we handle this love, and how we in turn respond to that love [which we set in motion]—there is a drama worthy of our novelists and playwrights: the same variations and intricacies and puzzles and surprises and pain and outrage and sadness that they have been representing for us over the centuries! A parent can show affection, encourage affection in return—but establish limits, let the child know that love is about control and sharing as well as possessiveness; or a parent can hold back too much, the well-known 'cold mother,' the father who withdraws from family life; and then there is the equally well-known parent who won't let go of the child, stirring up the feelings you and I learn of all the time in our work with the young."

Love's Offspring

I wanted us to go further, to pursue the relationship between parental affection and character development in children—only to realize that she'd more than hinted at what can get going when she probed love, explored its various aspects, its offspring, as it were, love as being "about control and sharing as well as possessiveness." Yet again, the parent has an opportunity to teach even a baby under one, and certainly a baby who is two or three, how to come to terms with those instincts, those wishes and yearnings, those times of disappointment and frustration that are part of love, of life. Some lucky babies have parents who show them love and who love in return, but do not become slaves, as it were, to their child's demands, nor to their own nervous wish, natural for all of us, to give as much as we have, and as often as we can, to our sons and daughters. Other parents are less sure of themselves, or are lacking in self-restraint, and so let concern and affection deteriorate into an indulgence that can turn a child's head. Too much of a good thing, and once more, a child's narcissism is hugely encouraged.

As Miss Freud mentioned, not a few conferences these days focus on such a turn of events — parents who in the name of offering love to their children give them the notion that what and whom they want is constantly available, leading to a grandiosity that becomes evident as a consequence of a petulance that has known no resistance. As for the distant or rejecting parent, a generation of child psychiatrists have spoken and written on the phenomenon, and the lessons learned are not too hard to consider: a curbed, cramped, hesitant response to the world; an inability to trust it, give oneself to it; a stinginess, so to speak, of feeling, that has a definite, obvious connection to the way a child is going to engage with others and think of them. Relatively unloved, a child knows far too little about how to embrace the world, and take to it with trust and without fear. On the other hand, a child who is loved possessively, too insistently, without the reservations that ought to characterize all human commitments ("I have others to attend and tasks that require my attention"), learns to love himself or herself too unreservedly, becomes the victim of a bloated parental "love" that may, as Miss Freud suggested, have more sinister (clinically worrisome) aspects to it — the possessiveness that masks apprehension, melancholy, even (ironically) disdain, scorn.

Who is the parent who can skirt all these hazards, take his or her young child through the complex kinds of human relatedness that occur in those preschool years, when children are fed, clothed, helped to gain mastery over their bodies, to walk, to go to the bathroom "in time"; when they are encouraged to speak and are spoken to and given evidence of a parent's regard and tenderness; and, too, when they meet the inevitable disappointments, the moments and times of disillusion that life and love are likely to bring at any age? The English pediatrician and child psychoanalyst D. W. Winnicott has given us the phrase "good enough mother," by which he intended to be not miserly or only reluctantly or qualifiedly hopeful, but rather, quite realistic. Of course, the word "good" moves us from psychology to ethics—but whereof this "goodness"? A doctor is demanding no perfection of mothers or fathers, only a sufficient degree of goodness, which is measured, one must stress, not by interviews or tests and their scores, but by a daily life that gets affirmed by a particular child, whose mother, we are quick to say, has been sufficiently kind and thoughtful and sensitive, sufficiently *present* to the baby, at pains through thick and thin to nurture and protect and assist, so that a reasonably confident and cheerful and assertive boy or girl grows and grows, affirming daily a lovable self, a more and more competent and capable self, all the result of love given and, too, the result of instruction given—the coaching by day and night that enables such a young person to impress himself or herself favorably upon the rest of us.

That coaching is a complex matter. Winicott's "good enough" parent has to be "good enough" not only to be a tender and devoted and attentive coach, who mostly summons the right word or gesture at the right moment, but also a coach willing and determined enough to withstand the child's impulsive and egoistic side, in order to bring the child into the world, so to speak—help it achieve mastery over its originally quite solipsistic nature, help it to learn to accept *no*, to understand *yes*, to comprehend as well as respond to the distinctions between those two words and all each one stands for. This is no small task for any adult, even the most caring of us—to begin, even in the first months of life to teach an infant that others count, that the best-intended beneficence sometimes will be experienced as thwarting, as baffling, as a defeat. I use lots of words here to describe all of this as it gets enacted in the "dyad" that some theorists use in referring to a baby and its mother or father (the rest of us use the ordinary word "family"). Dr. Winicott wasn't trying to be conceptual or highfalutin when he came up with that phrase "good enough" as it applies to a parent. Rather, he was invoking a quotidian psychology that becomes in its sum a kind of lived ethics: somehow one becomes "good enough" to start an infant on the road toward, yes, goodness. Again, the reciprocity of love, of attentiveness that enables someone who offers the good, the good enough, to receive back a child's goodness.

Might we specify the nature of that "goodness" in, say, a four- or five-year-old child on the verge of going to school, a budding goodness that "good enough" parents have enabled, nourished, permitted, encouraged? Such a goodness is obviously not something avowed, not words and more words uttered on behalf of "morality" or "ethical principles." Such a goodness isn't argued, isn't a philosophy asserted, refuted. Such a goodness begins to appear in the first months of life and is usually not called or thought of as goodness, but rather as a child's "nature" or "temperament": a lovely child, a gentle one, a responsive one. "All smiles and sweetness," I've heard certain mothers say, and they insist they are lucky, they haven't earned the bonus they've gotten, and so perhaps genetics is at work. I don't argue with them, for who knows how much of a baby's early presentation of itself is inherited, and how much a consequence of the treatment it has received day after day. Each of the above matters, it is safe to suppose: inheritance and a family's life, including, by the way, its values and ideals, the degree to which such values and ideals influence the behavior of those who espouse them. Even here, at the start of life, a parent has to practice what is preached, no small achievement for any of us in any aspect of our lives.

In any event, a "good-natured" baby smiles a lot, looks and looks at those who look at it, obviously delights, with coos, murmurs, giggles, in being touched and fondled and seems to enjoy its fellow human creatures, takes in with clear joy the food they offer, the warmth and excitement they also extend. The same baby gradually becomes more confident, is crawling and standing and, in time, taking its first steps, even as it utters its first words, and so doing receives encouragement and applause, responding to such with pleasure and new dedication: I'll continue walking down this path; I'm admired and loved, and I accept such feeling, I respond to it by persisting in certain directions, thereby generating more of that feeling. Language grows that way—a word, the pleasure it prompts, and then a renewed effort to speak, to offer listeners more words. All of that is understandably the province of psychology; yet a moral life is also on its way here, though we today may not be especially interested in seeing that to be the case.

A Moral Mutuality

A baby has learned to love, even as it has been loved, to reward with effort those who have exerted effort on its behalf, to accept and please those who have accepted it, have been so pleased by it. This reciprocity of feeling and behavior, this clear connectedness, as it broadens and enlarges all concerned, is an early expression of a shared respect, a mutuality of regard, a moral mutuality, a capacity of the baby no less than its parents (and other adults who appear from out of nowhere, it seems) to see the world through the eyes of others, to be grateful, to link arms in what becomes, really, a shared effort, parents doing their best, the baby doing its best. All of the above takes place so gradually and pleasurably and unself-consciously, with no abstract articulation of sentiment, no conceptual chatter (the "naturalness" of those early months and years) that one is apt to forget how much self-absorption is forsaken by most babies, in favor of an embrace of others, their hopes and their expectations: their *values*. The baby becomes a willing student who keeps its eyes quite literally on the teacher, senses what is wanted, offers it—joins a small community and earns its membership in it: a good citizen carrying his or her fair share of a family's weight.

Sometimes we take all of that for granted, until, maybe, we learn of a baby (a family, it really is) for whom such a chain of events, of breakthrough after breakthrough, doesn't happen. A baby doesn't respond to its parents with trustful coziness—indeed, can't tolerate the ordinary gestures of affection and affiliation the rest of us parents and children offer one another. A baby seems touchy, rather than touching; seems without interest in what others want for it, of it; cries when others would laugh, withdraws when others would come closer—and refuses, seemingly, to want any emotional or cognitive commerce with those who are its parents. No question, under such circumstances we adults will eventually mobilize psychiatric or neurological nomenclature in our desperate effort to comprehend what seems to be so strikingly irregular, so threatening to our sense of what is "normal" psychologically, but also, what is "right and proper." That is a worn phrase, often used by lawyers or rhetoricians, but I heard it used repeatedly by the mother of a baby of thirteen months who seemed already headed toward autism. The boy was withdrawn, all too indifferent when approached, quite disinterested in the solicitous overtures of his parents, and he was making no progress at crawling or early speaking. His mother was a political scientist, a political philosopher, really, and to no small degree a moralist. Once, as I tried with them to make as much sense as I could out of this perplexing and dismaying clinical situation, she interrupted me in exasperation and told me she was utterly overwhelmed by what seemed to her not "symptoms," not a psychiatric problem, not even a mysterious neurological one, but something "utterly beyond any understanding, even a doctor's," and then, this: "It's not right and proper, it's beyond what any person should have to contemplate—your own child, only a year old, withdrawing from the human community, becoming an exile, a stranger in a family. It's as if he's been sentenced by some inscrutable fate, some *judgment*, to the Inferno, to Hell itself, and we're with him. We're strangers to one another—that *is* Hell, and we've been sentenced there!"

A moral, almost religious judgment handed down, as if the word "disease" simply wasn't adequate to the situation at hand. The rest of us, graced with babies who, courtesy of genetics, neurology, and family life, seem almost effortlessly to prosper and grow and take on the world with increasing competence, forget the considerable accomplishments of our young ones, who learn to accommodate themselves to others, anticipate their wishes; who learn to speak to people and understand them; who learn to take care of their bodies in important ways, take responsibility for those bodies; who learn to deal with an array of intense emotions (desires, envies, rivalries, complex entanglements of feeling) directed at others with expanding tact and sensitivity and discretion, so that a child entering the first grade of school often enough knows the meaning of and readily uses "please" and "thank you," defers to the authority of the teacher, plays with others (there are inevitable lapses, admittedly), eats with some decorum, and manages his or her toilet quite well.

Civilization has taken root: a moral start of considerable proportions, and one not necessarily regarded as such by many of us who incline toward the language of psychology to describe what has happened. Still, some are ready to make a bow to parents in this way. I heard this message given by a first-grade teacher to the parents I have mentioned (they had invited her to one of our biweekly meetings): "I am an optimist, I guess, so I always see the bright side of things. I've heard some of you apologize for your children, and worry about them, and try to explain what you call 'their problems,' but here's how I see those children when I come into class each morning at eight-thirty: they say hello to me, they smile at me, they're immediately ready to work with me, to pay attention and try to cooperate and do their best and obey the rules and procedures and announcements. They eat well, clean up after themselves, help me keep the classroom neat. If one of them gets sick or is in trouble, the others (some more than others, but in general, most or all of them) worry about that person, and show that worry: they become alarmed and they want to be of help, and tell me so, quite directly. If *I'm* under the weather, they're also ready to be of help, and *my*, do they fret over me, and tell me how much they hope I feel better, and *soon*! True, some kids behave better than others, and even the best of them (of *us*!) have our bad days. But mostly, it is very impressive, and very touching, and if mostly I just take it all for granted, I have to tell you folks that sometimes, when I see an outpouring of sympathy on their part for one of their own, or for me, or when they'll on their own start cleaning up the room, getting ready for the next lesson or the next day, when they defer to one another, or tell me that they're upset, because so-and-so, not in our class, is sick, or got into an accident—well, I guess I'm trying to say that these are quite *upstanding citizens* you have sent off to school, and as the 'outsider' who first works with them in a school for a whole year, I'm very impressed and I'm appreciative, too."

Her remarks, spoken with obvious conviction—a summary of so very much—brought us all up short, reminded us that values begin being learned by children quite early on; that a long moral road has been traversed during those first years that precede kindergarten or the first grade; that these "good enough" mothers (and their "good enough" husbands) had managed not only Winicott's psychological feat, but a major moral one, as well, had given this world in these children some quite concrete and observable human goodness, reliably present in a public institution: young children already well on their way to becoming young citizens.

2

THE ELEMENTARY SCHOOL YEARS:
THE AGE OF CONSCIENCE

In elementary school, maybe as never before or afterward, given favorable family and neighborhood circumstances, the child becomes an intensely moral creature, quite interested in figuring out the reasons of this world: how and why things work, but also, how and why he or she should behave in various situations. "This is the age of conscience," Anna Freud once observed, and she went further: "This is the age that a child's conscience is built—or isn't; it is the time when a child's character is built and consolidated, or isn't." These are the years when a new world of knowledge and possibility arrives in the form of books, music, art, athletics, and, of course, the teachers and coaches who offer all this, the fellow students who share in the lessons, the experiences. These are years of magic, of the imagination stirred and fed in innumerable ways, of all that goes with a mind encouraged to explore the world, to try to make sense of it. These are years of eager, lively searching on the part of children, whose parents and teachers are often hard put to keep up with them as they try to understand things, to figure them out, but also to weigh the rights and wrongs of this life. This is the time for growth of the moral imagination, fueled constantly by the willingness, the eagerness of children to put themselves in the shoes of others, to experience that way their life.

At five or so, as the teacher quoted at the end of the preceding chapter so poignantly indicated, a child begins to engage in utter seriousness with the society, the nation to which he or she belongs. Until that time a boy or girl is listed in a town's or city's register of births, but that is all. Now, the world outside the home officially beckons, and in a way the home begins, as a matter of law and custom, to share with the community the responsibilities of bringing up the child. In the classroom the child meets teachers who begin to shape his thoughts, her way of seeing things; besides, there are dozens of children who are called upon to recite, who raise their hands to offer points of view, in a whole new world of factuality and reflection. Moreover, the mind is now ready for what is newly available to it: language has been consolidated and the body is bigger, stronger, its owner more surely in control of arms and legs.

The Bus as the Beginning: A Child's Whys

We are apt to forget, actually, what happens when a child gets on a school bus for the first time, or gets in a parent's car for that same destination, a classroom, or takes the walk that leads to a school building. An important psychological and moral lesson has been learned and absorbed, one all too easily described in the abstract as an aspect of socialization.

I prefer to call upon a mother who had just experienced a moment, "a time," as she put it, with her daughter—had taken her to the school bus for the first time. As she started to tell of that moment, she got choked up, and I fear I was quick to regard her as seized with the sadness that goes with loss, even if this type of loss is naturally an aspect of a huge gain: a child's first step on a particular ladder.

But the mother wasn't really interested in turning that occasion into an excuse for emotional catharsis. Rather, she was interested in what I only slowly realized to be a kind of civic introspection: "For several days, I talked to Jeanie about school. She knew about school, I guess, because she'd gone to 'nursery school,' but that was a small, private school in someone's home. Now, she was going to a building, a public building, and hundreds of other children will be coming there, and they'll all be on buses that are owned by our city—that's what happens when you go to school, I had to remind her a couple of times. You know why? She asked me *why*? She's always asking me *why* these days, and sometimes I can't take it any longer, and I say, please Jeanie, *later*. But this 'why' took me by surprise, because she'd obviously been giving some thought to the matter of transportation, more thought than I had realized. She asked, 'Why can't you just drive me there?' I said, 'Because—because there'd be a lot of cars there, too many, if all the mothers drove their kids.' But she pointed out that 'all the mothers' go to the supermarket, and go to nursery schools, to parades and playgrounds and movies, and the roads are big enough to handle the traffic. I thought: she's anxious about going to school for the first time, leaving home every weekday morning, and she knows this is a big deal, and she'd rather have me drive her. That's how I felt, too—I was anxious, and I'd much rather have looked forward to driving her!

"Anyway, I tried to get us off that track. I just said, 'It's the way it's done, everyone goes to school on the bus.' But she just kept up her whys. She wondered whether it could be optional—I would choose to drive her if I wanted. No, I said no. Well, *why*? I said *because*! I was *through* with this! She knew it was best to drop the matter, then. But an hour or so later, she's back with this: 'Mom, is there a law about it, that says that you have to put your kid on the school bus, and if you don't you could be in big trouble?' That one really got to me! I thought to myself: I don't know the answer. *Is* there a law, or is it just something you do as a parent: take your child to the place where the bus comes? I *could* drive her to school every once in a while, but you don't make that a habit. It makes the child special, different, and the point is for her to be with the other kids, right off, but I thought that there probably *is* some regulation that says parents should put their kids on the bus, rather than each kid being driven.

"Then, she threw me this curveball of a question: 'Mommie, do you think school starts on the bus, or when you go in the building?' Lord, *now* what to answer? I blurted out: 'When you go into the classroom, inside the school.' But I saw something on her face—she was doing some thinking, though she hadn't said a word yet. I said to myself, *you've* got to do some thinking, too! This kid won't settle for a brush-off! So, that's how we had our talk. I sat down with her. I said, 'Let me think!' I came around—I mean I turned around: I told Jeanie that in a way school *did* begin when you get on the bus. You're on your way to joining the world in a big way—it's a new part of your life, a very important part, that's how I put it. You're adding something on, a new, large room to the house you're building, your life! I actually picked up a pencil and drew her a house, and then added a wing to it. (I used to think I'd like to be an architect!) She liked that—the two of us at the kitchen table, with some chocolate-chip cookies and that sketch I made, and our talk about the bus and the school, and the school I went to when I was her age. She wanted to know about my teachers and I told her a lot—the ones I liked and the ones I didn't, and why! I had to tell her why—because 'why' is her favorite word. I hope her teacher is ready for her—all her 'whys'!"

School is a place where a child first joins a particular community outside the family as a participating citizen—acquires knowledge, yes, but also assumes responsibilities. No wonder that a child of five, off to school, is full of whys; they are our birthright as human beings, and once language arrives, it seems to be, for a blessed while, a servant of such curiosity, especially so when new circumstances arrive. Many parents of course feel more than taxed by the constant inquiries of their children, and some of us in psychiatry have offered explanations and interpretations for this constant search for answers on the part of our sons and daughters: they are a consequence of the sexual and emotional interests and attachments that puzzle and provoke and excite the mind, hence the effort to ask and ask about what is happening in the world—an indirect attempt to probe feelings and urges already known to be unsuitable for explicit discussion. No question, children of four or five want to discuss their family life, and struggle mightily at times with their possessiveness, their moments of envy, anger, desire, frustration and disappointment, all a consequence of how they and others who share with them the same roof manage to get along. But we are creatures of cognition as well as passion, and we are also purposeful creatures, intent on fitting together our knowledge and desires in such a way that this life we live makes some kind of sense.

Telescopic Vision, Moral Vision

For years, as I sat with boys and girls just embarked upon their school life, I tended to see them through the lens of my training in child psychiatry. I was interested in how they got on with their mothers and their fathers, their brothers and sisters, and thus regarding them I connected almost anything they said or told me they did to their evolving emotional life. All to the good, though there is much one overlooks or passes by too hastily, as I learned one day from a six-year-old boy who had already developed a keen interest in telescopes, and whom I was inclined, alas, to view as a budding voyeur of sorts. Consequently, I failed to learn, because I didn't ask, how much he had come to know about the heavens, the stars that populate it in such abundance. I asked him several times to draw a picture of himself, and he eagerly agreed to do so each time, and each time, he supplied his right hand with a telescope, and tilted his head upward toward a sky that he filled with celestial bodies: a sun, a whirling comet or two, and clusters of stars, a moon—as if night and day were one up there in the beyond he was creating. Finally, I wondered aloud whether he might want to lower his gaze a little—what might he then see, or be hoping, trying to see? "Well, I'd see what I see all the time," he answered.

I pressed the matter, looking for the content of his visual field, and he told me the obvious: that he'd see people, places, and things. Then, with patience and a bit of sympathy for me, he reminded me of the purpose of the telescope: to take one's vision elsewhere, away from the ordinary. "When I look in it it's like going on a long trip, and I'm far away, but I'm still here, too." All right, I thought—but *why* the urge for such travel? He must have realized, finally, what was crossing my mind, because he looked at me gravely, directly: "Why are you asking me so many questions about the telescope?" A moment's silence, as I tried to figure out a suitably evasive yet suggestive reply—one that would enable me to resume being the one who posed the questions. But he was a considerate, compassionate youngster, and he let me off the hook with another question and an offer: "Would you like to use the telescope? I could show you how."

Only later did I realize the full import of that exchange. He had let me know that even as I was putting questions to him, he might easily turn the tables on me, put a few queries in my path. If he had his unconscious reasons for being at six or seven a budding astronomer, I had my reasons (perhaps a few of them beyond my consciousness) for sitting with him, scanning his life closely. By implication he had tried to get both of us past that manner of seeing things—by suggesting that I take seriously *what* he was doing, not only the possible reasons for his particular interest, hobby, exploratory pursuit. When I started doing so, I found out more than I expected, learned of more than the facts a young, intelligent investigator had amassed. "Those stars," he told me, "are moving fast, even if it looks like they're not moving one inch." I nodded. Then he decided that I needed to know more: "A friend of mine said that God is keeping them from bumping into each other, but I told him no, God isn't like that. He lets things happen—he doesn't keep interfering! He made everything, and then everything is on its own, and people, too. In Sunday school, they say it's up to you, whether you'll be good or bad, and it's like that with the stars: they keep moving, and if they go off track, that's because something has gone wrong—it's an accident, it's not God falling asleep, or getting mad, something like that!"

He stopped to see whether I was following him. Yes, I was—and I nodded to indicate as much. He decided to complete his presentation: "Here it's different—there are people here. We're the star with people! That's why we could mess things up. The stars could hit each other—one star gets in the way of the other. That would be bad luck for the both of them! But we could do something bad to this place, this star—and it would be as bad as if another star hit it, worse even!"

Now I was looking at him more intently, as he noticed. I was wondering why he was bringing us close to such an apocalyptic moment—what had prompted this direction of fantasy, of speculation, of narrative exposition? He knew I wanted to hear more from him. He looked up at the sky for a moment, then returned earthward with his eyes, which came to rest on the television set in the kitchen. I immediately wondered what he had recently seen on that screen, what program may have stimulated this direction of our conversation. He told me without any prompting on my part: "I heard the man on the news say that there was a lot of bad stuff that got into the air." The nuclear accident at Chernobyl had taken place a week earlier. "If people don't learn the right thing to do they could get everyone in trouble, and that would ruin the earth. God might be upset, but I don't think He'd interfere. It's up to us to learn how to do things right—you can pray to Him, but you're the one who has got to find the best way, the right way to behave."

We had gravitated, as it were, downward from those other planets, made more accessible to sight by the telescope, to this earth, so troubled by forces and impulses sometimes even harder to see here than those at work on, say, far-distant Mars or Jupiter. Still, this boy was by no means blind to all of that, to the relationship, actually, between God and man and the planetary bodies, no small world to encompass intellectually and morally. In his own unpretentious, unassuming way he had let me know that no matter the "deep down" reasons for looking so intently at what is so far away (and no matter my reasons for looking so intently at his reasons), there was another line of inquiry for us both to pursue, one to which he, artful teacher that he was, eventually brought both of us: the matter of right and wrong, good and bad, as it arises anywhere, everywhere, in our lives. A boy seemingly detoured by intellectual inclination (and, I was speculating, by emotional inclination as well) from this planet's problems in favor of an abiding interest in other planets was quite interested in addressing the biggest questions confronting all of us human beings who live on this earth: how our behavior might influence the very nature of existence, of life as it exists here.

For me, that time of reflection with an elementary school child became more instructive than I imagined would be the case. He had taken me, courtesy of his telescope, on one kind of long voyage, but he had also enabled me to travel further into his mind, his life, and thereafter, into the thinking of other children than I had thought possible or desirable. I had been told by a boy then in the second grade that the abstract worlds of astronomy, theology, social ethics, and psychology were no unapproachable mysteries for him; that he was very much able to ponder the question of God's will, the matter of man's destructive possibilities, and to do so concretely, searchingly, suggestively, even if some adults might call his effort (sometimes dismissively) a passing interest or a season's whim or regard his concerns as evidence of "sublimation." In point of fact, this encounter taught me to be more generous to a particular child, and with his help, to other children with whom I was talking—to allow for their capacity to be ethically introspective citizens, at six or seven even, of this country, of the whole world.

The conscience is the voice within us that has really heard the voices of others (starting with our parents, of course) and so whispers and sometimes shouts oughts and naughts to us, guides us in our thinking and our doing. The conscience constantly presses its moral weight on our feeling lives, our imaginative life. Without doubt, most elementary school children are not only capable of discerning between right and wrong, they are vastly interested in how to do so—it's a real passion for them. At three or four, after all, a child has learned to oblige the world in important ways: has learned to care for himself, control herself, eat on his or her own, and with reasonable care and consideration for what others call manners; has learned to speak intelligibly and with proper respect for others, without which a two-way conversation won't long take place. All of the above, years in the making, has to do with an unself-conscious kind of character development, resulting in a child who has learned to go by the rules of the house, to "behave" himself or herself, mostly—a "good" child, at home and in the neighborhood.

Language for Opinion

A child attending elementary school is much more able than a preschooler to pause and look self-consciously at the world, wonder aloud and stop to think silently about it—to try to be good, yet also ponder the good, ask what "good" is, how it ought be expressed in the course of a life. Now, a more accomplished capacity for the utilization of language, a more skillful way with words, serves not only the purpose of communication but also introspection. Now children go to Sunday school or Hebrew school. Now they turn to science, as my young astronomer friend did, and as a consequence of the same whys that theologians in a different way ask of themselves, of us. Now they begin to read, to hear others read, and thereby their world is vastly increased. All sorts of others, long gone from this life (historical figures, for example) become remembered companions of sorts: their words, their stories, are taken up and in various ways, wittingly or unwittingly, are taken to heart. Now children have teachers to attend as well as parents, and scout masters and athletic directors or coaches, and of course, friends; and now they watch television, are taken to the movies. No wonder, then, that parents sometimes feel that they are losing a bit of control over their children, even as they are presumably glad to have their son or daughter get older—more rational, more capable physically, better able to follow directions and comply with instructions, better able to deal with the emotions that have a way of asserting themselves at the dining table, for instance, or in the family room, where people gather to be together and sometimes contend with each other as well as enjoy one another's company.

Now "yes" and "no" aren't so easy to impose upon a child, nor do many of us, certainly including teachers, want it to be otherwise. After all, the heart of the classroom, even in elementary school, has to do with (so one hopes) expression, consideration, discussion, amplification—not only the rote memorization of true and false, but reflection upon the complexity, ambiguity, inconsistency, and variation of this world's events, that side of the world's life that is waiting to be comprehended. Moreover, at school a child learns from classmates as well as from teachers and books—how someone of his or her age says something that may be unlike what a parent or a teacher has so far said, and therefore all the more unforgettable. This is a time when *opinion* comes to children—when language is not only for getting along with elders essentially on their terms, but for the assertion of the self: words a musculature at the beck and call of feeling, of concern and wonder, as they come to the young mind.

Betsy: The Introspective Speller

I sit in a third-grade classroom. These are eight-year-old children and the teacher wants them to know how to add and subtract, to read, to spell, to draw and paint, to look at maps with recognition of this or that country, city, region, ocean, range of mountains. They are doing spelling that morning, one of those more categorical subjects: correct or incorrect, and that is that. One girl is doing exceptionally well, to the point that the teacher not only applauds her but mentions a spelling bee that will be held, in which she might want to take part.

The girl does not seem pleased, however, at such a prospect. She lowers her head, frowns. The teacher notices this response, asks the student whether she is "all right." She doesn't say anything, and the teacher is obviously of two minds—to pursue the matter or let it drop and proceed with more words to be spelled, asked of more children. Something in the child's demeanor prompts the teacher to persist. She asks the child again whether she'd be interested down the line in representing the class in a "junior spelling bee," to be held at another school.

The child turns forthright: a firm shake of her head. The teacher is taken aback. So are some of the girl's classmates, who register surprise but also, I notice, a bit of pleasure: smiles appear on their faces. My mind quickly thinks of abstractions such as authority, disobedience—the girl's willingness to stand up to her teacher, the excitement such a posture generates in others. I am also not unmindful that a very bright or talented or capable child can stir envy and the anger associated with it in others, for whom classroom assignments, recitations, obligations are far less welcome and gratifying in their accomplishment. So I have in a flash rushed to a psychological conclusion about the student in question, and many of her classmates.

The teacher, too, has obviously moved from astonishment to concern. She hesitates a second. She has a choice: to move on and perhaps talk with the child later when they are alone, or to stay with this issue that has now arisen in the classroom, an issue directly connected to a subject matter being pursued. She decides to stick to her guns. She addresses the child courteously, but with a noticeable firmness to her delivery: Why does she not wish to "be part of" the spelling bee? The girl looks away toward the window. There is a hushed moment of suspense in the room, with all eyes on her, and then, suddenly, this: "My cousin is in high school, and he said a lot of spelling—it doesn't make any sense and they should make it easier to spell a lot of words."

The teacher obviously hadn't reckoned with that reply, and now it is her turn to look away toward the window for a second—after which she rallies to the defense of caution, of rules, of what *is*, tells the class that "some things we just accept, believe, go along with." The children don't argue with her; their silence is noticeable and, of course, provocatively enigmatic: What is each one thinking? The teacher, they realize, doesn't want to know what they think, as she indicated by her comment, and thus it will be: a compliant assent to the teacher's wishes, or so it seemed.

Suddenly, though, the teacher has a change of mind—of heart, maybe. She has looked at that bright girl, such a good speller, whose head is once more turned downward, and she has looked at the others in the class, who seem tensely tame, ready to heed her beck and call, but not especially cheerful or even interested. They are skeptical, suspicious, I speculate, my eyes wandering—on the lookout for clues in facial expressions, bodily moves, gestures. When I count three head scratches, I emphasize for myself the notion of perplexity: *Why*, they wonder, why *are* some words so hard to spell when they might be easier to spell? These students and George Bernard Shaw and William

James and Flannery O'Connor and God knows how many others have wondered this, I muse. All that thought has taken a second or two—interrupted by this from the teacher: "Let's talk about Betsy's cousin—let's see if you agree with Betsy's cousin!" Her manner of speaking, as much as her words, has opened up the class, and slowly, tentatively (a little fearfully I speculate, maybe wrongly) the children have their say, generating another lively discussion among school-children for me to record and, later, try to understand. I am impressed, right then and there—not to mention later, when I read what has been spoken—by the willingness of these children to give this subject thought, to show their hearts as well, and, not least, to mobilize for themselves a moral vocabulary that helped them decide what they believed to be best for Betsy, and for them as spellers, and by implication, for all of us, as readers and writers.

"You have to spell the words the way they've been spelled," said one girl, "or there'll be different people spelling in different ways." "Oh, maybe everyone could agree to change the spelling [of some words]. So they'll be easier [to spell]," another girl observed. Right away a boy beside her objected: "Just because something is *easy*, that doesn't mean it's right—that you should try to find the easiest way, and then choose it. You have to challenge yourself!" Another boy put the matter this way: "Who will decide what the best spelling is? What if people don't agree? How do you settle the argument? There could be a lot of trouble!" As for Betsy, she held back for quite a while, maybe a bit amazed by all that she'd gotten going. Finally she raised her hand, was called upon, spoke: "If they changed the spelling of a lot of words, we'd still have to learn how to spell them! I guess I'm a good speller, so far. But that's not what I'd like to be—a speller! I don't want to be bragging all the time—look at how I can spell! So I'd just as soon skip that 'bee' (whatever they call it)."

The class is now quite silent—the low-level noise of hands flung in the air indicating a desire to speak and of bodies moving about restlessly and of a whisper here and there dissipates completely, and the teacher notices the change right away. She coughs once, lightly—perhaps to interrupt this stunned hush: she, like the children, has to figure out what this leading student, this star speller, was trying to say, and what the rest of us are now to think and do. The children are obviously awaiting her signal. Until Betsy spoke, her classmates were vying with each other to have a say: a lively, inviting discussion, a sanctioned opportunity, as well, to have a bit of a fight. Now there seemed nothing left to consider. Betsy had taken the air out of the subject all too swiftly: hey, there will always be words to spell, this way or that. Moreover, she had raised with delicacy and without sly boasting the matter of *modesty*—a moral matter. She didn't want a spotlight on herself, didn't want to be identified as the one who was a first-rate speller. As she talked, one could feel her trying to be self-effacing—having her say quickly, then withdrawing from what was fast becoming a fray. I thought to myself: *here* is an ever-so-quietly demonstrated goodness, a refusal to show off, a willingness to reign in one's inevitable egoism (or "pride," in the biblical sense of the word) lest others feel diminished by comparison.

Finally the teacher interrupted our reveries, our collective perplexity, our charged time of self-consciousness: "You are right, Betsy, we'll always have spelling, even if it changes. I appreciate your desire not to be in the bee—we'd never want anyone to take part who didn't want to." She seemed to have more on her mind to say, but she stopped for a second—and then a hand was raised, and though she could easily have continued, she chose to recognize the boy, who rather tersely asked whether there ought "be a bee, anyway." The teacher appeared flustered, looked beyond the child who had asked the question, looked toward the door of the room and through its small windows, maybe, to the inviting hall. Finally she came down on the side of yes: "The bee has been going on for years and lots of children really like it." Another pause, then Betsy's name got mentioned: "Betsy just happens not to like it." At that Betsy flushed, and the teacher saw her doing so, and perhaps worried that the child had been unnecessarily embarrassed. She looked at Betsy a fairly long time, and finally Betsy spoke—maybe thinking that she was once more on center stage: "We'll all forget this pretty soon! The teacher in Sunday school told us your whole life goes fast as can be, and you never should forget that. She said God has it figured out (about us), but we can't know what it is—what He's figured."

Now more utter silence, until the teacher starts sorting out papers on her desk, clearly anxious to get the class going in another direction—and she does so: an arithmetic lesson.

Later, I have a chance to talk with Betsy, whose mother has been a member of the discussion group with which I've been meeting for over a year. We talk about that particular spelling class, and she is quick to tell me how glad she is that it is a thing of the past. I ask her for more of her thoughts on why she shunned the bee. She shrugs her shoulders. She repeats her classroom remark—that spelling was not especially her great interest. She goes back to a briefer, less didactic version of her Sunday school lesson: "Everyone will forget this, soon!" Perhaps she wanted to forget it all then and there—and wished I would as well. I say as much, planning an end to this aspect of our talk. She smiles, tells me this: "When I say my prayers, I ask God whether He wants me to be a good speller. I know you don't get answers, when you ask those questions [of God]. But there must be a reason I get all those words right! The teacher in Sunday school says you find your answers, after a while. Mom says it's just that I can [spell]. But my friends, both of them, can't, not too well—so I wonder, what's the difference, why?"

Later, driving home, I think of that eight-year-old girl, of ordinary, middle-class American background, her dad an engineer, her mom a hospital administrator and onetime nurse. Here was a child who already knew how to be genuinely modest, no small achievement in the life of anyone, of any age. She was, in her own fashion, trying to find a direction for herself, even as a third-grader—and she was willing, even publicly in a classroom, to connect a momentary introspective occasion to that larger vision of things she'd been hearing in an Episcopal, suburban Sunday school.

Thoughts on Pascal

For some reason my own mind kept going back to Pascal. Why Pascal? I had no immediate idea. As I drove, his name stuck in my thoughts, even prevailing over some engaging, lighthearted Cole Porter songs, sung by Ella Fitzgerald, which attempted to take me in quite another direction. I remembered my favorite college professor who'd been a tutor of mine, Perry Miller. He'd taught us Pascal in a course called "Classics of the Christian Tradition." But so what! Eventually, Pascal left me—until, at home, I "happened" to notice a book I'd read years, decades, ago: Pascal's *Pensées and the Provincial of Letters*, part of the Modern Library series. Next, I "happened" to pull it from the shelf—and soon I was noticing Pensée 205, which I'd heavily underlined: "When I consider the short duration of my life, swallowed up in the eternity before and after, the little space which I fill, and even can see, engulfed in the infinite immensity of spaces of which I am ignorant, and which know me not, I am frightened, and am astonished at being here rather than there; for there is no reason why here rather than there, why now rather than then. Who has put me here? By whose order and direction has this place and time been allotted me?"

A seventeenth-century Frenchman, a scientist and moral philosopher struggling to find his bearings, asking the great whys of existence in a most humble way—even as I had just heard a bright, knowing late-twentieth-century American girl similarly try to fathom the mystery of her particular life, its qualities and gifts, their ultimate meaning, if any. Pascal bowed before those two infinites, space and time, let them shadow his mind's struggle to find a home, a sense of purpose, an escape from a gnawing feeling of absurdity that any of us at various times might feel. Betsy was no stranger to a similar existential intuition: that correct spelling, loudly applauded, will hardly give her the moral satisfaction she already knew to seek.

She was, I began to realize, already doubly humble—no braggart in a class she was beginning to lead intellectually (her work in other subjects was also exemplary) and no cleverly, coyly, self-righteous scold, ready to bask in the washed virtue of her Sunday school lesson: here I am, remembering it and asking all of you, accordingly, to remember me. Rather, she was at pains to seek a spell of anonymity—let others take part in that bee—and she even dared wonder whether her gifted mind had the slightest moral significance in the mysterious scheme of things called life.

She had discomfited her teacher, after a fashion, I only gradually began to realize, by indicating no real interest in accepting proffered laurels, strutting before others as yet another big shot, a winner, a person headed upward. Rather, she worried what such a triumph would mean for her, for others, and even, yes, for the larger run of things—as Pascal might put it, *sub specie aeternitatis*.

A week after that school event her mother confirmed for me her daughter's "shyness," her lack of interest in the "spotlight." A humble way, also, for the mother to put the matter, rather than boasting about her daughter's essential humility and even capacity for moral inwardness. When I asked the mother about the daughter's favorite activity or hobby, she said that Betsy loved helping around the house and caring for the family dog—walks, gentle grooming, offering food twice a day. When I asked Betsy about her contribution to her family's daily life, she replied, "I do whatever is there waiting [to be done]." No lists, no lawyer's brief calculated to earn a congratulatory smile or remark—only a girl trying to be both competent and caring, a child who wouldn't want to talk about "values" or "goodness" or "virtue," only find ways to live up to what disquisitions on those words would surely spell out in elaborate detail.

I mention Betsy at some length because she was so quietly decent and kindly. I had to work a little hard to recognize and appreciate a certain ethical refinement in her—actually, to wade past the psychiatrist in me, all too ready to consign her to the ranks of the mildly irregular ones: this bashful, taciturn child who resisted the blandishments of academic success in favor of a bit of soul searching! Whence her "problem," after all! As her teacher also put it to me, covering her psychological bases: "I worry that Betsy can be a bit too reserved—she doesn't like the limelight one bit, not one bit!" I said nothing—because that was how my mind was also working. Maybe, I slowly began to think, Betsy's "problem" is *us*, people like her teacher and me who aren't as quick as we might be to spot a child's capacity, first, for ethical reflection, and, second, for trying to live up to ideas taken to heart.

At seven or eight, at nine or ten, children other than Betsy are fully capable of struggling with ethical questions—how much of one's pride, one's self-satisfaction, does one show in public, and at what cost? — and trying to do so in deed as well as word. Freud and his followers refer to those early school years as the latency period and mean by that a relative stability and quietude of instinctual life coupled with a relatively ascendant, well-muscled conscience. Babies, we all know, can be wildly out of order — demanding and impulsive and hard to reckon with. A child off to school has learned how to behave in ways not possible a few years earlier and has language under his or her belt, and so can be spoken to, and does so to himself or herself. "I told *myself* that," a seven-year-old boy told his mother, who in turn told us; her son's was a mind able to converse with itself, and more: wonder, speculate, worry, aspire, hope, despair, proclaim, denounce — the range of activity, intellectual and moral as well as emotional, that humans have within their heads. Later, during adolescence, the "instincts" will again assert themselves in the sexual fires of the teen years.

The Challenge: Possibilities and Dangers

How might we teachers and parents take up the challenge, respond to children of Betsy's age so that they become stronger morally in the way that matters: as an aspect of their daily activities? No question, in homes rich or poor, urban or rural, regardless of the ethnic or racial background of the family, it is in the very nature of a child this age to ask and ask, giving us to whom those inquiries are put a chance to provide direct and indirect answers, through what we say, through what we suggest or recommend, through the stories we tell, through the memories we share, through the experiences we offer as examples, through ourselves as talkers, as the ones who sift and sort memories and are able to articulate them.

These conversations, these exchanges on the spur of the moment or in a carefully planned encounter, these bedtime tales told, remembrances shared, these whispered moments or outbursts, terse orders or long and tendentious declarations, these casual comments over a meal or in a car or while working inside or outside the house, these statements in response to something heard on the radio, seen on television, these remarks overheard when spoken on the phone, these words expressed to animals and of course the way one *is* with them—all of that and more becomes part of the child's minute-by-minute moral experience: a take, slowly built up, on what matters and why, what doesn't matter, how one ought to talk and be with others, how one ought to think of them and of oneself, and, again, for what underlying reasons.

Family life is not a self-conscious seminar, with everyone constantly worrying about what to say or do, which explorations or suggestions or interpretations to offer, and when and with what tone of voice or choice of words. I can image (alas, I have witnessed!) an earnest botching up of a child's moral education at the hands of parents ever so eager to do right and teach their children what is right—to the point that an insufferable moral self-consciousness (and smugness) develops, a righteousness gone awry. Priggish, finger-pointing children (or adults) are, alas, not rare; neither are literal-minded moralists, ever ready to pounce on anyone who happens to fall in their way. Here humor truly can make a difference—humor and all that it implies: a sense of proportion and judgment, a relaxed sense of time as being reasonably plentiful, so that a day's events don't have to be seized relentlessly and seized for all they are worth.

Danger: The Child as Scold

Perhaps I ought to pursue further this potential (parodic) pitfall—a family so morally awake that the children are exhausted, tired of pieties pushed on them and, down the line, not unlikely to throw the whole regimen, in all its overwrought scrupulosity, down the drain. A teacher tells me of a child who takes up where she leaves off, remonstrating in the corridors or on the playground with the children who have stumbled, made a mistake in the way they behave, have whispered in class, copied another's paper, spoken out of turn.

This is fourth grade, and one wants to offer a little leeway to these kids, their teacher observes—and then comes a confession: she is really bothered by the scold she has just mentioned, whereas some of the boys and girls who demonstrate occasional wayward moments don't trouble her all that much, and sometimes cause her to smile to herself.

What do I make of this boy, I am finally asked, his willingness to more than risk his own fate (he has become decidedly unpopular) by becoming all too concerned with the fate of others? I am tempted to conclude that this boy is himself struggling more mightily than one might suspect with the very temptation to wrongdoing he observes in others. He admonishes them, therefore, to keep himself in check.

But no, something else is at work here, I eventually find—a family quite preoccupied with the very subject matter I am exploring in this book! This boy was constantly being cautioned about wrongdoing by a father who was not only a lawyer, but very legalistic. Drivers exceeding the speed limit or failing to signal an intention to turn left or right, people who don't say "please" or "thank you" in stores or restaurants, those of any age, anywhere, who swear and cuss—all were grist for this man's scrutiny. His explicit, energetic effort to strengthen his son's conscience, to help the boy to be alert to wrongdoing, to be sensitive to the insensitivity of others, had worked all right, and the result, alas, was a boy dryly, smugly preoccupied with the errors others can be observed making, to the point that his own moral acuity had become a source of more than pride to him; it had led to the vanity that can accompany achievement. I mention him and his father as a cautionary reminder: a certain zealous literalism can make a mockery of any effort, certainly including one that aims to nudge a family toward good deeds.

A Lesson from History: On Courage

I sit at a desk in a fourth-grade classroom where I am a volunteer teacher and feel the constant curiosity of the children, their evident desire to stretch the boundaries of both knowing and feeling. I ask them to take up our history book so that we can learn together about the founding and exploration of America and, later, the revolutionary war that established our nation's sovereignty. I am anxious that they know facts, dates, the names of the ships, the places where navigators first came ashore. I am anxious that we look at maps, try to know which land was occupied by which nation. I want us to talk about battles, wars, kings and queens who commissioned expeditions. I hope we'll learn as well about the *reasons* various people wanted to come here: their religious convictions; their lives as outcasts, even prisoners, in this or that European country; and of course their desire to start a new life, to strike it rich. Some of the children pay close attention; some of them pretend to do so; some are plainly indifferent or bored. I want to unite them in passionate interest, and so I resort to stories, show pictures, use maps. Suddenly a girl does my work for me with this question: "In those boats [that brought the first settlers here], do you think the people were happy to be there?"

I hadn't really thought about that matter—not ever, or not, certainly, in such a way. I'd thought of *why* the Pilgrims and Puritans, the Quakers and Catholics, had come to these shores, and of course, I knew that the journey was hard and long, that some died en route—but I hadn't tried to put myself in the *minds* of those men, women, and children, as this girl was asking us to do. Telling myself I was being coy, or reacting in the all too predictable manner of my psychiatric kind, I reflected the question back to the girl and her classmates: "What do you all think?"

Silence greeted all of us, and I got myself ready to ask again in a differently phrased way, or to speculate out loud and myself give an answer—probably say that I didn't think those folks back then thought about happiness so much as other aspects of existence: the right and the wrong. Just as that line of thinking crossed my mind, the girl who had asked the question decided to clarify her intent and, so doing, unwittingly confronted me with my (until then) unwitting condescension: "I was wondering if the Pilgrims, once they were aboard the ships, and once they were out to sea, if they thought to themselves: we did the best thing, we made the right decision."

Now the class caught fire—they had all been as stymied by that word "happy" as I had been! One girl said *yes*, emphatically, and then explained: "When you do something you know is right to do, you feel glad that you made the right choice, and you're going to be happy, even if the result is a lot of pain and trouble. My mom says, the worst thing, it's when you do something, and you know it's wrong, but you go ahead anyway." A boy across the aisle agrees by nodding as she talks, then picks up after she's stopped, as if he were her alter ego: "You feel worse, even though you've probably made your decision, thinking it would make you feel better! You know what my dad says? He says, 'The easiest way out can end up being the hardest, and vice versa'—you can make a tough choice and then you're so glad, real glad you did it!"

Across the room, another voice offered another angle of vision: "The way I look at it, those people were probably scared, real scared. I don't see them sitting there and being happy that they did the right thing. I see them being afraid that they made a mistake, and look what happened: they were going 'nowhere,' you could say! They left this life they had, and they didn't know what to expect, and they were out there on the ocean, and the trip would take forever—we forget how long it took—but even so, they'd made the decision, and they weren't going to turn back: no way. So, they worried, but they knew what they did, and why they did it, and they were 'happy' that way: they'd *decided*."

More silence, and I think we've exhausted this subject. I prepare to be the formal teacher and get into details of seventeenth-century American history—but another boy's hand has gone up and I nod to him, and he speaks: "I don't think they thought one way or the other about the rough trip, or the troubles they could have when the ship pulled into some harbor. I think they'd done what they knew they had to do—they were courageous. In Europe, no one complimented them—people criticized them for what they believed. But they knew what they should do; they had this idea of how to worship God, and they weren't going to surrender to other people, their idea of how you should [worship God]." He stops, and I decide to speak, though as I do I realize he may well have more to say, that I may be interrupting a train of thought: "That's your definition of courage—doing what you have to do?" He is quick to reply: "Courage is when you believe in something, you really do, so you go ahead and try to do what your beliefs tell you [to do], and if you're in danger, that way—well, you're not thinking 'I'm in danger.' You're thinking, this is right, this is important, and I'm going to go ahead, and that is that."

Now there is a flurry of hands raised, not to get permission to speculate on the emotions or beliefs of the Pilgrims and Puritans but to talk about courage, how one behaves in response to one's beliefs or values. These nine-year-old boys and girls are all fired up, ready to declaim, really, about what matters and how a person ought to prove a loyalty to what for him or her does matter. "If you believe something," another boy says, "but you won't risk anything—nothing!—for what you believe, then do you really believe in what you're saying [you do]? I don't think so! I think it's a lot of talk, then; but it's not believing—the person isn't believing." A girl in front of him shakes her head as she talks, and she waves her hand urgently: "It's not fair, to say you have to cross the ocean and you could die in the boat, or when you get there—to prove you're really believing something! I mean, you could believe in something, but that doesn't mean you have to jump over some rope to prove you do. The proof: it's for you to decide, what you'll do to show your belief is— is true. Maybe you don't have to do anything, or show anyone anything. Why should you have to prove yourself by *doing* something? Why not just have your belief, and it's your business, and no one else's?"

Much more discussion as the children attempt to clarify their sense of what a belief is, and how or whether it has truly taken hold in a given life. Another girl defends the boy who spoke of courage as connected to action and brings us back to the Pilgrims by saying this: "Look, it's not whether you do something. It's that those Pilgrims said it meant the whole world to them that they practice their religion the way they wanted to—and if they'd given up on that, wouldn't it mean that they weren't so into their faith? Wouldn't it? With us, here, you can have your ideas, your beliefs, and they're *yours*, so you don't have to prove yourself to anyone. You just have your ideas. But those Pilgrims had to prove themselves to God! I'm not saying you have to go *do* something, if you're going to have beliefs. I guess it depends on what the beliefs are. If the beliefs are—if you have to do something because of the beliefs, and you don't do it, because you're scared, so you don't practice your religion the way you believe you should, then I think you are not really living up to your beliefs. If you do live up to them, and you have to face a lot of trouble, then you're courageous, that's how you are. I don't think you believe in courage; I think you become courageous, you act courageous, because you really do believe something, and it's not just a lot of talk; you're not pretending, fooling yourself and other people, too."

I am enormously impressed. I glance at my tape recorder to see if the telltale light is on, a sign that I really want what I've just heard to be on the record; a sign, too, that I am so in awe of what I've heard that without that voice on tape I wonder whether I'll be scratching my head in incredulity! An elementary school child shows a capacity for probing moral analysis that encompasses the very nature of a belief, a value as it connects to a lived life. In this case, the value is courage, the capacity to put oneself on the line willingly, with apparent careless-ness (no matter what takes place deep within oneself) on behalf of what one believes, what one wants to protect or ensure as possible for oneself and for others. The point, we have been told, is not the estab-lishment of a kind of means test for courage, a rating system; the point is to understand what the issue is for each person—what sets of beliefs or values are at stake, and thus, how a person's courage might be man-ifested. The Pilgrims, we all agreed, had made their particular daily, weekly, religious practices the heart and soul of their lives, so to cross the ocean in pursuit of such a possibility took courage, that is, a full commitment to a set of ideals, of desired practices as an expression of those ideals. Courage, we were learning, may be defined as a determi-nation, no matter the obstacles or dangers, to live up to one's values rather than a capacity *per se* to face danger with apparent self-assurance. In other words, that girl, and with her the entire class, was intent on going beyond—beneath—the demonstration of a kind of be-havior to approach the sources of its inspiration, at least *some* sources.

We had not yet gotten into a realm of psychology that would entail discussion of behavior connected to, say, foolhardiness or vengefulness prompted by outrage or loss, states of mind that can prompt what can certainly come across as courageous behavior. When I did ask the class, in a good-bye to the discussion (the clock was running out) what other beliefs or values might prompt courage such as we'd been discussing, a chorus of suggestions, interestingly, descended on us—children speaking out directly, rather than raising their hands, politely waiting their turn: love of parents for children and children for parents came up in various forms of expression, as did love of country, loyalty to friends. These children had in effect declared their conviction that ties to family, friends, and country matter; that such bonds can or ought to or do command enough loyalty to enable the appearance of courage under various sets of circumstances. Put differently, courage became for this class a virtue that is prompted by other virtues—quite a contemplative exercise for all of us to have experienced!

I mention the above to indicate what young school-age children are able to muster collectively and individually in the way of moral reflection—not that we puffed ourselves up by attaching such a phrase to an informal and unexpectedly vigorous, and rewarding free-for-all. In that regard, we did well to stumble along, to let the casual, unpredictable rhythm of a classroom discussion rule the day. My hunch is that if I had asked more formally for an examination of courage, its antecedents, its sources in life, in the lives of one or another group of people, the children might have appeased my didacticism, but might also have been far less forthcoming in their approach to this historical moment, one to which they managed to find such a personal connection. So many younger schoolchildren are eager to embrace the imaginary—indeed, their minds are often afire with it. Given a choice, they will leap into one or another scenario, be it historical or contemporary, factual or fictional, and bring to it their very own moral or intellectual assumptions. Teachers have to control and regulate that tendency—help the children distinguish between themselves (as readers, as discussants) and the topic at hand. But such distinctions too strongly emphasized or enforced can stifle the willingness of boys and girls in a class to immerse themselves in, say, the life of seventeenth-century London from which the Pilgrims were embarking, and their willingness as well to think personally, confessionally—to level with themselves and others with respect to their own experiences as they give shape to a particular sense of what others once did, and why.

All the time, during these first school years, one hopes children are learning what is requested of them, how they must behave, what they must do, and one hopes, accordingly, that they come to school having already learned at home what is desirable, what is impermissible, what is utterly beyond the pale, and why. Under such circumstances, they are more interested in matters of right and wrong, virtue and vice, than we sometimes might acknowledge, either as parents or as teachers. They ache sometimes for a chance to sort out all of that, the mandates and warnings, the applause and the chastisement they have at various moments received. Moreover, what they have heard read to them, what they have learned to read, both at home and at school, has only encouraged them to wonder even more about ethical issues. Cinderella, Robin Hood, David and Goliath, Jack (of the Beanstalk), Goldilocks, the Pied Piper of Hamelin, Little Red Riding Hood, and those dogs and bunny rabbits, cats and chickens and frogs whom, anthropomorphically, various storytellers have handed over to young listeners and readers—all of them struggle for the good, contend with the bad, amid their adventures, the times of danger and peril that confront them. Moreover, parents, especially, make up their own stories to tell children, usually as they put them to bed, and in so doing commonly draw on family traditions and anecdotes, with no small resort to a cautionary lesson here, a saga of moral triumph there.

All of those times, in a bedroom or dining room or living room or kitchen, in a classroom, out in the playground, are often moral moments, however unacknowledged: opportunities for us adults to make yet again this or that point about how things go in the world, how they might go, how they should go. It is similar with history's moments, as demonstrated above. To offer another example from my classroom teaching (as a parent, I experienced a comparable experience), I still remember how the simple fact that Presidents Abraham Lincoln and John F. Kennedy were assassinated got to my class, to my own children. Both of these American leaders stand for so very much, the former as the one who took on the institution of slavery, the latter as a very young and explicitly hopeful, idealistic president who initiated the Peace Corps and gave national voice yet again to the pain of this nation's more vulnerable people. *Why*, so many children ask, were those two men cut down at the height of their power and influence? What is one to make of such tragedies? For that matter, what is one to think of the assassins, John Wilkes Booth and Lee Harvey Oswald, who almost exactly a century apart did similar deeds: a gun aimed, fired at a president? Here historical fatefulness can become a highly charged drama that deeply engages a child's developing moral sensibility. Here, a parent or a teacher, calling upon his or her own moral interests and, yes, sense of the dramatic can help a child or a group of children think about their own moral situation as they try to understand that of another, a president, an assassin.

Another Lesson from History—and a Family's Moral Conflict

In 1971, eight years after President Kennedy was shot dead, I sit with a nine-year-old boy, Tim, and his parents in a Boston child psychiatry outpatient clinic. The boy is unruly both at home and in a parochial school from which he has been told he may soon be expelled, hence his visit to a doctor. His parents make it clear that they're not great "believers in psychiatry." I congratulate them—an effort, I guess, to disarm suspicion with humor. But I emphasize that their son is more than occasionally "rebellious." They more than agree; they complain a good deal about Tim's constant "disobedience." When I ask them to give me specific instances, they cling to the abstract: he's a "rule breaker." I push, ask what rules get broken. They won't oblige. Rather, they persist with the general statement, telling me, "It's as if the lad wants to be different," and apparently spares no cost in the effort. Finally, I virtually beg for details—and, in so doing, notice belatedly that I have remonstrated with them: "Please, it's very helpful if you can give me some examples; I can't be of much help if you don't tell me specifically what's happening." They in turn bristle, fall into dead silence. I decide I'll find out for myself when I meet the boy, and take note of the developing unpleasantness, tension, in the room—a clue, perhaps, to what takes place between them and their son, in the sense that they may make general statements to him, and yet get hung up in some hard-to-express way on various particulars.

When the parents leave, I return with Tim to the impasse of sorts (so I felt it to be) that had just developed, with him as a silent other. He is quick both to acknowledge what has occurred and to guess at the direction that my mind has taken: "My mom and dad, my dad especially, they're always ready to give you the big picture, that's what they say: 'Here's the big picture.' But you can't pin them down. I try! You tried, too—and, well, you see what I mean?" I am struck by the comment, obviously, but made cautious by it: so swift a critical observation of his parents made to a virtual stranger. An invitation to a collusion of sorts?—so I worried. I decide to ask of him what I asked of his parents, an example or two. (After all, he had just mimicked them, albeit with some not so disguised impatience, disapproval.) But he too balked in the clutch, whereupon I surrendered, pursued other matters in his life—his favorite subject in school. History and current events, I learn. Again, I look for the specific, ask what topics have most interested him. He tells me that he enjoyed reading and hearing about President John F. Kennedy, "the first Catholic to get into the White House."

I note the choice, pick up on it: "How did he do it?" For a second Tim is taken aback, throws me a look, retreats into conventionality. "He got elected." Then, an amplification: "There was tough politics, the sister said: they almost stole the election." Who is "they," I want to know. "The people who were afraid of Kennedy," I am told. Why the fear, I ask. "Oh, he was a Catholic," I hear. I chalk that up to "the sister," maybe, or the boy's parents, even as I want to continue, press *my* understanding of that 1960 election—that there may have been irregularities on both sides, though no huge effort to thwart a *Catholic*, as this boy saw that event of a decade or so before. I stop short of asking a question that might by implication broach that view of mine. I might have simply wondered aloud whether it wasn't a struggle between two

political parties, rather than a religious confrontation. The boy, however, has seen skepticism on my face. (Sometimes we're better at controlling our tongues than our appearance.) He asks me a question
before I put one to him: "Do you think they tried to keep Kennedy out
of the White House because he was a Catholic?" I decide not to be evasive in that ticlike way of my ilk: throw the question back at the asker. I
say tersely, "No." I'm ready to expand, but the boy is a step ahead of me:
"I agree—you could be right." Now I am taken aback by this abrupt reversal. The boy notices me hesitating, senses that I'm perplexed. He ex-
plains himself. "Our teacher, she is very strict. If you don't tell her [in
answering her questions, or on tests] exactly what she said, you flunk.
My dad's like that, too. My mom says, 'He hands down the law.' I guess
it's right [that he do so], he's a lawyer. When the teacher said that people tried to keep President Kennedy from being elected, Daddy said,
'Yes.' My mom said it was just 'politics as usual.' But Daddy said it was
different, so she went along."

With that, I start to learn about authority and power in a family as
they connect with a child. I am beginning to see a family's way of seeing things (the struggles that precede a settled point of view), though it
will require time before I'm ready to take up the matter head-on with
the boy. Instead, I let us talk about history, about its lessons—about
President Kennedy, and his assassin, a matter the child himself has let
me know means a lot to him. We talk at length about those "Thousand
Days" of the Kennedy years, and their terrible ending in Dallas. Tim
asks me directly why "that man (what's his name?) killed the president." I try not to be, again, reflexive (and coy); I try to say what I think,
rather than quickly turn the tables on the boy with that old chorus-line
weighted with significance: "What do you think . . . ?" I say I doubt that
anyone will ever be able to answer that question. The assassin, after all,
was himself killed before he could be interrogated. But the boy comes
back with this: "Well, he'd been to Russia, and he was a Communist,
and he hated Kennedy, because he was the enemy, an American, and
he was a Catholic."

I don't immediately reply. I am ready to let the matter drop, although
I don't agree in my mind that Oswald, in his mind, was likely thinking

of Kennedy's religion before and as he pulled the trigger. Tim is once more quite aware of cues I didn't know I was sending—yet another look of skepticism, no doubt, or maybe an extra pause that indicated consternation, if not doubt. He says to me quite simply, quite disarmingly: "You don't believe that." I say, "Yes, I don't quite." He further gets to me, puzzles me, with this: "You wouldn't be a good teacher!" I see a smile on his face, even as words such as "hostility" come to mind (more reflexes at work!). I do ask him, now, for an explanation, and he obliges: "A teacher is supposed to say yes or no—not maybe!" "Oh?" I say. "Yes," he says. "All teachers?" I say. "Yup," he says. "Well, I've met some teachers," I say, "who subscribe to 'maybe' every once in a while." Then a most startling answer: "I don't always like this *yes, no*, people give you." "People?" I ask. "When I'm home, they say, 'It's either right or wrong, and there's no in-between.' The same [goes] at school. I get in trouble with them if I don't agree."

There was more, much more, during that meeting and others that followed. I can only give a hint here of a certain developing moral direction, so to speak, in a child's life—a way of looking at this world, its rights and wrongs, its reasons, its tragedies, at least some of them. The important gist of our talks was that this boy had been taught at home and at school to think only one way, in a clear-cut decisive manner: either/or, yes/no, without resort to qualification, emendation, supposition, speculation. Tim's "rebelliousness" had to do, significantly, with a failure on his part to learn by example, to take in without protest what he'd seen and heard and make it his own. Most children do exactly that, watch how their elders behave, hear what they say, and follow suit. This boy was having trouble doing so—because, as I soon enough learned, his mother didn't agree with much of what he heard from his father, and with some of what his teachers said in class. She was a Protestant who had converted to Catholicism without great conviction—"to make peace" I would hear her say, eventually; "to keep a united front," she also once said. Easier said than done: her son would figure out her disagreements, her reservations, her dissents, unexpressed or conveyed in disguised (sometimes, thinly so) offhand remarks. Her secret doubts, really, became his. He took on her moral qualms, her capacity for ambiguity, her interest in having a second thought or two, but he also tried hard to obey his dad and his teachers—tried hard, but unsuccessfully. Consequently his interest in Oswald, in the mind of an assassin, was in no small way (months of clinical work here risk the glib reductionist caricature of condensation, of explication) that of someone striving to think one way, yet driven by forces at work in a family, now become forces at work in himself, to think another way.

Once in a breathtaking self-observation, worth more than many remarks I'd made meant to clarify and interpret, Tim noted: "It doesn't pay to watch everyone too carefully—you could get into trouble." I wanted to know, unsurprisingly, who "everyone" was and what kind of "trouble" he had in mind. He was unprepared to take himself, us, into the land of specificity. But a couple of months later we returned to that comment, because he uttered it again, and this time we could indeed discuss the different ways his parents not only talked but acted: the father the one who gave orders to people, the mother the one who asked people if "they might be of help," those people being men and women who came to the house routinely to work in it or on special occasions when repairs were being done.

A psychological crisis, then, was in a certain rock-bottom way a moral one: a clash of values as well as one of opinion. The boy had tried his very best to resolve the conflict, to agree with those who issued caveats and conclusions in no uncertain terms, but he also had his afterthoughts, some of them by no means in agreement with the statements that prompted them. The longer I talked with him, the more I came to understand how sensitively he mirrored not so much his parents' words as their deeds. One moment he could be brusque, demanding, all too provocatively sure of himself; the next he was solicitous of others, tried hard to comprehend them, showed a humility that seemed quite sincere and not overdone. His combative outbursts with his teachers, a reaction to their times of insistence, were in fact deeply held protests on behalf of his mother's values—she who would so often emphasize the significance of complexity, uncertainty. "My mom says let's turn the coin over and see what's there," this boy once let me know as we were getting toward the end of our work together, and then told me his dad's invariable rejoinder: "What you see is what you get, so why look for trouble!"

Their son not only heard such conflicting remarks, he also tried to reconcile these aphoristic, parental hand-downs, and was powerfully persuaded to do so, because his parents lived up to what they said: the father gruff and commanding at home, in stores, with friends, neighbors, employees; the mother sweet-tempered, ever ready to listen to others, hear their side of things, apologize for her lapses, her mistakes of judgment. To be sure, I had to take notice of the emotional side of all this—the boy's desire to be a man like his father, even as he strongly loved his mother. But this boy already saw rather clearly the ethical questions at stake, the implications for his behavioral life (not to mention his interior or feeling one) of his father's values versus his mother's.

In a telling and hard-to-forget moment that Tim eventually relayed to me, he found himself letting a maid know that she'd overlooked dusting a room, had failed to empty a wastebasket filled with Kleenex he'd used while he had a bad cold. His father had smiled upon hearing him speak as he did—Tim as a general ordering a soldier to shape up fast. But his mother lowered her head and said nothing—until later, when she took him aside to point out that the maid had her own "rhythm of housecleaning," that she eventually would have attended to all that he'd rapped her for not noticing, whereupon he lowered *his* head, only to become quite difficult the next school day with a teacher who, by his own description, kept telling the class that she wanted "law and order" at all costs, and anyone who denied her that blissful state would be severely punished. "All I did was raise my hand," Tim remembered, "and she went ballistic!" After some conversation between us, he also remembered that the teacher had been discussing grammar, the rights and wrongs of it, had told the class she wanted "no ifs, ands, or buts," simply compliance with the rules she was about to promulgate. But he had a "but" in his mind—a big one: he was hoping to ask "who made those rules," and so started waving his hand all too resolutely in the air, even as the teacher began her disquisition. The two had already had several showdowns resulting from a pupil's reluctance to accept certain matters on faith, and this time the teacher lost all her patience. "When she banged that book she was holding down on the desk," the boy recalled, "I thought she was going to explode—and she did: she came and got me and pulled me out of my seat and then out of the room, and she told me I had to stand there for ten minutes. When I told her I didn't have a watch, so how could I know, she got all red, she just went inside the room and slammed the door so hard, you would have thought that someone fired a gun!"

There he was, I thought, an outsider literally, a loner, with the rage symbolized by a fired bullet in his mind, an echo in one of our last meetings of a discussion we'd had in our very first one about Lee Harvey Oswald and his motives as an assassin. A boy who had taken to heart a family's split moral imperatives as they got lived day by day had developed a split, an aching heart. A teacher had told his mother: "When he gets rebellious, you can see his eyes filling up." The parents had trouble figuring out that particular "symptom," as they called it. I appreciated their obliging gesture towards psychopathology, but I thought to myself at the time, and with Tim's help would come to know, that this issue was not only clinical but, again, deeply moral: how to reconcile different, even contrasting or opposing values that are both spoken and enacted by one's parents. The solution: to be defiant, peremptory, though with tears of regret and sadness, sullen words, a contentiously waving hand, modified by expressively knowing, mournful eyes, eager to undo what has been said or done.

Mixed Moral Messages

So many of us (not entirely to the extent of that boy, perhaps) carry around such mixed moral messages and mandates, and struggle long and hard for a way to reconcile them. We heed various voices within ourselves, the remembered words of our parents, teachers, kin, as they were spoken to us as little children; and especially, we remember the specific acts, the nods and nays, the conduct of those giant moral figures in our lives: how they behaved, how they carried and comported themselves, how they steered their course in life, how they managed to do so when others came into sight, how they acquitted themselves: true to their prior words and injunctions or in contradiction to them.

No question, the early school years that precede the onset of adolescence (grades one to six, say) matter a great deal, morally—and not only as a consequence of home life. At this time, the voices and actions of teachers and coaches and the parents of friends become alternative examples, complementary and supplementary and sometimes contradictory in nature, to the substance of what is implied, suggested, enacted, with respect to values at home.

"My children come home and say so-and-so said *this*, and they heard someone else say *that*," a mother tells me as we talk about her daughter's constant questioning of her and her husband. I ask for the details, of course, and yet again hear of a child who is trying ever so strenuously to reconcile various notions of right and wrong, to the point that at eight she has announced that she doesn't want *a* career, but *three* of them, to be embraced in a carefully staged succession: first, she will be a nurse who works in a distant, war-plagued country (Bosnia was on her mind, at the time); then a businesswoman here in the United States; and finally, an artist who lives out West someplace. I am interested and a bit taken aback by the specificity and ambitiousness of what is being proposed, perhaps annoyed a mite by a certain presumptuousness in such a projected life, the sense of entitlement implicit in its delineation. I wonder aloud about the rationale, with a careful politeness, I notice, that no doubt belies a bemused skepticism—or is it a populist grudge, that so very much is possible, even in fantasy, for a certain few, relatively speaking, while others her age dare dream, maybe, of plentiful food and a permanent roof over their heads?

Soon enough I realize that my own preconceptions and blind spots and prejudices, my *values*, are in my way, are endangering my usefulness as a clinician. Here was a girl, I would realize, already shaky as a consequence of the enormous demands placed upon her at home by parents who did everything, it seemed, and were both dazzling in their aspirations and accomplishments. Here was a child whose skin troubles (intermittent hives) and eating troubles (she was "picky" with food, had a host of preferences and dislikes) spoke a good deal about a teetering accommodation to such a fiercely successful life. Why should I now deny her a concerned empathy, whereas at other moments I mobilize the greatest of concern for children far away from this office, where I sit? As I struggle, so does she, to answer my questions and, really, to answer her own inquiries, such as this one: "Maybe it's wrong to want so many careers—maybe I should stick with one of them, but I don't know which one! My dad is a businessman, but he's the head of a hospital and he says *that's* what's really important [to be connected to a hospital]; and my mom is a professor of economics, but she's big with the museum, so you see, they are 'all over the map.' " Her father was the chairman of the hospital's trustees, and her mother was a trustee of the Boston Museum of Fine Arts.

That phrase "all over the map" comes from both parents: it's their way of saying that they each do an enormous amount of work, both in their respective professions and as vigorously committed volunteers. Consequently, their daughter and her younger brother see little of them but spend a lot of time with them in fantasy, as it were—hence this girl's effort to draw on her parents' contemporary commitments in order to fashion some for herself.

The more I got to know of all this, the more I realized that "values education," or "character education" was going on all the time in that household, albeit informally and by implication rather than as a structured part of a school curriculum. And let's face it, we can all rather quickly and conveniently forget moral abstractions, even their advocacy in a classroom, in a book or two; but the day in, day out embrace of values and ideals that gets called life—*there* children get a visible, an audible, a palpable "character-in-action" lesson: what their parents say, why they say it, what they do, how they speak of what they do, if they speak about it.

It is important for us as parents or teachers to "talk a good line," to espouse various virtues, to try that way to build up the character of our children in hopes that they will be patient, thoughtful, sensitive, responsive to others and honest, law-abiding, conscientious, kind-hearted, generous souls. Especially we should talk about what we value and uphold, and why, as we sit with our children in order to read them stories. Mostly, though, I have to keep insisting, we teach by example — a teaching that happens unself-consciously all the time, and a teaching that sometimes has to become more thought out by all of us who are parents or teachers: what do we really want our awake and aware children or students to believe in, to learn from what we say and, yes, most powerfully, influentially, from what we all the time do?

In point of fact, we are constantly answering that portentous question by indirection, and not rarely, unbeknownst to ourselves, through the conduct we offer to our witnessing children. The girl mentioned above fashioned an imaginary life for herself, dreamed of three careers for herself, on the basis of what she saw her parents doing, their joint commitment to hospital work, business, the arts. When I asked her which of her three stated goals would most please her, which she'd *choose* if she had to do so, she balked: she couldn't pick "only one." All right, I said. We moved on. A half hour later, we were nearing the end of our time together, and she brought up the subject, ironically, of time — how fast it goes, especially for her parents, who, she said, are "always rushing, rushing, rushing." I looked interested, curious, and she was enough "onto" my way of so indicating my feelings, my attitudes (a tilt of the head, a rise of the brow, a widening of the eyes) that she gave me an example, offered me, really, a moral fable that was also a family's story, even legend: "My dad had to go to a hospital meeting, and he was way, way, way behind [in his schedule]. He came home late, grabbed some food, made some calls, and he said a quick good-bye to everyone. My mom wasn't home, so when he left, Clara [the family's nanny] said, 'Your father drove off so fast, I worry he'll get into an accident.' That's when I said that if he did he could hurt someone besides himself, and Clara said, we mustn't think like that. But I said, if everyone was taken to Daddy's hospital, they'd all get the best care."

In their own way Clara and the child (shades of some of John Cheever's short fiction) had together sensed and given expression to a huge irony: the speeding hospital benefactor putting someone's, anyone's, his own, life in danger—drumming up business, it could be said, sardonically, for the institution he so insistently served, while the value of such service was put a bit in jeopardy by the dangerous, potentially quite destructive driving that enabled his presence at an early evening meeting. Meanwhile it is left for others, in particular his daughter, to make sense of all that; to figure out which values to embrace, with what degree of passion, and what kind of character to develop, with what attempt at consistency: the tireless, rushed philanthropist; the driver who really cares for others, thinks of their safety, not to mention his own; the person who is at the top and can't be bothered by the small, bothersome details; the person who drives as if she is everyone's good neighbor and Samaritan and, yes, equal, lest she become hurtful, regardless of the merit of her destination.

These are big matters for a child to sort out, settle for herself—for all of us, of whatever age, to try to confront. These are matters my own son posed to me during *our* rush to the hospital mentioned earlier. They are matters that address our very humanity, our capacity through language to wonder *why, whither, to what purpose.* At times, an elementary school child can seem so vulnerable, so needy of us who are parents and teachers—so little at a remove from the early childhood years that precede attendance in kindergarten or the first grade. At other times, however, those same children appear virtually to be adults, with their feisty independence, their determination to explore, to see and hear and ask and try to fathom, to flex their body's muscles even as they stretch the range of their conceptual and perceptual selves. That is what the phrase "magic years" as applied to this age means: an inclination to leap, to break the bounds that soon enough settle on those called adults; an imagination that pries and pokes, that extends itself, that soars, not only in pursuit of a growing factuality or in response to the urges and tensions of a particular emotional life, but to some end, an intention that the child seeks. Our range of awareness, our way with words, our time consciousness, all conspire to make us not only wonder but worry about the pursuit by children of definition, of limits, of structure. What to do, where, in which way, and to what aim—such inquiry requires knowledge and character alike, even as we adults need to supply an overall *direction*, a way of seeing, of being, that also addresses both those sides of the young humanity entrusted to us, the capacity to acquire information and the capacity to look inward and outward ethically. Such a distinction will be all too quickly needed. In no time, after all, the "magic" of those elementary school years gives way to another kind of "magic," the sexual life come alive, and with it a host of moral quandaries.

3

ADOLESCENCE

Young people coming of age quite naturally command a good deal of our notice. They are understandably self-conscious, hence apt to call attention to themselves while often claiming to want no such thing, and they bring us back to our own momentous time of adolescence, a time that is like a second birth of sorts, only now accompanied by a blaze of self-awareness. Perhaps no other aspect of our life has prompted more writing on the part of our novelists, social scientists, journalists—it is as if these youths, in their habits, their interests, their language and dress, their music and politics, and not least, their developing sexuality, have a hold on us that is tied to our own memories as much as to the day-to-day reality presented to parents and teachers.

It is a commonplace that our concern about teenagers is more often than not unwelcomed by them, seen by them as a clinging intrusion that predictably stirs defiance on the part of young men and women anxious and determined to achieve a growing measure of independence. This search for independence is of course both encouraged and resisted in various ways by parents and teachers, by our society as well. We know deep down that our children ought to leave us and build their own life, yet we also want them to stay close. They are, after all, reminders of *our* life, and they are our legatees, long-standing witnesses to our lives—hence the power of our attachment to them. Still, they yearn to be their own persons, and we, their elders, by turn courteously or reluctantly, learn to accommodate them. Nor is that yearning of our young for their own lives only emotional in nature. Psychology abhors a vacuum, craves a social, a cultural, and ultimately, a moral vocabulary, as teenagers (and we who are their parents, or teach them, or work with them as doctors, or observe and write about them) surely know. Thus, the importance of the music, the clothing, the language, the food, the reading, the movies, the television programs that a so-called "youth culture" embraces.

Moral Alienation

Such choices, we correctly know, tell us of rebelliousness, of stubborn assertiveness, of isolation and loneliness, of melancholy, the familiar story of adolescence: young men and women trying things out, embracing a cynicism toward the rest of us, often feeling alone, a touch peculiar, sad, and, not least, angry. Such choices also have their moral consequences, their moral analogues. If the achievement of independence is the defining task and goal of adolescence, and if the pursuit of that independence can prompt the familiar moody isolation, the cliquishness, the defiant otherness that we older folk are often at a loss to fathom, there are moral consequences and risks too: a moral alienation that asserts itself openly or gets variously disguised. Indeed, this chapter aims at examining that moral aspect of adolescence, the ways young people struggle to break away from us morally, while at the same time holding on to us for dear life (holding on, that is, to the sense of what matters, learned from us). The result of such a struggle can often be a moral paralysis, a sense of moral drift, unnerving, hard to shake.

I have sat with groups of parents of teenagers in several cities over the years, heard them worry and, most of all, heard them express a host of fears—especially that of a kind of estrangement: fear that they will be unable to be heard respectfully by their sons and daughters, and also that they as adults will lose a capacity to understand those same off-spring, no matter the decade and more that all parties have spent under the same roof. Most recently, sitting in my hometown listening to reasonably well-educated, quite sincere and devoted parents (and teachers, too) speak of adolescents (their own children, and those who belong to neighbors or, more abstractly, to the world at large), I sometimes feel we are discussing an alien tribe of sorts, elusive, unpredictable, errant.

"Most of the time we get on fine—but that's because we've learned to keep out of one another's way," a mother of two teenagers, a daughter of sixteen and a son of fourteen, tells us, and her husband nods a bit too emphatically, as if to assert not only agreement but decided resentment. I look at him with concern, friendliness, empathy, and sympathy, or so I hope, but immediate and strong memories of a family's recent struggles deny him a relaxed, reflective response. Instead, he tries valiantly to keep his cool, even as he tells us of tensions, misunderstandings, raised voices, slammed doors; his voice brings it all near at hand: a high-pitched tremulousness, a mix of apprehension and anger that (apart from the content of his remarks) stirs us, unnerves us. Finally, an observation that is also an implied question and without a doubt a plea for assistance: "It is a 'stage,' I know it is, people keep saying that it must be! But it's not natural that people who belong to the same family have such different values!"

I was struck right off by that way of putting the matter—a different cry from the usual one, which emphasizes a psychological antagonism that somehow, so it is hoped, with the right series of interpretations, will yield to a rapprochement. I perk up, ask about those "different values." The father, an engineer, quickly apologizes for using what he thinks I think are the wrong words and switches to a psychological vein: "I'm sorry, I didn't make myself clear. My children—well, that's it: they insist all the time that they're not children anymore, and that my wife and I are still treating them like they're our kids. 'We've grown up,' they keep telling us. The next thing you know, there's another argument: about how late they can come home on weekdays, and how much freedom on weekends, and all that! We just don't agree!"

Arguing with Moral Authority

I hold on to his use of the word "values." I say that he has some firm beliefs, I assume, that form the basis of his position that his two teenagers be back by a certain hour, that they dress in certain ways rather than others, that they shoulder certain responsibilities at home, in the neighborhood. He agrees, but doesn't really seem to want a discussion on morals; he comes back to psychology, to the arguments and fights that keep occurring. The two youths are "rebellious," we are told, and he has a hard time putting up with that wide, highly energized streak in both of them. Saying so, he turns to the others in our room, located in the basement of a church, as if they are fellow sufferers, but also as if they will help him in some way. One of them, a father of two teenage sons, eighteen and seventeen, tries to oblige: "You have to watch your every word; that's what I've discovered. If you walk as if there's glass all over, it can pay off—you avoid those confrontations!"

A mother doesn't like what she has just heard and says so forthrightly: "I disagree. I think that you've got to put your ideas right out there, and the kids, too [they should do likewise]." She is about to continue but is interrupted by another mother, who takes immediate, strong, lengthy issue. "You get nowhere pushing teenagers with those frank talks—you end up making bad go to worse that way. They love to argue—believe me, I know! That's what being a teenager is—in America! I mean, argue, argue with moral authority—with everyone who has it. That's all I hear from my son [who's sixteen]: authority this and authority that! I've had those 'knockdowns'—we've said *everything*, and you know what? Once you do that, you don't forget what you've heard! I'm not just blaming him—I'm talking about myself. I've gotten so upset, I've lost my temper. I've told my son that his problem is that he's got an easy, comfortable life, so he can be one of these teenagers who is 'in rebellion.' If he had to go to work so he wouldn't starve to death he'd not be 'in rebellion'; he'd be glad to have a job and obey the people over him! My father grew up in the Depression and he had to work and work, and he brought home money from doing errands and delivering newspapers, and he wasn't out there fighting with his parents, and complaining about how grown-ups were treating him, and how they're abusing their 'authority'! He was glad to *slave* away—at school or in the jobs he found, and he handed his money over to his parents and felt honored to be able to do that! They *struggled*, those people; now it's gotten so easy for our kids that they don't know how lucky they are!"

She stopped only to gather momentum to continue, and no one seemed willing to intervene. When she resumed she shifted direction, explicitly and dramatically: "Look, I'm not going to give you folks the speech you thought you'd be getting from me. I tried telling my son long ago what I just told you—plenty of that! In one ear, out the other. Oh, I'm not being very fair to him. He let me know: his life isn't his grandfather's, and there's no point in trying to say that it is. I began to realize that *my* life isn't (it wasn't ever) the same as my mom's and dad's. They sent me to Europe when I was in college—unthinkable for them! They bought me a car—unthinkable for them that your parents buy you a car! That's why you've got to do some heavy thinking, each of you and your husband or your wife, about the differences between the generations, what they're about, and how you should handle them. You're coming at all this from your life, and they've grown up with theirs, and you don't need a head-on collision. You need to figure out how to get your views across—you've got to be *heard*. It's a problem of *communication*, that's what I'm saying, communication and psychology."

Everyone seems to be agreeing with her, including the person whose remarks got her going so forcefully. I realize I am expected to put a kind of *imprimatur* on this line of reasoning—the purest common sense of our time! I think to myself as I sit there: the grandfather who worked so hard as a teenager never thought of "psychology" or "communication" when bringing up his family, even as *his* parents and grandparents surely didn't, either. In fact (and in contrast), his daughter and her son have that in common—they both know those two words very well. His daughter had essentially told us that she and her son share a point of view about life (and the experiences that go with such a point of view) that is quite at variance with her father's, his grandfather's—and I decide to mention this, to say that *beliefs* and *experiences* and, yes, *values* matter here, not only "psychology and communication."

I have a long speech in me, but withhold it, eager to see if perhaps one or two others will take the cue, respond out of their lives (talking about "psychology"!). I am not disappointed. Another mother, one of the more reticent ones in our bimonthly, two-hour meetings (which have extended on occasion to over three hours) speaks up: "I think my daughter and I really do understand each other, and we have a good relationship—but there are disagreements we have, and as my husband keeps on saying [he is a lawyer], they are 'substantive.' I mean, if you want an example, I don't want my daughter [she is sixteen] to be sleeping with a boy, any boy, even if he's very nice and even if they've known each other for a long time, and they're good friends. Some of my friends will say that—they'll say if they're really good friends, and he's a good boy, then it's all right, it's natural, it's inevitable: that's what they say, and then if I disagree, they look at me as if *I'm* the one who's got 'problems'—I'm a 'puritan,' or 'uptight'! I say I have certain beliefs, principles, call them what you will, values, and one of them is that a mother has an obligation to be more than a listener to her kids, ready to take in what they say, and more than someone who is always ready to *understand* them, keep on *understanding* them! A mother is an authority figure, and so is a father, and they always will be, and they damn well should be. I have a friend—her daughter keeps saying she's [the mother] trying to be an 'authority figure,' and she [the daughter] doesn't like it. I said, hey, your problem is—this is what I thought, I'll just say here what I said there to her, I said: 'Excuse me, I don't mean to be rude, but if you're just *trying* to be an "authority figure" with a sixteen or seventeen-year-old, then *that's* a "problem" right there! You *are* one, or you *should* be one, or if you're not one, then—there's a *big* problem all right, never mind what you're arguing about!'

"I sit down with my daughter, don't get me wrong. I talk with her—and talk with her. I don't shout and scream; I'm not against 'psychology' or 'communication.' I read the newspaper and the magazines; I try to keep up with things. But I tell my daughter what I believe in, and why, and I don't mince words. I try to be a straight shooter with her. I'm not afraid of the word 'right' and the word 'wrong.' "

She pauses, and a mom sitting beside her quickly poses a question to her: "What about sex, what about abstinence? Why do you believe in it—I mean, what do you tell her and does she listen?"

Asserting Moral Authority

We are all quite attentive—this is pay-dirt time. The mother doesn't need a long stretch to gather her thoughts; she's right there, ready with this: "She listens; she doesn't always agree with me. But she knows that I believe in something and that I want her to hear me out, and she knows I want her to go along with me. That's right, *obey* me on certain matters, even if she doesn't agree with me. I know this sounds strange to a lot of people these days—to some of you, here—but I feel my daughter shouldn't be having sex, sexual intercourse, as a high school girl, no matter what (I mean, no matter with whom). I think she's too young; she needs time to learn about herself and others, and I feel it's my job to talk with her, try to persuade her, hear her out, try hard to persuade her, but also to say no, to really come down loud and clear and hard, finally: *no*—for all the reasons we've discussed. I'm not afraid to bring in my moral values, my husband's, what we believe: we do go to [an Episcopal] church, and we do have some religious and moral beliefs. I know, you could have a talk with Episcopal ministers, and maybe some of them wouldn't agree with me on my view [about abstinence during the high school years], or some would, and they'd say it's God's will. I don't know whether God has ever expressed Himself specifically on this issue (maybe He has), but I think He'd want us parents to enlist Him on the side of waiting, and letting yourself become a grown-up who's out in the world, in college, or working, in your twenties, and He'd want us to give our beliefs to our kids, stand up for them, I mean, when talking with them."

Her position, its specifics, predictably stirs comments, criticism. Across the room, a father points out that she is "hedging her bets," that she seems reluctant to say "out and out" that she favors "abstinence" ("What's wrong with that word?"), and that she does so out of her "religious faith." "Yes," says a mother next to him: "You're saying it's not psychology or communication, but you're not going to say no because that's what the Bible says—you're probably afraid your daughter just won't listen to you! I'm not blaming you, mind you! I'm with you! I know what my kids will accept, and what they'll just shrug off and laugh at!"

The mother rises to her own defense, attempts to refute the implication that she is some kind of clever, agile diplomat, ready to cloak her convictions in the very psychology she denounces when summoned by others. She insists that she has "never before" used the Bible as an explicit instrument of affirmation or condemnation with her children; that they know of her church attendance, her faith, yet also know that when she tells them of her beliefs and convictions, they are offered as *hers* and her husband's, as *theirs*, really: *we* expect this, *we* insist upon this.

All right, others say, but what if your daughter out and out "disagrees"? The mother is ready for that line of questioning, pursued by several of her fellow parents. She points out that if one doesn't define one's views, explain them, and ultimately, *insist* upon them, then one is accepting right off more than the possibility that the youth will "disagree," will go his or her way, but will now by implication be encouraged to do so by a parent who refuses to give "something badly needed," namely, "opposition" to what "seems popular," what "they and their friends" think is "cool," and is being advocated and practiced by "everyone." We are now in the midst of a complex, necessary discussion—how to convey one's moral principles to an adolescent bent on independence, on asserting his or her personal initiatives and ideas, in such a way that one is heard, heeded, both. I am asked for suggestions—and am reminded by particular parents of their failures, their efforts to enforce this or that rule, regulation, principle, that foundered on a son's, a daughter's refusal, noncompliance, defiance. I smile nervously, confess a major inability. No words, however convincingly stated, can wipe out the individuality of every family's past, its moral as well as emotional past, nor guarantee, along one or another lines, its future. By the time a child begins becoming an adolescent, becoming a young man, a young woman, a person not only prompted by sexual interests and desires but sanctioned by the society as increasingly able to work, to have opinions and values and rights (teenagers acquire certain legal rights at sixteen and eighteen), a lot has happened between a given parent, or set of parents, and that youth, a lot that will very much give shape to the way my "advice," my remarks, anyone's, spoken or written, are understood and greeted and shared (by a parent listening to me, a youth doing so).

Moral Loneliness, Moral Vulnerability

With that caveat, a big one, I nod to the mother who has spoken of her effort to enforce explicit sexual limits for her daughter. I tell of what I believe adolescents, all of us, need so very much—standards, values, by which I hope I mean not easy rhetoric, including the psychological kind forthcoming from my kind all too readily and welcomed by many rather too readily. I tell of the loneliness many young people feel, even if they have a good number of friends and seem to be in the very midst of things. It's a loneliness that has to do with a self-imposed judgment of sorts: I am pushed and pulled by an array of urges, yearnings, worries, fears, that I can't share with anyone, really—and don't wish to, even as I wonder about others, their thoughts, their emotions. This sense of utter difference, this sense of peculiarity, even as one at the same time realizes one's kinship with family members, one's substantial affiliation with and resemblance to various friends, makes for a certain moodiness well known among adolescents, who are, after all, constantly trying to figure out exactly how they ought to and might live—where, doing what, and with whom.

I call upon some past teachers of mine, including youths who in their often tense, nearly mute manner can convey so very much. I remember out loud a young man of fifteen who engaged in light banter, only to shut down, shake his head, refuse to talk at all when his own life and troubles became the subject at hand. He had stopped going to school, begun using large amounts of pot; he sat in his room for hours listening to rock music, the door closed. To myself I called him a host of psychiatric names: withdrawn, depressed, possibly psychotic; finally I asked him about his head-shaking behavior: I wondered whom he was thereby addressing. He replied: "No one." I hesitated, gulped a bit as I took a chance: "Not yourself?" He looked right at me now in a sustained stare, for the first time. "Why do you say that?"

I felt that much was at stake now—I knew I'd come close to something, to someone, yet I also knew that this youth might for that very reason be scared mightily, and so more than inclined to run fast and far. I decided not to answer the question in the manner that I was trained to reply, had become accustomed to reply: an account of what I had surmised about him, what I thought was happening inside him: his moral vulnerability, his self-arraignment at the hands of an overbearing conscience, which was naysaying him and everyone else, hence his extreme solitude. Not that I'd have gotten into psychiatric specifics. I would have been, I hope, gently interpretive, would perhaps have commented on the "hard time" I thought he was giving himself, in the hope that maybe he'd take over and tell me about the hard time that he was having, in that way confirming my sense of things. Instead, with some unease (I could always attribute that to the patient, *his* unease as picked up by me!) I heard myself saying this: "I've been there; I remember being there—remember when I felt I couldn't say a word to anyone. I guess I was saying that to myself, that I had no idea what to make of myself, say to myself."

I can still remember those words, still remember feeling that I ought not to have spoken them: it was a breach in "technique." Not that they worked, triumphantly—hence my resort to them with those parents, and now, here: a not-so-sly kind of self-affirmation, if not congratulation. The young man kept staring at me, didn't speak, at least with his mouth. When he took out his handkerchief and wiped his eyes, I realized they had begun to fill.

I plunged on, worried that *I* was talking, afraid that I was becoming "too personal," concerned about what one or another of the supervisors who had taught me child and adolescent psychiatry might think, say, were he or she there (they are, naturally, always "there," in one's worrying mind). I told the teenager sitting before me of my own adolescence, some of it—how I had been so cut off at moments from others, even those in my own family or, rather, especially them. I added this: "Often I wanted to strike out at the world, but I didn't." From him I heard, "Why?" I answered: "I think I must have known at the time that the trouble wasn't outside of me, it was inside."

I had tried to put myself back in time, put myself in my own youthful shoes. I wanted at all costs to avoid coming off as the smart aleck who even back then was on his way to becoming a shrink. I wanted to call upon the truest memory that I could muster, speak out of my heart, offer this locked-up youth some sense of companionship: that is how it went for me, and that is how it can go for any number of us at such a time in life. On the other hand, I was "editing" my life, as it were—commenting on it from the distance of my then late thirties: trying to interpret a bit how I felt, why I had behaved as I once did. As all of that rumbled through my head (only in retrospect does it have the conceptual clarity I have just tried to summon) the youth opposite me sat quietly, his handkerchief now back in his pocket. Finally, I had to tell him that our time was up, that I hoped that we could meet again at the same time next week. As he got up to leave, he kept looking at me, but in silence. He did, however, make one gesture that gave me a bit of hope: he nodded once—a significant turnaround, I couldn't help but feel (and hope) as against his head-shaking of before.

That time turned out to be our lowest spell together—from there we began a very gradual climb upward, step by step, out of the "slough of despond," his as it was then being lived, mine in retrospect as I was asked to share it with him. I abbreviated a lot of all that for my fellow parents at that meeting, as I now do in the retelling, here—I wanted (I now want) not to offer the details of something called, these days, "psychotherapy with a depressed adolescent," but rather, to indicate the great challenge that a troubled teenager can sometimes present to himself or herself, never mind us adults, be we parents, teachers, doctors. How to put in words such a mix of feelings, of apprehensions and misgivings and longings and appetites for oneself, never mind the ears of another? I now understand that this youth had confronted me with his quite singular self, his seemingly impenetrable aloneness. Perhaps I might have gotten to him in a more conventional psychiatric way, our tensely wordless, seemingly confrontational encounters yielding to a degree of (desperate) trust that would have enabled the give and take of communication. But something in me must have doubted such an outcome—or maybe, doubted the *value* of such an outcome. Doctors have *their* values too, and one of them is the conviction that clarification of another's thought can be of decided help—and so it can, *sometimes*. I think I had come to feel in my bones or gut, more than in my head, that this young man's determined solitude might be reached only by an evocation on my part of another solitude, mine of yore. Eventually, as we got to talk, I learned of a teenager who was angry, withdrawn, contemptuous of any number of prevailing moral and social standards, who in fact appeared headed for an encounter with the law because of his marijuana use—yet, he went after himself with more insistence than even the sternest of prosecutors or judges would do. The key to his "success" as a self-accuser was his brilliance as a social observer: he spotted anyone's, everyone's, failures, missteps, hypocrisies, pretenses. A master at unmasking others, he couldn't let the matter stop there; with no one left to expose, he turned on himself, made mincemeat of what he saw. The one who mocked the world's phoniness joined it— the nearest he could come to being in the company of others.

Anna Freud on the Adolescent Conscience

I brought him up at that parents' meeting, and do so now, because I don't think I've ever met a tyrannical conscience so thoroughly masked. A young man who could unmask others, and himself with them, wasn't (nevertheless, and ironically) able to comprehend the imperial intensity of his own conscience. Nor was he all that unique. Here is Anna Freud speaking on the subject and drawing on her many years of psychoanalytic work with adolescents:

"For many adults, adolescence is a time of rebelliousness, we all know. Parents often first come to see me alone about their children—before they even broach the subject [of seeing a psychoanalyst with their son or daughter]. I am not saying that what I hear is always the same. When I say *that* I'll be ready to retire! No, each parent has something new and different to tell, but there *are* certain themes that keep coming to my mind as I listen to these mothers and fathers—they are often quite distraught. Over and over I'm told that a child is terribly 'difficult,' extremely 'rebellious.' I ask for details, and get plenty of them—and as I listen I begin to understand the parents' sense of what is going on, but I have to admit (and I do, to them!) that I hear something else, commonly; I hear a demanding conscience at work [in the adolescent], with the rebelliousness a reaction to it. This can come as a surprise to the parents—who have been pronouncing their own children virtually lawless, without moral standards, at the mercy of their every whim and fancy! So, we can have some spirited conversations; and this is the beginning of treatment for the adolescent, I firmly believe: that the parents understand why there is so much showing of the teeth and shaking of the fist and throwing down the gauntlet.

"All the no's the child has learned are still there inside; all the values and standards—but society has made such a big thing out of the independence; and the drives, the instincts, are newly influential, and these young people don't quite know, some of them, what to do! A lot of them, I find, talk a big game [of rebelliousness], scare their parents and themselves, but don't go get themselves into a lot of trouble. Some stumble into it [this or that kind of difficulty]. Others end up in serious trouble; and when some of us talk to them, get to know them, we can, even with them, find a youth who is tormented by his conscience, which he's tried to rid himself of—projected it upon others, then fought it that way! I know all of this sounds very complicated, and it *is* very complicated, especially, for parents and teachers, who aren't studying the mind the way we do, with a bit of detachment. But I do believe that it is important for all of us not to regard adolescents, most of them, as lawless, as beyond the kind of moral anxiety that most of us have learned to have—[that] *they* have been brought up to have.

Often, to make this point [with parents] I have to get personal; I tell them of my own adolescence—not a big outpouring of autobiography, but a description of a time when I felt quite alone, and constructed 'showdowns' of my own, [on behalf of] which I often fought very hard!"

I was a bit taken aback at first by that—the willing surrender by a distinguished authority, Anna Freud, of her near-mythological aura of psychological perfection, itself of course, one of those "shadows" (or halos) we imagine out of our need to gain our own authority, our sense of competence, through the embrace of the purported brilliance, the unchallengable savvy of another. Then I turned back, quickly, to our earlier conversation, and realized that, like some of the parents she had been describing, I had been making quite a to-do about a contemporary version of adolescence as especially provocative, prone to waywardness, if not outright deviance: weird clothes, music, hairstyles and hair colors, not to mention resort to drugs, an unapologetic, thoroughly advocated sexuality, some of it quite unconventional. She didn't want to disagree; she did, though, worry that I had lost my bearings a bit, not descriptively, but analytically: the whys of what I perceived, described. She had tried to move beyond the constant shifts of cultural expression, bring us a little closer to the moral as well as emotional heart of adolescence, as she did with her patients on occasion, when she introduced herself into the discussions she had with them.

Anna Freud on Trying for Connection

All right, then—what to do next, after one has reminisced, delved below another's surface with the aid of one's own life as a snorkel of sorts! In a guarded, fearful, tentative way, I asked that of Miss Freud, only to hear her quite directly address my concern and curiosity: "We are here [in this field of psychoanalysis] to listen and learn—and to be able to do so with children and adolescents (who may not be as anxious to come see us as their parents are that we see them!). We may have to reach out as best we can. You are afraid that we won't succeed—the suspicious, sullen, resentful adolescent might clam up, or refuse to come back. That has happened; that will happen! We are not miracle workers who can say something, and, presto!, the trouble in a life has vanished! But I have noticed that in most of the adolescents that I see (and I see the ones far more troubled, far more 'on the edge' than most their age), in most of them a real effort at *understanding* on my part, a gesture that shows that I'm at least *trying* to understand, and that I've been in *some* of the distress they're experiencing, hard as that might be for them to believe (or for some of my colleagues, or at certain times of the day, for *me*!)—all of that can go a long way. The adolescent will be interested long enough to want to continue our meetings; and as you know, that is all-important: we have another chance, and another still, to sort out some of these difficulties and figure out what is happening."

A second's silence, while she catches her breath, and then she gives a bit more: "I guess I'm agreeing with you that adolescents can be as touchy and irritable and suspicious and disobedient and heedless of convention as you say—*some* of them, remember. But I do feel that if we make the effort to indicate that *we* are not the policeman and the judge, and not the ones with whom they've already fought, and not the ones they are *looking* to for a fight, but are like them in some way, have known at least some of what they are experiencing, the loneliness, and sincerely want to be in touch with them, want a *connection* with them in a way that might be useful, helpful (whatever the right word is here!)—then that might well (often does) happen."

There was more, much more. We shifted into the theoretical mode, itself an escape of sorts from those tough, vexing clinical challenges that confront psychiatrists all the time. Still, that word "connection" stuck in my mind, and her commonsense reminder that most adolescents don't go through an especially worrisome time of it, and that those whom we doctors see, as is so often the case, are apt to be relatively the most in pain, and cause most alarm and pain to others. Nevertheless, the parents sitting with me clearly wanted more, wanted "guidelines," wanted advice and direction (even as, perhaps, you, the reader, now do). So I sensed, and so I learned, this way, from a father: "You mention Miss Freud a lot. I read some of her work in law school. She worked with the people at Yale Law School, I think, on children's issues, if I remember correctly. I respect her, as you do, but I wonder what she'd have done *as a parent.* She never had to face that, the way we do. My wife and I, we read these books one after the other, and they tell you something, they sure do. If it's a good book, you get up, you walk away a little smarter. I don't mean 'smarter,' actually—wrong word! You've been taught something, and it's there, in your mind— ready for you to think about when there's the need. But then your kids come into the house, into the room where you've been sitting and reading that book and saying to yourself, 'Yes, interesting, yes, very in- teresting, yes, that makes sense' (or 'Maybe to do that, to say that, will be of help')—and suddenly it's a whole new ball game. You're not read- ing a book; you're *you, there,* and with your kids—and you've got a whole family history that you're carrying on your shoulders, all you've said and done, and I guess I should add, all you haven't said and haven't done.

"I mean, a couple of years ago, when Margie [his daughter, then fif- teen] was just beginning to 'sprout,' as my wife used to put it, we thought we should talk with her. My wife already *had,* mother to daughter. This was supposed to be a bigger, a more general discussion, not about sex itself, really, but about how you behave, now that you're getting older and can be more on your own: a what's right and what's wrong discussion, and a practical one, too. How do you handle these guys, for instance, who come hanging around you, and what time do you come home (a set time or no set time?), or what kind of responsi- bilities do you start picking up in the house, that kind of talk. Well, I had this book inside me, and I told myself now was the time to use it, and so I started talking to Margie. I told her we knew she was going through a lot, this 'adolescence,' and we want to talk with her, and we want to do the best by her, and she should understand that—that we're really trying to understand her. I kept talking. I made some of the points that the author made, and I even told her about the book, and said that she might want to read it, too. My wife wasn't as high on the book as me; she's skeptical of people who give a lot of advice. 'I'd like to be a fly on the wall in their house, and see how they follow their own words, if they do, and see what the result is,' that's what she'll say when

I put on her desk a magazine or book that tells you how to tackle some family problem. But she backed me up. She said I'd been worried, and so had she, and we both wanted her to know, Margie, that we're always going to be her parents, and we're always going to be there for her, and if she has any questions, or wants to have a good old talk with us, we're there, we're *there* for her.

"I know this sounds fine, what I just said, what I said to Margie. But you know, it went over like the proverbial lead balloon, a complete dud. There was something in my voice, something on my face, in the way I talked—my daughter started looking at me as if I wasn't me, as if *I* was the one who needed 'help,' and she and her mom were there to talk with me! When I stopped talking, she said: 'Dad, are you O.K., are you all right?' I didn't know what to say. Sally tried to rescue me. She said we were both trying to be good parents, and we know she's becoming more and more a grown-up (we tried to avoid using that word 'teenager,' because in the book they said it can be a put-down, many kids think.) So, we just wanted to sit and talk with her, and let her know that we're here and we are ready to discuss anything she wants, anytime.

"That's when I added my two cents, my stupid two cents; I said, 'We want to open a "dialogue," Margie.' She laughed, but she didn't think what I said was funny. She asked where I got that 'dialogue stuff' from, and I said I'd been doing some reading; and she said she thought there was too much talk about 'teenagers,' and we should just go on as we've been, and not get into all these 'discussions.' She had a look of scorn on her face when she used that word, and I wasn't going to say a word, and my wife was very quick to get us all out of this jam. She said we're having her dad over, and she needed to do some shopping, and she asked us if we'd both like to come along. I said yes, of course; but Margie said, no, she couldn't, because she had an 'appointment.' I sure wanted to know with whom. But there you have it, I can't be the busybody I used to be, at least I can't *reveal* that I am (my true colors!) because Margie *is* older, and she has every right to keep things from us. Later, my wife and I were at the supermarket, and we were discussing which kind of cheese to buy, and we sort of looked at each other. We both were thinking the same thing: this is the beginning of a new kind of family life for us, in a way. Sure, you can make too much of it, but you can 'whistle Dixie' and get into trouble just as easily—forget that your daughter is becoming a woman, and whether you want to notice or not, others do: those guys."

He stops, then apologizes—he didn't mean to be "crude." He goes further, wonders in a long monologue whether parents don't sometimes "overworry"—become all too aware of possible hurdles and hazards awaiting their adolescent sons and daughters around one or another corner, when in fact "most kids" do "O.K., mostly" when they get to middle school, to high school. That is how he remembers his own adolescence, after all, so he kept telling his wife: he was an athlete (baseball), a good student, held a job as a stock boy in a supermarket not unlike the one that he and his wife had visited after that, for them, momentous talk with their daughter. He offers his wife's thoughts on the subject of adolescence as his final word: she had come up with one of her favorite phrases: "It's wait-and-see pudding."

His experience, relayed at such rambling length and with such a mix of perplexity and earnest interest in what to do, how to do it, prompted a great deal of discussion—and wary questions. Again and again these mothers and fathers struggle with the same polarity of sorts that this father evoked with his comments: a desire to address adolescence as a phenomenon directly, knowingly, through resort to reading and reflection, and, ultimately, family discussion, as against a sense that such a course of action may well be difficult, even futile—get new problems going, actually. At a certain point I tried to be of help, to talk about adolescence as a time of endocrinological change, and psychological change, yes, but as a time, also, of inevitably heightened moral awareness: sexuality and a more active citizenship both arrive, and each youth will have a particular way of dealing with those new possibilities in life. Of course, this father had essentially warned us about "advice," be it written or spoken, and all of us had *that* message very much in mind. Certainly I did as I edged toward a bit of persuasion, guidance, instruction. I pointed out the obvious, that a certain truth emerges in adolescence—it could be called the hatching of eggs: earlier attitudes, troubles, achievements, difficulties, and hang-ups have a way of becoming newly significant, as young men and women hold on to what they have got and who they have been for dear life, even as they venture into new and often fearful territory. No wonder that matters of right and wrong, the heart of moral thinking, can take on powerful meaning at this time—often expressed indirectly, through pointed questions, through refutations of the conventional as a means of finding for oneself something "better," something more "real."

Stranded by Moral Seriousness

I had brought with me tapes of interviews I had conducted with young men and women, all high-schoolers. Some lived in crowded urban areas; some lived in suburbs; some came from quite well-to-do families and had been sent off to private schools. We listened together to the voices of those youths. We heard them talk about the traditional subjects of adolescence, how they were trying to deal with their families, their friends, their sexual life, but also heard them talk about their lonely struggles for "meaning in life." Indeed, they often connected their loneliness to the intensity of that search for meaning, as if they felt alone, stranded by their ethical inquiry—and the rest of the world was uninterested. Those youths brought up various ethical questions: not only how they should behave but why, in accordance with what larger scheme of things. Here they revealed a tenacious moral seriousness, even as they weren't sure what to do with it, where to take it, so to speak. "My parents, they're ready to talk about sex at the drop of a hat," a sixteen-year-old girl from a well-to-do, well-educated family observed, and then she gave us the details: discussions of contraception, discussions, as she put it, of *whether, when, with whom, how much*! She told her friends in that room the details of those talks, told of her boredom, by now, with the subject. Then she became both ironic and sad: "You know, there are times when I think that my folks are more into all that than I am! They've read all these books, they've talked with doctors, and my mother is seeing a shrink, and they're ready—wow, are they ready!—to sit with me and talk about 'options,' and 'psychology,' and the 'stages' I'm going through, and 'women,' and how it's different being female, and you have to understand that, and 'men,' and what *they* are like: I've heard it all! Even our minister—he talks about that stuff all the time! I went to a 'sexuality' course, a seminar he ran at the church. He and my parents, they talk exactly alike! I got out of those meetings, and I thought, this is *something!* You can't take a breath if you're a teenager without someone coming at you and telling you that you're going through this 'cycle,' and you should 'share your feelings.' My grandmother—she told me that when she was my age she was trying to do well in school and hold down a job, and her dad was sick, so she worried about him, and no one seemed to be worrying about her, or talking with her, *and that was fine!*

"What I wish: I wish a lot of people who are worrying about us 'teenagers'—I wish they'd be worrying about themselves! I feel so damn odd and peculiar—as though I'm the only one I know in my family who's trying to figure things out, as if I'm walking on this street and there's no one in sight. I wish my folks would stop turning me into one more reason *not* to worry about themselves, that's what I wish! I look at them sometimes, and I think: Lord, they're in a sorry way, even if we do have this big house, and this heated swimming pool, and my dad plays golf and wins the trophies, and he goes racing in his sailboat, and he wins the trophies: a lot of the time, he looks just plain *down*, but no one, not Mom, not even her, can say a word to him, ask him anything."

I asked what she would ask him. "What would I ask him? I'd ask him—hey, Dad, why are you being this way, what for? I mean, what do you *believe* in? Anything? Nothing? Your job and your hobbies and us, your family? I'd ask him if he thought, if he wished he'd be living like he does now, back when he was my age? I'd ask him what really counts. He goes to church with Mom every once in a while, and she says he's almost fast asleep most of the time! That's what I remember, when I used to go—how he'd be bored, he'd be going through the motions, that's all. When I stopped going, Mom was upset, but Dad just shrugged his shoulders. You want to know what I think? I think he shrugs his shoulders a lot—at life! He's 'made it.' He's in the seven-figure bracket, his 'estate,' it's way up there. He brings home the bacon. He's a fat cat. He plays golf pretty good—hits par, below. He's a 'tough sailor,' the guys call him, and he beams! *That's* what he believes in, that's what he wants out of life: a hole-in-one, a shrewd, fast tack that brings him in ahead of all his buddies; an income-tax shelter; that Jim [her brother] and me both go to Yale so he can announce it in his class notes section of the alumni magazine there; and now, that Mom finally stops seeing that shrink! He hates it, that she goes once a week into the city to see him—'a total stranger, and she tells him everything I'll bet, and what do they know anyway!'

"I think Mom's troubles got him interested in Jim and me—he started worrying about us: 'You're teenagers! Is there anything you want to talk about? This sex urge—you've got to be aware of it, you can't just ignore it.' That's the way he talks. Mom says 'psychology' has made '*some* inroads' in Dad—but not much! But she's more like him than she realizes! She's *very* smart about psychology. Unlike him, she's being coached! She'd talk my ear off about sex if I let her."

"You don't let her?" I asked. "I don't. I don't, because that's not the big point for me. What is? It's this life—what does it mean? *That's* what I keep asking myself—that's what I'd like to be finding out, figuring out. I ask my mother about that and she gets this far-off look. She'd much rather talk with me about my boyfriend, and my friends, and their boyfriends. She'd like me to help her with her garden. She'd like me to learn to cook all these exotic foods, the way she's been learning in that course. She'd like me to be better at tennis: 'We could play doubles to-gether; we'd make a spectacular team—*smashing*!' She says tennis clears her head. She says that her shrink gives her 'food for thought.' I asked her *what* food, *what* thought. She smiled and told me I wasn't to know—it had to do with 'your mother and dad's private business.' Sex again! Relationships! 'How are you doing with your friends?' She asks me that once a week, at least—once a day! I'd like to think I'm headed for more than this, a repeat of it! I really would!"

The Root of Adolescent Cynicism

Much shuffling and squirming, I notice, as the tape machine whirls around, and a voice I remember as vigorous, lively, comes across as curiously strained, a victim, maybe, of the machine's static, its distortion of sound, its capacity to contain spoken life in the world of a small, thin, black case. In no time, however, a distant spell (the interview was done a year earlier, a hundred miles away) catches hold, spreads—as parents of youths her age are at pains to worry about her, her parents, themselves, their children, and not least, America. "I'll bet most people would say that family has *everything*," a father also well on his way to getting, having, "everything" observes with some puzzlement, irritation, but in the end, sympathy: "Why all the complaining? She's knocking her life, but I'll bet she'd miss it if it was suddenly taken away from her! I guess there's an emptiness there—that's what she's saying. Leave it to our kids to spot all our warts, all our mistakes. You know what—I think adolescents are master skeptics, or cynics, and they have super-vision, better than twenty/twenty. They see everything, and they let you know they do! Fine! But after a while you want to say *enough*! Hey, you get your kicks out of our failures—but, please, stop and think about *yourself*! Turn that laser eye back on your own life and on your friends—who can do no wrong, while if I cough once, I'm a really 'sick' guy, and not just in my lungs!"

He had much more to say, but the gist of his remarks were understandably self-protective, as if he feared at any moment being arrested, arraigned, put on trial, convicted, sentenced. It took one mother's terse, blunt intervention to stop minutes and minutes of such self-defensiveness: "I think we're all overreacting! We're turning our own children into our worst critics, our enemies, virtually! Give our kids a break! Give ourselves a break! Teenagers are looking for something to believe in, that's what is going on. When they become cynical and fault-finding, that tells you something. They've got a conscience working inside them—or they wouldn't have the slightest interest in finding fault with anyone, anywhere! They feel critical and 'out of it' because they're noticing a lot; they're not missing the tricks lots of us try to brush aside. I get tired sometimes when my son won't let up on something. He can be so contemptuous of certain people; he calls them arrogant and he doesn't see his own arrogance, the way he dismisses those people out of hand! But I stop myself from shouting at him. I say, look: he's sixteen years old and he's trying to find something to believe in. He goes to a lot of movies; in my opinion, too many! He'll think about them, though, and he'll talk to us about them, and it's then that I realize this boy is a man. This son of mine is looking at the world and trying to sort out all he sees, and most of all, he's looking for some goals, some path to take. That's what it means to be an 'adolescent,' I believe. You're not yet an adult, you haven't chosen your spouse, and you haven't chosen your occupation, your profession, but you're in the process of doing that, so you have to be a little critical and dismissive, because that is what 'choice' is all about. I realize some people don't have the choices our children have, I do [the matter of race and class had been brought up], but for a lot of us there are so many choices that it can be a big problem in itself, a buffet so full you can't decide what to eat!"

Adolescence as a Second Chance

This woman's remarks on "fault-finding" struck a big chord in all of us, helped us consider contemporary adolescence, in its bourgeois American and European expression, at least, with some fresh insight. She was of course emphasizing the moral aspect of adolescence, the building of a conscience that takes place then. As she talked I remembered Anna Freud's important book *The Ego and Mechanisms of Defense*. In it she gives a lively, compelling account, quite personal in nature, of adolescence, emphasizing the capacity youths have to turn on themselves and others, an aspect of a conscience very much bent on displaying its muscles.

In 1970, while talking with her at Yale, I heard this comment on adolescence that also came to mind as I listened to that mother's words:

"Unfortunately, many people—including many psychoanalysts!—have succumbed to the popular notion that we *are* who we *were*: that early childhood, the first four or five years, determines our psychological fate. My father emphasized those early years, but you have to remember why—you have to understand the assumptions of those who lived in the last years of the nineteenth century and the first years of the twentieth century. At that time young children were believed to be 'innocents'—though I remember my father once saying that lots of parents knew better, because every day their little boys and girls taught them better! What he said—well, he told the world in his books and articles that even nursery-age children have desires, wishes, likes and dislikes. He knew what mothers and fathers knew who kept their eyes and ears open and dared think for themselves and follow their observations to rational conclusions: that children have strong feelings, urges, and that they generally learn some control over them. That is the beginning of civilization.

"All of that is now common knowledge, but it has been distorted to the point that an emphasis on early childhood has been turned by many into something else: everything of importance happens there, and the rest of life is simply a reworking of that past, the first years. Not so! We keep learning as we grow, obviously—or at least there is a possibility for us [to do so]. In adolescence, especially, there is a new and heightened [psychological] drama: the defensive stand of the superego [the conscience] and the ego [the part of our mind that accommodates us to the world's reality in various ways] in response to the new instinctual pressures, and that [struggle] gives each adolescent a second chance, you could say. I mean, a child old enough to enter school has come to terms with his family life, figured out more or less how to comply with certain demands and rules and customs. In adolescence, that same person has to go through a similar kind of accommodation, but now it is not only the family that he has to deal with, but the world outside it. I often think of young people as caught in the middle: on one side is the body, on the other side society—and they're trying to come to terms with both."

She went on, spoke at length, as she had before in our talks, of the loneliness that many youths feel—to some extent a consequence, she pointed out, of the trouble they are having in understanding what is happening to them, hence a withdrawal from others. She told of some of her patients, how hard it was for her to stay connected with them. She even became a bit rhetorical, a rare moment for her, and told me how important it can be for adolescents to be in touch with at least one adult in some candid and trusting way, even though many young people deny having any interest in such a relationship. She told me of a sixteen-year-old girl who came to see her weekly only to denounce the whole adult world as "crooked" or "rotten." After such condemnatory comments, which lasted about half an hour, she almost feverishly tried to get the answers to various questions that were obviously on her mind, while all the while saying that they were inquiries put to her by others, the answers to which she already knew but wanted to compare with anything Miss Freud might have to say. The moral of all of this: many youths want so very much to rely upon at least one older person, even as they dismiss out of hand all of those whose age is over this or that number. "Whenever I hear teenagers being especially scornful of their elders," Miss Freud observed, "I know they are in need of exactly what—of whom—they are most scorning." She concluded on this cautiously upbeat note: "If they can find that person—well, there's a possible second chance: to try to work things out once more."

Among adolescents, so-called "body talk" can be a major topic of discussion. This is the time when the body arrives to greet its owner, and how to respond to it is of obvious significance. With ease and enjoyment? With fear and constraint? With abandon, if not reckless abandon? Often, the way a teenager has learned to regard his or her body, its urges and requirements, turns out to be the way he or she treats others. Miss Freud again: "If you have it in for yourself, others will pay for it; if you have some respect for yourself, others will be the beneficiaries." I was struck by her blunt, terse use of the vernacular, a measure, I suddenly realized, of the passion she felt, no doubt the cumulative result of years of difficult, demanding clinical work with adolescents who often

had nothing good to say about anyone a few years older than themselves, yet who secretly, unbeknownst to themselves, let alone others,
yearned for someone (at a bit of a remove from what they were experiencing) with whom to share some thoughts, worries, concerns.

Much later, as we were saying good-bye, she repeated herself, as if all
of us who work with teenagers need to hear this: "The more I hear a
young person say that he [or she] doesn't trust anyone who isn't his [or
her] age, the more I know the need of that person for someone to share
things with!"

Paul's Second Chance

She was insisting that adolescents have their own quite strong requirement of privacy, of independence—but not at the expense, ultimately,
of their ties to kin, to neighbors and teachers, to those who, one hopes,
have hitherto meant so very much to them as parents and grandparents, uncles and aunts; as coaches and scout leaders, and school nurses
or doctors; as social workers or storekeepers—that web of adults whom
children get to know in the course of their lives. In that regard, I had
shared a clinical story with Miss Freud: that of a sixteen-year-old boy,
Paul, the son of well-to-do and well-educated parents, both doctors, actually, who turned resolutely, defiantly on them—declared them lacking in "understanding" (and worse). He was experimenting with drugs
(pot, as well as beer and wine), and talked of leaving school for a year
or two with his girlfriend, in order to "see the country." No one, meaning no adult, could engage this youth in a heart-to-heart conversation,
or so it seemed.

Eventually, however, Paul's mother learned that someone was, in
fact, having long talks with her son: a middle-aged woman who worked
in the town library, its head librarian. She'd known Paul since he first
came to the children's room for books; now, as he contemplated various volumes and borrowed them from the high school and adult sec-
tions of the library, he got into talks with her, often ones that connected
with the subject matter of the books—self-help manuals directed at

people who were struggling with addictions. It turned out that this librarian was the person who tried to persuade the youth to expand the range of his trust with respect to the adult world—to talk with his parents. He refused to do so, but did get going in casual but quite serious conversations with a much-liked and trusted aunt, and through her came to see us at a hospital clinic intended for youths like him who were struggling with personal troubles, chief among them being a severe distancing from the immediate family.

Not that Paul wanted to regard his difficulties as "psychological." Again and again he shunned that way of thinking, insisted on the moral/legal approach: for instance, should or should not marijuana be legalized? It was important for us (the social worker, then me) to respect that point of view, to speak with this young man on his own terms, to avoid, as much as possible, the mannerisms of the clinic, the peculiar condescension that some of us in such a place show to anyone who shuns our language, our way of putting (seeing) things. To be sure, we did not abandon our interest in his considerable "problems," but we tried to remind ourselves, constantly, of his fearful skittishness with respect to us, and our kind of work, and tried to establish, as we always try to do with patients, some measure of trust. Once that objective began to be realized, we were surprised at how readily (hungrily, in fact), this seemingly "resistant" youth took to forthright conversations about his hopes and worries and, too, his conflicts at home and at school.

For example, Paul's passionate advocacy of the legalization of marijuana was connected to a no less passionate advocacy of "personal liberation," by which he meant his own independence from his parents. The more we talked, though, the more he brought up moral matters— how he ought to behave sexually with his girlfriend, what his obligations to her were "in the long run," not to mention his responsibilities to himself, his future. Put differently, a youth who was very much rebellious, who was well on his way to a drug problem, who was more than flirting with the idea of "taking off" and doing so with a girlfriend (who was also psychologically at odds with and estranged from her similarly affluent suburban family) turned out to be also a youth full of moral questions, qualms, and doubts: what long-term influence marijuana might have on his brain and mind, for instance, and what would happen were he and his girlfriend to travel together—what, that is, would they thereby be saying to each other, to the world?

Moral Companionship

No question, all of the above was more than grist for a psychological mill—yet we in that clinic had to keep reminding ourselves how "touchy" this youth was, quick to make judgments, quick to pounce on others and, not least, himself. As we learned to take our cues from Paul, meet him on his own turf, that of moral introspection, we began, gradually, to earn a bit of leeway psychologically: he let us talk not only about what he *should* do (or society, meaning adults, should do), but what he felt like doing or worried about doing or having to do and why. A strange irony, we began to realize: generations ago, adolescents had to struggle with the serious moral constraints imposed by (learned from) their families and of course those coming from outside the home. Today, many teenagers have parents who are more interested in psychology than moral inquiry, and the secular society is significantly (overwhelmingly, some would insist) relativistic in its moral outlook, even as it falls back on psychology and psychiatry with ease, if not abandon. Consequently, this high-schooler came across as a challenging anachronism—though perhaps the problem was ours, not his. Paul wanted from us an interest in his ethical quandaries. As Miss Freud one day pointed out to me, he wanted "an alliance between us and his superego," *that* kind of (for him) crucial psychological initiative. He and other teenagers are ever so vulnerable and needy in that regard. They are struggling hard to figure out how to behave, what to do, and why; they are interested in obtaining for themselves certain credible moral fundamentals—a set of values that strike them as convincing and that, they hope, will give them some reliable and worthy direction. They seek, to put it differently, a kind of moral companionship from an adult or two, be the older person a parent, a teacher, a relative, a friend's kin— whomever they can find who is ready to "level" with them.

"Please, I'd like you to level with me," Paul said to me once. I realized in retrospect that I had been verging toward the "authoritative expert" in my dealings with him, handing over (handing *down*, I fear) advice masked as thoughts. He wanted a bit more equality. He wanted me to be nearer his "level," less high and mighty. Young people like him often feel grown enough to be entitled to more parity than they feel they are receiving. But of course they also, many of them, crave candor—a willingness on the part of their elders to put ourselves more directly on the line, "level" with them. When I thought I made a mistake one morning, talking with Paul—I told him I wasn't really ready to argue "rationally" against the legalization of marijuana, but rather, on the basis of "a gut feeling," I felt a parent's fear of drugs and more drugs as a (legal) part of our society—he instead visibly relaxed, stopped battling me (we were haggling, really, as determined legal antagonists), smiled, and told me for the first time that he could "see how you [I] would feel that way." I thanked him for putting himself in my shoes for a moment or two, and asked if he'd mind if I tried to do so with respect to him. A smile (the first) and a nod (the first), then abruptly a qualification, meant to warn me to watch my step and go slow: "Be sure you're trying to get into my shoes, not take me out of mine!" Now I smiled, said, "Fair enough," and warned myself that sometimes I did veer in the very direction he worried I might find more than tempting.

I don't underestimate the desire that many youths have to put their hands over their ears when any adult approaches, a critical tongue at the ready. For a while, actually, I thought Miss Freud a bit naive. I looked on *her* as perhaps many teenagers do with regard to their parents: she was an old-fashioned moralist, no matter her psychoanalytic training with its inevitable emphasis on "understanding" rather than judgment, and so she couldn't help herself; she had to let her young patients know her firm positions on various matters, then justify (or rationalize!) such behavior on her part as therapeutically necessary or desirable (talk about a patronizing attitude, mine!). Only in time (no small amount of it) did I begin to see that these youths sitting across the room from me in a room called an office wanted (as Miss Freud had in-

sisted) my help in sizing up some very real moral as well as psychological matters in their lives: whether to use or reject liquor or drugs; how
far to go with a girlfriend, a boyfriend; how to deal with vague or not so
vague stirrings directed at those of the same sex; and in school, how to
handle their competitive side, their envies and rivalries, especially as
they could prod one toward cheating in class or being "unfair" at this or
that sport.

To interpret such "problems" psychologically can be quite valuable,
quite helpful, though often the youth in question still is haunted by a
conscience that is very much geared to the practicalities of *choice*: what
exactly to do, and with what ethical rationale. Moreover, many of the
options available to the young come at them not from within (the pressure of instinct, of desire, fueling a search for expression) but from
without (social and cultural possibilities from a consumerist society
ever ready to pester, entice, seduce an audience, an "age group").
Young people, to repeat, take in values from that world, from the music
they hear, the movies and television they see, from the fashion, adver-
tising, and magazine industries as they influence what gets worn, what
gets said, how hair is cut or colored, what hobbies are pursued.

Alice's First Step

I always go back in my mind to the clinical work I did with a seventeen-
year-old girl, Alice, from a comfortable suburban home. She felt all
kinds of tugs from the so-called "youth culture," from her own interest in
it—to the point that, as she succumbed to the imperatives of fashion, she
herself knew to call herself "weird-looking." It's no wonder that she could
say one afternoon that the most "relaxing times" for her each week were
her stints of field hockey. Then Alice *had* to dress a certain way, play a
certain way, be a certain (traditional) person—a big relief to someone
trying to be "with it," to keep up with the moral demands of an aspect of
late-twentieth-century America as it exerts its unmistakable influence on
its young citizens: talk like this, dress like that, play these tapes and discs,
be sure to see (and gab about) these programs and movies. In that regard,

one last moment with Miss Freud on adolescence: "Young people don't really abandon their wish for moral allegiances, so much as *switch* allegiances (sometimes). They will become obliging, obedient, slavishly so, to what their parents or teachers call fads. They obey those fads—and get called disobedient by parents who don't want them to [do so]. There is still a desire to do what is 'right,' but the one who calls the tune (literally!) may be a rock star, not the parent!"

The more we stop and think about matters along the lines that Miss Freud suggested, the more I suspect we will hold our breaths, keep our eyes on the longer distance, the larger picture, try hard to find ways to stay in touch with our fast-growing sons and daughters. Alice's mother was having one devil of a time finding a halfway amicable moment with her daughter, whom she understandably called "rebellious," "hostile," "stubbornly silent," "provocative." I knew about all the "psychodynamics" that awaited me if I were to explore with that young lady her interests and worries and difficulties—that is, *if* she would be willing to sit with me week after week in the implicit agreement that we ought do such exploration, have such discussions. We went back and forth for a couple of weeks, teetered on the edge of such an agreement, but found ourselves unable to seal the deal, as it were. Finally I came up with an idea, born of frustration, desperation, and a sense of failure on my part at my inability to reach Alice in a way that augured well for a therapeutic engagement between us. I would meet with the mother and see if a talk with her might be of any use.

As the mother folded and unfolded her hands, crossed and uncrossed her legs, made clear her quite worried state of mind, I reached for something, anything, a series of dos and don'ts, maybe, that would appease her momentarily, maybe even (who knows!) prove a bit helpful. But in my heart of hearts I knew that a list of rules or suggestions or tips, however appealing and clever to me, and however attractive (out of desperation) to her, was an evasion of sorts. The heart of the matter was an estrangement between mother and daughter: How to ameliorate and heal it and help find for her and her daughter a companionship of mind and heart sorely missing? I heard myself make one suggestion with some tentativeness: perhaps she ought go to some of those field hockey games, as some (not many) of the parents did. The mother raised obstacles, things she had to do on the days those games were played. But she "shuffled things around," and joked with me: her *life* was being shuffled around by dint of the troubles between her and her daughter. No magical rapprochement occurred. Still, Alice noticed her mother's presence, threw her an occasional look of acknowledgment, then in time, a smile. Also, very important, the mother felt a bit less panicky about and angry at her daughter after seeing her dressed "normally," playing by the rules of a game, behaving with some conventionality, however limited and temporary.

Additionally, the mother saw with her own eyes her daughter's still quite powerful and evident desire to set goals, as well as achieve them in a particular game—to work with her teammates, to show motivation and energy on behalf of a cause. She "felt better" about her daughter, and so the confrontation between the two of them became less strident, more muted, and for long stretches abated altogether. "I believe Alice has taken a first step back toward us," the mother averred, even as I thought to myself that she wasn't giving herself due credit for having taken that step herself. Trouble there still was—a defiant young lady who much resented what she knew in our psychological age to call her "controlling mother," her "ambivalent father" (who, she insisted, talked one way as a moralist but acted another, she knew, because she'd learned from her mother, of all people, of two affairs he'd had). Still, on that playing field a team member and an observer, a daughter and a mother, a youth and a middle-aged parent found a bit of distraction from their confrontational selves, some limited reason to feel in psychological and moral harmony with one another. The youth sure wanted to win, and the mother sure wanted her to win—a companionship of sorts, however limited in nature and duration, that would mean a lot to each of them and would be a prelude, we eventually learned, to a gradual waning of mistrust, distrust. So it can sometimes go, the challenge for all of us (adolescents and grown-ups): to figure out how (and for how long) we can stay in some touch, share a similar view of what is desirable, link arms, thereby, as moral comrades, our eyes on particular, shared ambitions, purposes, goals.

III

LETTER TO
PARENTS AND
TEACHERS

By now I hope it has become clear to you, the reader, that our sons and daughters, our students, of whatever age, are on the lookout for moral (as well as psychological, cognitive, or intellectual) direction. Babies need to learn no and yes; elementary school children need to learn how to get along with others, how to engage with them (in the tradition of the Golden Rule) as one would hope to be engaged by them; teenagers need to figure out how to regard their newly capable, yearning bodies and, too, the various interests and preferences and attitudes constantly being thrust upon them, by friends, by advertisements, by actors and actresses, announcers, singers and musicians, by sports heroes. How ought we, you and I, as parents or as teachers (parents are, again, always teachers) to do the best possible job of handing our principles and convictions and values to this next generation, which belongs to our children or students?

No question, some of us don't really stop and think about such a challenge until some trouble arrives at our door—then come the moral alarm and anxiety: What to say, what to do? We may forget that prior to a particular time of crisis or concern we have all along been making certain moral points to our children, sending them messages directly or by implication: in their sum, our notion of how one ought to behave under a variety of circumstances. Much of all that—the day-by-day encounters with children, during which we say yes or no, smile or frown, advocate one or another line of thought, course of action—is done quite naturally, by "instinct," that is, with no great amount of deliberative energy expended. We possess in our hearts, our bones, our guts (wherever our particular anatomy of moral intuition would locate it) an ethical sense of things, and we draw on it constantly. We also know way down within ourselves how eagerly most children look for moral clues from their parents, their teachers. For years, as a volunteer teacher in an elementary school, I have used the Tolstoy story offered and discussed at the beginning of this book—and witnessed firsthand a moral fable's magical power to prompt a young reader's empathic response. Some of those readers (charmingly, instructively, poignantly) want us all to take Tolstoy's story to heart by literally living it out: "We could be told to eat in some corner, out of a dishpan, and, wow, we'd sure remember what that was like," so a girl of ten insisted.

Another year, a boy of nine was more elaborate: "Half of us would eat at a table and there would be a tablecloth, and the nice dishes, and half would be on the floor, in the corners, or someplace, with the dishpan. Then we could all switch—and then we would know!"

What would we know? the eager teacher asks. "We'd know what it feels like the one way, and then the other," the wide-eyed boy, filled with a kind of adventurous enthusiasm, replied.

That same year, a girl has her version of a kind of moral theater: "We could throw dice or something, so if you have bad luck, you'll get the dishpan treatment. Then, you'll really feel sorry for yourself, and you won't just forget." She seems finished with her scenario—only to add this: "We should try to help the person with the dishpan. I mean, if I was on the floor, and I was getting my food that way, and it wasn't as good, the food, as the food others were getting, eating in good dishes at a table, and then someone came over, and she offered to give me a better dish, or better food, and told me I could stand up and sit with the rest of the people at the dining room table—then I'd sure be grateful to that person, and if I saw someone else sitting over there on the floor, in the corner, and they (she) was eating bread and water, like that, from a dishpan (or he), then I'd want to go and help them, I know I would; I'd want to invite them over and give them a nice dish, because if you've been there, in trouble, you'll know, you'll remember, and you'll want to help the next guy who's there, I think."

A more skeptical girl, also nine, wasn't, alas, so sure that such would inevitably be the case—and did *she* get us all going: a real gift. "How do you know," she wondered aloud, "if someone would remember the dishpan a year later?" We didn't "know," of course—but she continued her inquiry, expanded it in this manner: "What if someone got really mad sitting on the floor, and she said to herself, I'm here, now, eating out of the dishpan, but if I get lucky and I get out of this, or if I work my way out of it—if somehow this ends, what's happened to me, then I'll get even with the people, because they did this to me, I'll make *them* eat out of the dishpan, or I'll just try to forget all this! I'll say, don't remind me of all my troubles; they're gone! Couldn't that be the way, the way it could work out?"

To play that portion o̅f a tape-recorded class discussion is to bring to the listener a reminder: the variousness of our possible responses to an affecting, compelling moral fable, the work of a master, a giant among writers. That girl, just quoted, was quite in touch with her own family's world, as she let us know with this terse, final comment: "My father says it's best to forget pain, once it's over." The children nod readily—and why not? "Who wants to hold on to pain?" another girl asked, asserted, seconded. Nor was I quick to take exception. A long spell of quiet, however, gave me time to think—and think and think: How to get us into a kind of reflection that would bring us back to the Tolstoyan spirit we'd initially embraced upon reading his short, morally evocative story? My eventual comment: "One way, I guess, to deal with pain is to try to learn how to spare others what you've gone through yourself." No response, and I can hear in retrospect my pietistic bullying: I want you kids to look at this story *my* way, and by God, I'll get you to do so with this comment, or if it doesn't "take," with another one! Finally, a hand in the air and this: "Yes, but if you keep worrying about other people, their pain, you won't forget the pain, so it's still bothering you." Again, nods of agreement, not universal nods, but plenty of them. What to say now? How to justify, actually, my saying more—a continued effort to steer this moral discussion in a direction that pleases me, in a direction that confronts critically an attitude or position that doesn't at all please me, or that, at the least, worries me?

I nod; I thereby agree with what has just been said, though other thoughts race through my mind, even as I realize I can't (shouldn't) speak them, at least not in the way they came to me. Hey, to forget something is sometimes to give it a lot of authority, grant it a hold on you. Better to let a memory stay alive; better, really, to put it to some redemptive use, hence Tolstoy's suggestion that a remembered experience can change the way we live—meaning, live with others, behave toward them. On the other hand, to be fair, I'm loading this matter up to suit my own taste, *my* values. Why not forget pain? Isn't that what makes it possible for all of us to keep going? To be sure, psychoanalysts (my ilk) have a big stake in the recovery of memory, in the respectful, insistent examination of it. We are not ones to brush something aside, especially something painful. But more important, I kept worrying that a major difference of opinion was out there, hanging over us, *within* us, and that I didn't know how to (maybe, didn't want to) come to terms with it. Empathy can most definitely be costly; it surely can amount to the assumption of someone else's pain. Why do so? When to do so? When to say, *enough*? These questions pressed upon me, even as the threat of condescension edged toward me: How to bring up such issues with my fifth-grade class? (When my mind goes down that road, a warning sign ought be posted: "Beware, you are hiding from your own inadequacy by stressing the supposed age-related inadequacy of your students.")

A rescue—a girl who raises her hand and speaks simultaneously, before I have a chance to recognize her: "Pain is no good, but sometimes it just has to happen." Why? An immediate rejoinder: "Because," the girl replies—but no follow-up, and I feel dejected, tempted to give a disquisition tailored to the age of my class. I'm still not able to accept the moral vitality of these children, their willingness, their capacity to delve into the very matters Tolstoy has explored—and expressly for fellow human beings of their age, no less! Again, a deliverance, from another girl: "Because—because that's what it's like sometimes." "What do you mean, what are you talking about?" The boy is relentless, I think—he'll be a lawyer, a prosecuting attorney one day. But the girl is undeterred, unfazed, quite sure of herself: "See, there are times when it's true—'No pain, no gain,' that's what my dad says. My mom—she told me you can't be born without your mother being in pain."

While that pointed example settles in, I feel pleased—and suddenly, quite admiring of this class, its moral possibilities, capability. (More self-serving condescension?) Then, the sharp rejoinder: "That's different. That's the body, in the body. We're talking about something different here." He stops. I await a well-muscled reply to him, shirtsleeves rolled up—from someone. But silence rules—until he bears his own, further strength, prowess: "You want people to be born, but if you keep worrying about *everyone*, then you'll need someone to worry about you, because that's all you'll be doing. See?"

I feel admiration for this lad—he *will* be a solid, able, adroit, fast-thinking lawyer! The class is now more than silenced. The stillness of bodies, the rapt attention directed at the last speaker, from the girl who had taken him on, from me (I realize) speaks volumes: he has reminded us that we can outdo ourselves, become undone in the name of virtue, and at a cost to those near and dear to us. Their empathy will now need to be directed toward us empathic ones! Oh, I make too much of this, I think—or rather, *he* does! Why push us to that extent—why not just accept Tolstoy's wise, succinct parable, feel its punch, pick ourselves up and resolve to seize the day's invitation to be better sons, better daughters-in-law to our ailing parents, so that our Mishas will get the message and, come the time, the day of our own reckoning, will be there for us with the cups and saucers and forks and spoons of their kitchen tables, dining-room tables?

I look at the clock—just a few minutes before the bell tells us to stop, prepare to go have our lunch. How to end this discussion? Rather, how to nudge it further, so it *won't* end, so it will live in the minds of the boys and girls, so that it won't be forgotten, no matter the "relief" such a disappearance from awareness, such a loss of memory, might provide? But

I am at a loss to know what to say—I feel the considerable temptation of exhortation, and try hard to resist it. The devil arrives, however—with the familiar rationalizations: this is an elementary school class, and I ought not to forget *that*; an effort of "closure" will help us all; try to give a reasonably fair summary of what has taken place, and trust in the spirit of the children, their already apparent, infectious enthusiasm for this kind of reflective activity. I prepare to make my remarks, only to see a boy's hesitant hand up in the air, his forlorn face looking half at me, half away toward the window: "I'm sorry, what is a 'dishpan'? Is that the kind of bowl that dogs use?" The class stirs; chuckles are launched; rules are set aside. One yes, another yes, with no hands raised for permission. Then a no—Tolstoy didn't mean to imply *that*: "A dishpan— it's something you put on the floor, maybe. I don't know—does it have to be for a dog or a cat?" (The future lawyer's perplexity.) I realize that we haven't defined the word at all. I think to myself: a dishpan—it's a pan that holds dishes, a sink for them, most likely used, and so in need of cleansing. This student is right in a certain way—a lowly thing, and not for regular dinner-table use. I blurt out my thoughts. A girl says her classmate is right, as well—such a dish or pan is of the kind dogs and cats, indeed, use. She tells us how her mother took a "casserole dish," converted it into a "water bowl" for their dog, Spanky. Yes, yes, we all say to ourselves or out loud—and then, the bell.

As the children explode into recess noise, I wonder what our intense discussion will mean to them, if anything, a few hours hence, never mind a week or two down the line. A question impossible to answer. The mystery of this life (of how we respond over the course of it to what we have heard and seen, experienced) makes a mockery out of our all too human desire to gain mastery over the future. There I sat, after all, remembering my own fifth-grade teacher, her great effort to inspire us by teaching us about Abraham Lincoln with enormous emotional and intellectual and moral energy, to the point that he haunted that class-room, even as we stared at various pictures of him hanging on the walls, memorized words of his written on the blackboard, sat quite still, mesmerized, stunned, by the utter seriousness, passionate, and even, at times fearful, of this ordinarily cheerful, even breezy teacher of ours, as she told us of that extraordinary American president, whom she brought so alive, warts and all. Indeed, it was Lincoln's struggles, his frail side, his unexceptional side, that got us so hooked—someone who made mistakes, made compromises, and ultimately, made amends, a sequence, I now understand, we had even then come to know. Getting to know him, we got to know ourselves, our parents—writ large, yes; but such an acquaintance is not to be confused with worshiping a hero. Lincoln only gradually became that—in a sense, we were learning what heroism is: not a saint who arrives from on high, but someone who stumbles, is tempted, turns away from evil, toward good, only with some struggle, a heroism, it can be said, that is first *within* (a moral and psychological struggle), and only later lived on one or another public stage.

There I sat, too, remembering my eighth-grade teacher, who taught us to respect language, be careful with words, endeavor to say what we mean, mean what we say, a holiness of thought and expression both, and all of that, he made clear, a kind of self-respect: "You are a human being, the one species who speaks, writes, listens to words and sends them on their way to others." He never told us to memorize that statement, but all of us did, because he himself had convinced us, by example, that heart and soul he spoke out of earnest conviction, told us exactly what was on his mind. Now, decades later, I was a witness that morning to the moral energy given by children to a teacher's life, even as, surely, many of us have memories of moments when one or both of our parents said something, did something that stuck fast to us, helped shape who we have become.

Finally, as I watched those children politely file out of the room (the control quite evident that harnessed their desire to run, run, run with joy, with relief, to that cafeteria, that playground), I remembered someone approximately their age (he was ten) whom I knew a long time ago; remembered what he taught me about the capacity of a "mere child" for ethical contemplation, for spiritual inwardness. The boy was gravely ill with leukemia. Since I had trained in pediatrics as well as child psychiatry, I was asked to consider the young patient's psychological situation, because I'd worked with such children medically, had some idea

of what happened to their bodies, and how such developments sometimes influenced their mental condition. This lad, David, had started
asking the doctors and nurses attending him whether they ever prayed
for their patients, him included. Those earnest, hardworking, well-
trained men and women were taken aback by that line of inquiry.
(David told them he was praying for them!) Hence the request that I
"evaluate" him, see what was "troubling" him. In no time I obliged,
and my response to this boy was perhaps more telling about me (my
values, assumptions, way of thinking) than him. I told his doctors in the
note I wrote that he was a bright, sensitive child who was assailed by
anxiety and fear. He was trying to understand what was happening to
him—yet in his heart of hearts, he knew this: he would soon enough
die. With obvious desperation, he was praying to God that he somehow
would survive, so I thought—though he actually didn't emphasize that
rather unsurprising, even conventional, kind of appeal to higher authority. Rather, he prayed hard for the doctors who were treating him,
in various ways, at various times. He even told me that he felt sorry for
the doctors: theirs was an uphill fight, and they might lose, and, as he
put it, "No one likes to lose." Immediately I thought to myself: *he* will
be the loser—and he is *really* worried about himself, not us doctors.
Shouldn't I help him to see clearly what is preoccupying him; isn't it
my job to do so?

One morning, with such a mission vaguely in mind—that of clarify-
ing for David his present situation, his clinical prospects—I sat with
him in his room and asked him how things were going and, more to the
point (*my* point!), how he felt. The boy looked weak, tired; yet light
shone in his eyes, and he managed a wan but determined smile. He
told me that he was "O.K.," but that he was worried about the doctors
and nurses: "They're working so hard, and they seem discouraged." A
pause, then this, again: "I'm praying for them." Needless to say (yet I repeat), I was convinced that such comments told of the boy's self-
concern—an unacknowledged apprehension that his battle for life
wasn't going to be won. I decided to circle around that matter, see if
David and I eventually might talk more openly, directly, about what

was going through his mind, on the theory that to do so would be of some help to him in the midst of this quite fearful and sad time. I asked him what he said in the prayers he offered for the hospital staff— expecting that he was praying that those men and women, somehow, might be able to pull him through a terrible ordeal. I heard from him this: "I ask God to be nice to them, so they don't feel too bad if us kids here go meet Him." Another pause, and then this afterthought: "When I meet God I'll put in a good word for the people [who work] in this hospital. I told the doctor [his pediatric oncologist] I would, and he smiled."

I was finally beginning to realize, as I listened to David, how important his religious faith was to him, how earnestly he had tried to connect it to his life's experiences, his grim fate. I still think of him when I talk with children who contend with various obstacles or difficulties and who try to understand what is happening to them through religious or spiritual reflection. David and other children like him I've met taught me a lifelong clinical lesson: that children very much need a sense of purpose and direction in life, a set of values grounded in moral introspection—a spiritual life that is given sanction by their parents and others in the adult world.

Since I got to know David, long ago, I've spent years talking with children whose parents are Catholic, Protestant, Jewish, Muslim, here and abroad; and as well, children whose parents subscribe to no faith, yet are deeply concerned with contemplating the whys of this life, the oughts and naughts, too. Again and again I have come to realize that even preschool children are constantly trying to comprehend how they should think about this gift of life given them, what they should do with it. People like me, trained in medicine, often emphasize the psychological aspects of such a phenomenon and, not rarely, throw around reductionist labels, as if a child can't stop and think about this life's meaning without being a candidate for a doctor's scrutiny. In fact, moral exploration, not to mention wonder about this life's various mysteries, its ironies and ambiguities, its complexities and paradoxes— such activity of the mind and heart make for the experience of what a human being is: the creature of awareness who, through language, our distinctive capability, probes for patterns and themes, for the significance of things.

No wonder so many Americans go eagerly, routinely, to churches and synagogues. No wonder even agnostic and atheist parents have told me (as they tell their children) that it truly matters for one to have beliefs and ideals—that we must respectfully stand in awe of this existence granted to us so fatefully, even as we probe harder and harder to gain material mastery over the world around us. Unfortunately, all too many of us in contemporary America feel troubled by the matter of religion as it connects with our children's life, in school and at home and in the neighborhood, as if the subject in some ways is puzzling, confusing, even a threat to this nation's secular society. Yet children constantly ask their whys, seek the moral reasons upon which to gird their present and future life—the heart of spirituality: to look inward in search of meaning and purpose; to seek an understanding of what truly matters and for which reasons, an activity that need not take place under formal religious or institutional purposes and that can be encouraged by reading stories and poems, by learning through scientific contemplation of this awesome, wondrously enchanting (as well as fearfully vulnerable) planet, whose many secrets still elude us.

In retrospect, I realize that the boy David was an important teacher of mine. Back then, I was yet another well-trained doctor whose innocence was blunted by a child's savvy. His spirituality enabled me to contemplate the spirituality of other children—and to realize, eventually, that we honor our children by taking the moral and spiritual side of their lives seriously and by thinking how we might respond to it with tact and intelligence. If David at ten taught me a lot decades ago, another young person, ten years David's elder, on the outside edge of adolescence, taught me a lot more recently, and prompted me to take up, yet again, the central issue this book addresses: how we might help one another to live in such a manner that espoused ideals get enacted in the way we get along with others whom we meet.

Every time I think of that student, Marian, I think of Ralph Waldo Emerson, whose work she much admired. Over a hundred and fifty years ago Emerson, in his "American Scholar" address and essay, made a distinction, a comparison, a judgment that culminated in a terse assertion: "Character is higher then intellect." Even then, a prominent man of letters, an intellectual, was worried (as many other writers and thinkers of succeeding generations would be) about the limits of knowledge and the nature of a college's, a university's mission. The intellect can grow and grow, he knew—in a person who is smug, ungenerous, even cruel. Institutions originally founded so that their graduates become good and decent, as well as broadly, deeply literate can abandon that joint mission in favor of a driven, narrow book learning, a course of study in no way designed to lead to connections between ideas and theories on the one hand and our lives as we live them on the other.

Students have their own way of realizing and trying to come to terms with the split of sorts that Emerson and others have noticed. Four years ago, Marian, a sophomore student of mine, came to see me in great anguish. She had arrived at Harvard with a Midwestern, working-class background. She was trying hard to work her way through college, and to do so cleaned the rooms of her fellow students. Again and again she met classmates, college mates, who apparently had forgotten the meaning of "please" and "thank you," despite their high S.A.T. scores, and who did not hesitate to be rude, even crude toward her. One day she was not so subtly propositioned by a young man she knew to be very bright, a successful pre-med student and already an accomplished journalist. This was not the first time that such an overture had been made, but now a breaking point had arrived. She quit her job and was preparing to quit going to school in what she called "fancy, phony Cambridge." She came to see me full of anxiety and anger, and soon enough, she was sobbing hard. She had been part of a seminar I teach on Raymond Carver's fiction and poetry and Edward Hopper's paintings and drawings—the thematic convergence of a literary and artistic sensibility: American loneliness explored, its social and personal aspects, both. Soon she had quieted down, and we were remembering the old days of that class. But she wanted to discuss some weighty present-day matters that were on her mind, and I would eventually hear a detailed, sardonic account of college life as viewed by someone all too vulnerable, and quite hard-pressed by it. At one point this observation was made to me: "That guy [who had pressured her sexually] gets all A's. He tells people he's in Group I [the top academic category]. I've taken two moral reasoning courses with him, and I'm sure he's gotten A's in both of them—and look at how he behaves with me, and I'm sure with others."

Marian stopped for a moment, to let me take in what I'd heard. I happened to know the young man, and could only concur with her judgment, even as I wasn't totally surprised by what she'd experienced while trying to tidy up his room. I was at a loss to know what to say, although she had no trouble letting me know what was on her mind. A philosophy major with a strong interest in literature (she was combining the two fields), Marian had taken a course on the Holocaust, its origins, its ultimate nature: mass murder of unparalleled historical proportion in a nation hitherto known as one of the most civilized in the world, with a citizenry as well educated as that of any country. Drawing on her education, Marian put before me names such as Martin Heidegger, Carl Jung, Paul de Man, Ezra Pound—men who were brilliant and accomplished (a philosopher, a psychoanalyst, a literary critic, a poet), and who had consorted with the hate that was Nazism, fascism, during the 1930s. She reminded me of the willingness of the universities to do likewise in Germany and Italy, of the countless doctors and lawyers and judges and journalists and schoolteachers and, yes, even the clergy, all of them able to accommodate themselves to murderous thugs because the thugs had political power: morality bowing to that power all too readily, and no doubt with clever rationalizations. She pointedly made mention, too, of the Soviet gulag, that expanse of prisons to which millions of honorable people were sent by Stalin and his brutish accomplices—staffed, commonly, by psychiatrists who were quite eager to call these victims of a vicious totalitarian state an assortment of psychiatric names, then shoot them up with drugs meant to reduce them to zombies.

When Marian left my office I was exhausted and saddened—and brought up short. I had tried hard toward the end of a conversation that had lasted almost two hours to salvage something for her, for myself, and not least for a college I much respect, even as I know its limitations and worse (and which institution is without them!). I had suggested that if she had learned at Harvard what she had just shared with me—why, *that* was itself a valuable education acquired. She smiled, gave me credit for a "nice try," but remained unconvinced. She put this tough, pointed, unnerving question to me: "I've been taking all these philosophy courses, and we talk about what's true, what's important, what's *good*—well, how do you teach people to *be* good?" Then her amplification: "What's the point of *knowing* good, if you don't keep trying to become a good person?"

All along sympathetic to her, to the indignation she had been directing at certain of the students whose rooms she cleaned and to her critical examination of the limits of abstract knowledge, I suddenly found myself on the defensive. Schools are schools, colleges are colleges, I averred, a complaisant and smug accommodation in my voice as much as my words. I topped off a kind of surrender to the status quo with a shrug of my shoulders, which Marian noticed and to which she responded with a barely concealed anger, which she did not put into words but rather expressed through a knowing look, meant to announce that she'd taken full moral measure of me. Suddenly she was up on her feet. She told me she had to go meet someone. I realized that I'd stumbled badly. I wanted to pursue the discussion further. I wanted to applaud her for taking on a large subject in a forthright, incisive manner, tell her she was "right on," had hit the matter hard: *moral reasoning is not to be equated with moral conduct*. I wanted, really, to explain my shrug—point out that there is only so much that any of us can do, that institutional life has its own momentum, authority. But she had no interest in that line of argument, that kind of self-justification, as she let me know in an unforgettable aside as she departed my office: "I wonder whether Emerson was just being 'smart' in that lecture he gave here. I wonder if he ever had any ideas about what to *do* about what was worrying him—or did he think he'd done enough because he'd spelled the problem out to those Harvard professors?"

She was pointedly reminding me that she hadn't forgotten my repeated references to the "American Scholar" essay, to the emphasis its author (in a speech delivered at the very institution that she and I at that moment called ours) placed on character, the distinction he made between it and intellect. She was implying that even such a clarification, such an insistence, could all too readily become an aspect of the very problem Emerson was discussing—the intellect at work, analyzing its relationship to the lived life of conduct (character), with no apparent acknowledgment of (unease with respect to) the double irony of it all! The irony that the study of philosophy, say, even moral philosophy or moral reasoning, doesn't by any means necessarily prompt in either the teacher or the student a daily enacted goodness; and the further irony that a discussion of that very irony can prove equally sterile, in the sense that yet again one is being clever—with no apparent consequences, so far as one's everyday actions go.

How to address the matter of how we teachers might encourage our students (encourage *ourselves*) to take that big step from thought to action, from moral analysis to fulfilled moral commitments? Rather obviously, community service offers us all a chance to put our money where our mouths are, and of course such service can be connected to reflection, can even liven it up: a reading of Ralph Ellison's *Invisible Man* (literature) or Elliot Liebow's *Tally's Corner* (sociology and anthropology) or Erik Erikson's *Childhood and Society* (psychology and psychoanalysis) takes on new meaning after some time spent in a ghetto school or a clinic. By the same token, such books can prompt a reader who is a volunteer in one or another service program to stop and think, by which I mean think not only in the abstract, but concretely: How might Ralph Ellison's wisdom, say, worked into his fiction, help shape the way I get along with the children I'm tutoring—affect, that is, my attitude toward them, my understanding of them, the things I say to them, do with them? I might ask him to become a mentor, might try hard to call upon his earthy common sense and humorous canniness in my teaching life.

Classroom discussion, then, can be of help in this matter, the skepticism of that student of mine notwithstanding. Marian pushed me hard, to the point that her story, the ironies she noted while cleaning those dormitory rooms and attending particular college courses, really hit home. In my college classes I started making reference again and again to what she had observed and learned and my students more than got the message. Her moral righteousness, her shrewd eye and ear for hypocrisy, hovered over us, made us uneasy, goaded us. When all of us in a seminar devoted to moral introspection (courtesy of St. Augustine and Pascal, Tolstoy and Bonhoeffer, and, yes, Emerson) took ourselves to a nearby elementary school to work as tutors with certain boys and girls, we had Marian as well as the writers and thinkers to thank, a final irony: her intellect, energized by that "work-study" experience in those dormitory rooms, became an encouraging, goading instrument for us, an intellectual provocation that became a spur to activity. I suppose that we had at last figured out (the intellect at work!) that such activity was the only "correct answer" to the moral problem being posed.

The events described above—a student's experience and a teacher's stunned, then alarmed, even desperate, response to it—have actually given me a measure of hope with respect to the possibility that moral reasoning and reflection can somehow be integrated into a student's and a teacher's lived life. All too often those who read or teach books don't think to pose for themselves the kind of ironic dilemmas discussed above. In a sense, that student became the teacher of all of us in my seminar: she challenged us to prove that what we think and uphold intellectually can be connected to our daily deeds. For some of us, again, such a connection was established through community service. But that is not the only way. I asked the students to write papers that told of their particular effort to honor through action, through example, as it were, the high thoughts we were discussing. Thus prompted (thus stirred to a certain self-consciousness, I suppose), various students made various efforts, the best of which were, I felt, small victories, brief epiphanies, that otherwise might have been overlooked but had great significance for the particular individuals in question. "I thanked someone serving me food [in the college cafeteria], and then we got to talking, the first time," one student wrote—seemingly a passing moment of no great consequence, yet for her a decisive break with an indifference to others hitherto abstractly regarded as "people who work on the serving line." In her mind she had thereby gained much—she had learned about another's life, even as she had tried to show respect for that life. Marian, who challenged me with her angry, melancholy story, had pushed me to teach differently. Now, I made an explicit issue of the very matter she had brought to my attention: the more than occasional disparity between thinking and doing. Now, I asked all of us to consider how we might bridge that disparity and then to reflect upon (in discussion, in writing) any effort made to do so. To be sure, this is a report on a mere beginning. The task of connecting intellect to character is daunting, as Emerson and others well knew, and any of us can lapse into cynicism, turn the moral challenge of a seminar into yet another moment of opportunism: I'll get an A this time, by writing a paper cannily extolling myself as a doer of this or that "good deed"! Still, for a number of us in that seminar, reflection had gotten linked to experience in a way that had touched us, even as we shared stories of what had happened to us and what we hoped might be the result, so far as our future daily lives are concerned.

Of course, parents don't routinely ask their children to write compositions or do community service—though I sure remember my mom putting little stars that she bought in Woolworth's on a card when I fulfilled certain household responsibilities, and when enough of them accumulated she bought me or my brother a present or two in that same five-and-dime store (at a time when those coins actually had some value). Bribery as a means of encouraging moral behavior in the young? Obviously, not a recommended course of action, but I believe our mother was making quite clear to us what she held high and dear, and she was showing us how hard she would work to convey her values to us, how imaginative or inventive she'd try to be, how responsive to *our* humanity, even as she was putting her own on the line. To this day I can remember her pleasure as she licked those stars, put them on the cards with our names on them: the smile on her face, the lilt to her voice. I also can remember the sadness, the regret on her face, the quick glance at the cards tacked to her bulletin board when they had been untouched of late! She wanted so much for us to learn to carry our fair share of a family's chores, responsibilities; she wanted us to learn to use those words "thank you" and "please," not out of some smug superficial rote resort to manners, not out of a parent's pedantry, as we sometimes thought (we learners, entitled to our frustrations, our disappointment in ourselves, followed by a surge of irritation with her—the old sequence of turning on others when faced with one's own limitations!), but out of a genuine desire on her part that we learn to break the hold of the holy self, so insistent on its own gratification, in favor of a turn, a bow, to others.

"We matter to one another," a refrain we heard and heard. But what really mattered was the constant evidence our mom showed us of what mattered to *her*—and that evidence consisted of her willingness (not in a showy or didactic or self-important manner, but in a quite casual manner) to use those words "please" and "thank you" and mean them. She went out of her way to try to be considerate of others, to ask of them with tact and sensitivity, to tell them of her considerable gratitude for any help they may have offered her or us or others she knew. No question, I risk sentimentality in this ode of sorts to a mother, sung so long after the fact, so to speak—a self-indulgent and self-serving romanticization. Still, I well remember words spoken at her funeral a few years ago by friends of hers, neighbors and fellow volunteers in the service activities she pursued to the very end of her life—some of those folks were people I scarcely knew. Hearing their tributes to her, it turned out, brought back to me the very memories I now find myself putting on the record for you, the reader—the evocation of a person who kept saying that she wanted my brother and me to "make room in your mind for others," an interesting spatial way of putting it: we ought to shuffle our life's furniture a bit, work hard at a kind of accommodation, lest we be all too full of ourselves. We failed repeatedly, of course, and she took all our failures to heart, we knew—but she did not undo all she was trying to accomplish by turning on us in such a way that the person who asked for "please" and "thank you" would become cold, imperious, unable to give us the benefit of the doubt, unable to remember how slow and hard it can be for all of us to get to various moral destinations held up to us as important during childhood.

She knew how to be patient, obviously; but, more fundamentally, she knew how to be patient not only with us but with herself. To heighten the psychology a bit, she knew the meaning of forgiveness—as it pertained to her, never mind us. How do I know that? I know that because I remember her letting us know how "forgetful" she could be—telling us that she'd sometimes be "mortified" because she took something (or someone!) for granted. Then we'd hear a particular story, not told in a way that we got scared for her and, of course, for ourselves; not told so that she'd emerge, craftily, as the impossibly good person, so good she even confessed her sins to us; but told in a comradely fashion, as if she and we were in something together, something that was of importance to all of us and, yes, to those others whom we needed to remember to think of, through the words we used, "please," "thank you," words she now made sure she used in her speaking to us: so very important, so unforgettably, silently, instructive.

I also remember her talking with us about what can go wrong, and why, with respect to human behavior. Our mother told us stories of courage, stories of fear. She read us stories, too—but the moments we anticipated most eagerly were those that came after the reading, when she spoke to us out of her own life, shared memories with us and, too, remembered feelings: times when she was scared, or moved to tears, times when she'd been inspired, excited by someone, by something done. Dad, too, was a great storyteller, at the dining-room table and at our bedsides, when he was saying goodnight. His stories, like those of our mother, were frequently autobiographical, but were not mere indulgence in what George Eliot (his great love, as Tolstoy was Mother's) would call "unreflecting egoism." No, he told us of *others*, of his childhood "chums" (he grew up in Yorkshire, England), or of his favorite uncle, who was killed while in the English army during the battle of Ypres, a place of terrible slaughter amid the First World War, or indeed of his older brother, also killed in that battle. He told us of his big sickness, of the tuberculosis he contracted at the age of sixteen, and of the kindly, life-saving care he received at the hands of the Benedictines, to whose monastery he was sent as a youth.

Those monks became of great interest to us. We soon enough realized that had it not been for their success—well, we'd not ever have had a chance to live. So, they had not only saved our dad, they had enabled us to be! How had they done their most important work? Not by administering drugs or performing surgery, not, that is, by being smart and technologically proficient, but by dint of, by *virtue* of, their various virtues, of which we were told not through abstract lists but through reports of deeds done: delicious food, brought to his room with care, affection, smiles; lovely rides by horse and carriage, with so very much pointed out as the monk and he passed through the countryside; learning pursued with him, for him; a modest regimen of exercise, carefully implemented with the help of a particular "brother," Dad's mainstay of bedrest notwithstanding. All in all, we got a picture of thoughtfulness, of generosity, of concern—and such qualities, we kept on realizing, because discreetly but most definitely we were told so, had made all the difference, had resulted in his eventual cure, his visit to America so that he could go to college, his chance encounter with a woman at a dance who would become his wife and, eventually, the mother of his children. I tell this to indicate (now, the abstract!) the existentialist character of some of that storytelling, its powerful pull on our attention, interest, memory. Our very lives depended on the goodness of heart, the purposeful, reliable openheartedness of those monks whose behavior we heard described. Dad's stories were tales of danger and pain, of levity, too; they were, I now realize, informally told "character-sketches."

My father was a scientist, and, during his English youth, a great walker. He carried his love for walking across the Atlantic, and all during my childhood and beyond, he and I took long walks together. I can't imagine myself being the person I am had those ambulatory times together not happened. On them he'd ask me about my life, my current interests, hopes, activities. He'd share with me—he'd share so very much with me. The years that separated us seemed to dissolve as we walked, long hikes that turned us into pals, though, always, he was my dad, too. I learned from him about his own childhood, about his experience with the sickness that I've already mentioned, about his decision to study the basic sciences and ultimately to do so in the United States, at M.I.T. But, very important, he told me of people he had known, those he liked and did not like and why. His reasons for liking or disliking particular individuals, I would eventually realize, were, in their declared sum, his values offered unself-consciously, in a continuing narrative, to me, our legs moving, moving—an assist, perhaps, to the candor that befell him, and me, too, because as his loving and admiring and grateful son, I followed suit, told him of my buddies, the pals I liked, the guys I didn't like, and why. Later on, naturally, there would be girls I'd mention, even as he'd meet them. His highest compliment, I came to know, was this: "A good person, a really good person!" His most critical remark would be "Not a very good person." His understated phrases always had great weight for me—such a contrast with all the daily hype that afflicts us these days. In a sense, a big part of a son's moral upbringing took place during those walking expeditions—miles and miles of stories told, a father's ideas and ideals, his values, worked into them.

By the time I was a teenager I had learned not only what kind of person my father liked or didn't like, but the ethical principles that informed his choices, his decisions. He much respected, for example, a teacher of his at M.I.T., a man who was reticent, retiring, modest, unaffected, much given to museum visits, attendance at symphony concerts. As I heard this teacher described, I realized how much of him had been absorbed by my dad, including his highest compliment for that teacher—and to this day I can hear every single word of it being spoken, when the subject of that teacher somehow came up: "He was a good person; he knew how to look out for us students as well as himself." No big, discursive deal there; no elaborate, overwrought, intense, philosophically subtle, highly complex argument; no psychologically clever and intricate statement, full of the unobvious, therefore (assuredly) quite original, brilliant. A father was telling his son, through the sharing of a memory of a revered teacher, what it is that matters to him, the qualities that make a distinctive moral difference to him on the plus side. As for the downside, to repeat, I heard about that, too— the qualities Dad disliked in certain people. He himself was not without blemishes; he could be cranky, shy to the point of reclusiveness, all too sardonic and, thereby, all too smugly self-satisfied. It was important for my brother and me to realize his limitations and those of our mother: a step on the road to moral awareness—though, Lord knows, there weren't those self-conscious psychological "steps" hovering over us in those days. My father, actually, was his own best (and worst) critic; he could be clear and candid about what was "wrong" with himself: his "arrogant aloofness," we'd hear, as he tried hard to keep us (literally and symbolically, both) walking on paths untrodden by others. With pain, even today, I recall his dismissive references to "all those people"—this from a man who claimed to like "ordinary folks" as against the "snotty elites." With pain I realize how thoroughly his faults have become mine.

Orwell was Dad's hero, and he had Orwell's clay feet (who is without them?). Now, I teach Orwell, explore with students that wonderfully lucid, compelling essayist's adventures, contradictions, inconsistencies, flaws—and think of Dad, and our walks, and him talking of Orwell back then. Now, I realize what they had in common: a moral passion that informed their thinking, a passion that in Orwell's case has reached so many of us, worked itself into our lives, our thoughts and commitments. My dad exerted that kind of influence on his family and on those with whom he worked as a volunteer for twenty years after he retired, at sixty-five: constant visits to needy, elderly people, whom I'm sure (I was told so by the people who ran the agency to which he gave his time, his energy) heard the same kind of wry, bemused observations on "life," on how one "ought live it," that my brother Bill and I heard, not to mention our mother who, surprisingly, filled in certain details that Dad omitted—and vice versa for her life. So it goes with all of us: what we don't confide, can't say, tells so very much about who we are.

She was the one, actually, who let us know about the good and kind M.I.T. professor whom Dad so revered, and why. The professor had noticed an able student's homesickness, his sad manner—the youth was all too far away from his home city of York, in Yorkshire. And so the older person asked the younger one to go take a walk, with coffee as the destination, the ostensible purpose. One walk would lead to another: not "psychology" there, not "counseling," not the wordy talk of "isolation" or "depression," but rather, an old-fashioned morality: I recognize you, I sense things about you, I will try to befriend you—the gesture of a teacher who felt moved to, obliged to, extend himself toward another human being.

One of my dad's flaws, I used to think when I was a resident in psychiatry in a Boston hospital, was his only too apparent dislike of the social sciences, especially psychology and psychiatry: a real blind spot on his part, an aspect of fear, of "resistance," as it is put by us in psychoanalysis. True, no doubt, to some extent—but of late I have realized the moral side to his worries, to his misgivings, to his strenuous doubts. He was more interested in that professor's gesture toward him, an expressed courtesy and kindness, a respectful attentiveness shown a student, than he was in toting up for recall his various psychological vulnerabilities of the time. My mother had once put it to me this way: "Your dad isn't altogether disinterested in psychology! He loves it, when George Eliot is practicing it; and he often talks about 'moral psychology'; *that* is the kind he wants to poke about in." For me that was a big moment—it got me wondering what in the world "moral psychology" can possibly be. I need only have looked to his hero, Orwell, of course, or to his other hero, George Eliot, or, yes, to that M.I.T. professor—these were people who examined motives eagerly, relentlessly, but they were moral motives, or as Dad unashamedly put it, "moral instincts," by which he meant our "desire for purpose in life, our sense of how we should behave toward people."

Dad was no naïf about the unconscious, however—the main repository, in my psychoanalytic mode of thinking, for the "instincts"; but he chose to do his kind of analytic work in a different realm, that of action, rather than thought, fantasy, dreams. I quote from a letter he once wrote to me (he wrote letters constantly, to his family in England, to us here, even if I was only a few miles away in school, and with a telephone in my room, or later, living with my family nearby): "I can see how you folks [psychiatrists and psychoanalysts] would be interested in figuring out why people have the thoughts they do, and the feelings they do. But I say to you [a familiar way of his putting something to me!]—what truly distinguishes people is how they behave toward one another, no matter what crosses their bedeviled minds. You see [another of his literary mannerisms], your own Dr. Freud has told us what

we've known since Sophocles and Shakespeare, at the very least: the secret vices we all carry, vices of our imagination, they are. So, why all
the hoopla? What matters is how all that trouble you folks explore is put
to use in the world. Think of the ironic possibilities: for instance, the
psychoanalyst who understands everyone and everything, and isn't a
very nice person at home, or in the neighborhood, the community; or
the thoroughly mixed-up fellow who badly needs 'treatment,' but who
is out there on some moral assembly line, working like the proverbial
dog on behalf of some cause (and you folks would say, out of his neu-
rosis); and all sorts of folks in between [those two polarities, of sorts, he
had spelled out]."

So much to ponder there for me: how a certain perspective can inform our view of people and, by implication, the way we get along with
them, and teach them, including the manner in which we bring them
up if they are our children, our students. My parents, I am saying, were
interested in specific moral goals for us. They wanted us to "behave."
They meant for us to obey the laws that are on the society's books, as it
were, but also moral laws they were at pains to specify quite explicitly.
When we fell flat on our faces, as we did, we were not immediately
thrown a psychiatric lifeline, thereby shifting the entire discussion, the
heart of the matter, from morals to emotions.

I hope I am not painting my father and mother, and now myself into
some corner all too conveniently labeled, these days, "out-of-date" (to
say the least). My folks and the teachers I still hold high and dear in my
life knew how to be psychologically sensitive and responsive—this is a
kind of knowledge, anyway, that by no means only belongs to this century of ours. I remember my mother reading both Freuds, reading Karl
Menninger and A. A. Brill and Lawrence Kubie and Karen Horney and
Clara Thompson and, not least, Erik H. Erikson. She even asked my
dad to do likewise, and not to his derisive refusal, or his patient tolera-
tion of a weakness in her. I can recall looks, many of them, in their eyes
that bespoke of a psychological understanding—extended in my direction, or that of someone else (and toward each other, of course). Indeed, my mom and dad were right there with Erikson when he titled
his book *Insight and Responsibility*, talking about psychological sub-

tlety: at some point an examined inwardness has to step into a world of duty and obligation toward others, toward our neighborhoods, our nation. They were right there, as well, earlier on, with Erikson's bold challenge to an increasingly psychological and "value-free" culture, not to mention his psychoanalytic colleagues, in those last powerful moments of *Childhood and Society*:

> We know today that communication is by no means primarily a verbal matter: words are only the tools of meanings. In a more enlightened world and under much more complicated historical conditions the analyst must face once more the whole problem of judicious partnership which expresses the spirit of analytic work more creatively than does apathetic tolerance or autocratic guidance. The various identities which at first lent themselves to a fusion with the new identity of the analyst— identities based on talmudic argument, on messianic zeal, on punitive orthodoxy, on faddish sensationalism, on professional and social ambition—all these identities and their cultural origins must now become part of the analyst's analysis, so that he may be able to discard archaic rituals of control and learn to identify with the lasting value of his job of enlightenment. Only thus can he set free in himself and in his patient that remnant of judicious indignation without which a cure is but a straw in the changeable wind of history.

"Indignation" is, needless to say, an intensely moral word—the prophets of Israel, Jeremiah and Isaiah and Amos and Micah, raising their voices unapologetically in opposition to the reigning "principalities and powers," never mind the wrongdoing they saw about them on the part of their next-door fellow human beings (sinners). The "indignant" one doesn't only stop to wonder what their "problem" is, those who are behaving in this or that wrong way; rather, the point is an aroused sense of judgment, a decision to condemn, and mightily so, and do so not in a cool, slippery, even-handed fashion that implies an all too oblique criticism, usually called "concern": I hear where you're coming from, and I worry about you! Erikson's challenge, in contrast, is that of the necessity for moral outrage—its absence, ironically, a judgment all its own on the very "psychology" that is pressing us all the time to be wary of such spells of alarm, of anger, of outright disgust and horror (what do such "outbursts" *mean*, tell us about ourselves, the incantory questions go, scaring us into a discreet, self-conscious silence). He was claiming, as a child psychoanalyst, that children need beliefs and moral commitments that, if threatened, violated, require a defense, the prelude to it being the energy generated by indignation, meaning an ethical determination that one has made.

Once I asked Erikson how we might move toward the moral arousal he was postulating as a final arbiter of sorts, one well above the various psychoanalytic paradigms he'd both studied and (as a training analyst) taught for so many years. "Oh," he answered, with considerable reluctance, "I wouldn't want to prescribe," and then the sly, ironic addition, "or proscribe." He was worried, always, about a righteousness that could turn, all of a sudden, pedantic, literal-minded, reflexive, proprietary, rote, arrogant, smug, a righteousness become self-righteous. He saw me still wanting something, wanting more—the hungry, needy, searching self so many of us carry within our more methodically practical, workaday selves. But silence claimed me—I sat there struggling for a direction to our conversation.

Suddenly a former patient came to mind. " 'Ours not to reason why, ours but to do or die,' " that patient once said out loud to me: his embrace of Tennyson's version of the Crimean disaster was meant to let me know something of his own obligatory drivenness, as it largely determined his lock-step life. Then, the moment of reconsideration: "I do sometimes wonder why—a dozen whys, but I'm not very good at going further, asking the full questions, finding the answers to them. I stop with why—and it becomes an exclamation, not a question! I wish I had the language [for the full question], or really, I guess I wish I wasn't made so damn anxious at the thought of putting the questions to myself. Maybe if I'd had more *experience*; maybe experiences give you the right questions, and the answers to your whys"—and there he faltered, dropped off. I found myself telling Erikson of him, of what I'd heard from him, learned from him—and Erikson now became visibly more relaxed, less guarded. He smiled, told me I'd already been given an answer to my question by one of my patients, and I "seemed to know it," even if I said I didn't, by the way I was telling him that story: "A patient can sometimes be the very doctor [for us] we most need." Well— enough of that psychological version of the Delphic oracle! I wanted from Erikson some pedagogical specifics. Our sons were becoming school-age children, and every once in a while I wanted to scream, I was made so frustrated and anxious by something one of them did, or didn't do—get into a fight, dress like a slob, leave his room messy every day, swear like a trooper, forget and forget to say "please" and "thank you"! He saw my impatience, Erikson clearly did, so I knew when I heard him say, "It's a long haul, bringing up our children to be good; you have to keep doing that, *bring them up*, and that means *bringing things up* with them: asking; telling; sounding them out; sounding off yourself; teaching them how to go beyond *why*, as your patient said he wishes he knew how to [do], and that means trying it all out by your-self—finding through experience your own words, your own way of putting them together. You have to learn where you stand—and by God, you won't budge from there. You have to make sure your kids learn that [where you stand], understand why, and soon, you hope, they'll be standing there beside you, with you, and it'll be patience that gets them there, day-by-day work, the patience to do it: *moral work*, based upon speaking those moral sentences that you hope your kids will learn from you, for themselves—their own version, though!"

I could see that we weren't going to go any further. He'd delivered a bit of a sermon to me—and how we need them, sometimes, from someone we trust and respect, someone who is willing to do as he said we ought to do as parents: take a stand, no matter one's shaky, doubtful moments! He was being respectful of himself and me, steering both of us away from the overly precise, away from the temptation for the for-mulated, in favor (more elusively) of a *tone*, an *emphasis*, a *direction*: the moral call as each of us has to listen for it ourselves, sound it for others. Then, abruptly, we left behind the above matter, turned to a discussion of his undergraduate course in which I taught; talked of his analyst Anna Freud, whom I was then getting to visit, and from whom I was learning quite a bit. Suddenly he stopped us both in our tracks and remembered moments from his first years as an analysand of Miss Freud's, as a student at the Vienna Psychoanalytic Institute. He remembered her lectures to parents and teachers, how she tried to impart a point of view, rather than spell out *the* answers to the questions (so many of them) that her listeners, she knew, wanted to pose. Once she had said to him, in response to some rather specific questioning of his own, that she couldn't give him "the detailed answers" he seemed to want, "only a way of tackling the questions." I laughed—said that a lot of us parents and teachers want to "tackle" not only some questions, but our own children and those of others (our students). "Yes, yes," he answered, "and that's when we have to struggle to be kind—we have to tackle ourselves so we can do the best for them."

I wouldn't, couldn't, let that word "best" go unnoticed, unremarked upon. I tried to use it in order to get this wise, wise old man to tell me more, give me more, settle me down a bit as a parent, a teacher, ground me in his accumulated knowledge, wisdom. *How* do we do "the best for them"? What *is* "the best for them"? I posed those anxious questions, pretending to be "cool" about it all by laughing, mocking my very inquiry—yet another worried, literal-minded father, teacher. "I told you," he addressed me, he reminded me, " 'to be kind,' that's what we have to be, to *do*: show by how we behave that we're interested in others and want the best for them." Now he slumped a bit, and so did I—we both realized, I thought then, I still think, that we weren't considering a specific act, or a series of acts, a routine, a set of rules, a strategy, but rather, a way of being to which one first aspires, then works, day by day, to find for oneself, to share with others.

Henry James's nephew, the son of William James, once asked the great and thoughtful novelist what he ought to do with his life, how he ought live it. The nephew (who today might be regarded as going through Erikson's identity crisis) received this advice: "Three things in human life are important. The first is to be kind. The second is to be kind. And the third is to be kind." The issue here is the hortatory verb, "be," as well as the adjective—the insistence that one find an existence that enables one to *be kind*. How to do so? By wading in, over and over, with that purpose in mind, with a willingness to sail on, tacking and tacking again, helped by those we aim to help, guided by our moral yearnings on behalf of others, on behalf of ourselves with others: a commitment to others, to oneself as linked to others, that won't avoid squalls and periods of seeming drift, but that will become the heart of the journey itself, with its ups and downs, a journey that is, after all, the destination—moral commitment given the life of moral companionship.

APPENDIX

I have mentioned at some length in this book a Tolstoy story, "The Old Grandfather and the Grandson," and a movie, *A Bronx Tale*. I've made passing reference to the familiar legends we share with our young children—the moral implications of, say, Robin Hood or Cinderella. Fortunately, there are books that offer us parents and teachers all the reading matter we could ever wish to have as we try to ponder ethical questions with our sons and daughters and students—so this appendix can be, I think, helpful but mercifully brief. In 1993 William J. Bennett gave us *The Book of Virtues*, a huge resource, a large and most valuable companion for parental moral inquiry, not to mention that of the classroom. In 1994, William Kilpatrick, Gregory Wolfe, and Suzanne Wolfe gave us *Books That Build Character*. In 1995 Mr. Bennett gave us even more to ponder, to summon and use, with *The Moral Compass: Stories for a Life's Journey*. In that same year Colin Greer and Herbert Kohl gave us *A Call to Character*, with even more reading matter for our family life, our school life. Then, there are more Tolstoy fables. Some, such as "How Much Land Does a Man Need," or "Master and Man" can be read to children and by them and can also serve well to stir the moral imagination of high-schoolers, college students, and even students in professional and graduate schools. Of course, so many of our great novelists and playwrights and poets serve us well in the same way, give us plenty of moral pause. I have mentioned George Eliot's *Middlemarch* in these pages—and respectfully refer the reader interested in further fiction of similar moral suggestiveness to a book I wrote a few years back, *The Call of Stories: Teaching and the Moral Imagination*.

Movies are, naturally, always at one's beck and call, and some of them can powerfully prod us to look inward, wonder about how to live this life. I would especially mention, here, Mel Gibson's *The Man Without a Face*, a film about a former teacher, disfigured in an automobile accident, and now become a feared, mistrusted outsider in a Maine seaside town. A boy of eleven or so gets to know him, and what they teach one another has a lot to tell us about "moral intelligence"—a child's growing capacity to understand others with fairness, honesty, concern, generosity of spirit. I have used that movie to great effect with my middle school and high school students; it is not at all preachy, yet they are provoked to consider the ways we judge others, the reasons we accept or turn away from them. Of course, as my students keep reminding me, there are few Westerns that don't offer the chance for a viewer to consider the various rights and wrongs of this world, and the same holds for many so-called detective stories put to film—not to mention plenty of adaptations of good novels on film.

Yet, with all due respect for what books and movies can do to stir moral reflection, several fourth- and fifth-grade teachers in a Boston school where I worked taught me a lesson about the way we might help develop the moral conduct, the moral experience of our children—the point of this book's discussion. With no great fanfare, these teachers took their classes to a nearby nursing home so that the boys and girls could visit with the elderly and incapacitated folks who lived there—talk with them, listen to them, help serve them snacks. On other occasions, the children helped clean up a nearby playground. A sixth-grade teacher in the same school had some of her students reading to the blind, getting to know about their lives.

As I watched such efforts take place, traveled with these youngsters and their teachers to particular destinations for an occasional visit or "clean-up time," I began to realize that I had become witness to what might be called a "moral curriculum"—a sanctioned and encouraged realization in deeds of the ethical possibilities these young people possessed. Surely, we who have learned to take our children through various cognitive loops, to guide them through any number of emotional hurdles, can also give thought to how we might join those teachers of elementary school and older students in developing further modest additions to such a moral curriculum, even as we who are parents can take notice, follow suit.

INDEX

accommodation, mutual, 85
action:
  choices of, 57–59
  courage and, 119–20
  ideals and, 178
  moving from awareness into, 24–25
  translating words into, 16–17, 182–84, 190
  see also behavior
adolescents, 135–66
  Alice's case, 164–66
  alienation of, 136–37
  anger of, 136, 137
  antisocial, 32–34, 57
  authority asserted by, 141–43
  authority challenged by, 138–41
  beliefs and, 140, 141, 156–57
  "body talk" of, 159
  choices of, 157, 169
  as clinical specialty, 32
  communication with, 139–40, 146, 150–52, 165–66
  in the community, 143
  companionship of, 162–64
  conflicts in, 158, 164
  confrontation avoided with, 49–50, 138, 162
  connectedness and, 148–53, 159, 165–66
  consciences of, 146–48, 156–57, 158, 164
  the Crowd, 41–51
  cynicism of, 136, 156–57
  deviant behavior of, 148
  disobedience of, 142
  equality sought by, 163
  estrangements with, 165–66
  ethics of, 153, 162, 164
  fads of, 165
  focus of, 154
  gangs of, 53, 54, 57
  goals sought by, 157, 166
  head-shaking of, 143–45
  independence sought by, 135–36, 142, 153–55, 160–62
  interviews with, 153–57
  isolation of, 136, 146, 148, 159
  legal rights of, 143

adolescents (cont'd):
  loneliness of, 136, 143–46, 149, 153,
    155, 159
  Margie, 150–52
  Marian, 178–84
  mentors sought by, 159–60, 162–64
  moods of, 136, 143
  moral aspect of, 157
  moral seriousness of, 153–55
  as mothers, 51–56
  needs of, 162
  parents of, 137, 138–43, 147, 150–52,
    153–57, 165–66, 188
  Paul's case, 160–64
  peers' influence on, 142, 143
  privacy needed by, 160–62
  psychology and, 32, 139–40
  questions of, 159
  rebelliousness of, 136–37, 138, 147,
    165
  responsibilities of, 150, 161
  role models of, 165, 169
  second chance for, 157–64
  self-consciousness of, 135
  self-respect of, 159
  sexual activity in, 51–56, 59, 114, 141,
    143, 153–55, 161
  in trouble, 147
  trust and, 146, 160, 161
  values of, 45, 140, 162, 164
  as victims, 57
  world outside and, 158
  youth culture of, 136, 164–66
adults:
  behavior of, 5, 7, 58–59
  direction supplied by, 134
  hypocrisy of, 42–43
  as learning from children, 8–10
  as mentors, 159–60, 162–64
  morality of, 5
  questions answered by, 114
  reliance on, 58
  trust of, 58

  values of, 58, 127–29
  see also parents
Aicchorn, August, 32, 33
Alice (field hockey player), 164–66
alienation, moral, 136–37
allegiances, switching of, 165
aloneness, moral, 57
American history:
  lessons from, 116–29, 174–75
  Pilgrims and Puritans in, 117–20
  reasons for immigration in, 117
  revolutionary war, 116–17
"American Scholar" (Emerson), 179,
    181–82
amplification, in classroom, 106–7
anal stage of development (toilet
    training), 86
analysis, moral, 120
anger, of adolescents, 136, 137
animals, learning from, 81–85
anthropology, cultural, 69
antisocial behavior, 27, 28, 32–34, 57
anxiety, moral, 147–48, 169–70, 193
apathy, and teaching limits, 84
appetites, curbing of, 87
archaeology, moral, see moral
    archaeology
arousal, moral, 193
assumptions, moral, 34
attention, need for, 17, 65, 66, 67
attentiveness, reciprocity of, 93
attitudes, moral, 34
Auden, W. H., 51
Augustine, Saint, 183
authority:
  arguing with, 138–41
  cavalier attitude toward, 73
  delegation of, 44
  of experts, 163
  in family, 125, 127–28, 140, 141–43
  independent thinking and, 107–8
  mixed messages from, 129–34
  moral, 24–25, 43, 44, 58, 138–41

moral crossroads of, 43–45
of teachers, 96, 126, 128–29
autism, 95
awareness:
moving to action from, 24–25
range of, 133
Axelrod, Howie, 13

babies, *see* infants
"bad" person:
behavior of, 29–30, 192
delinquents, 28, 32–34
development of, 5
infant as, 65, 67
law and, 27, 28
qualities of, 28
as stony-hearted, 25–26, 28–30
subjective judgment of, 27
behavior:
of adults, 5, 7, 58–59
antisocial, 27, 28, 32–34, 57
attention-getting, 17, 65, 66, 67
of "bad" person, 29–30, 192
character and, 16
consequences of, 15, 16
converting virtues into, 16–17,
182–84, 190
courage and, 120–21
development of, 3, 10, 81, 93
deviant, 148
distracting, 23
of elementary school children, 122
of "good" person, 4, 6, 29
head-shaking, 143–45
ideals and, 178
imitation of, 83
of infants, 64–65, 66, 72–73, 79, 93,
94–95
justification for, 43
learning of, 5, 162
mind and, 7, 10, 17
moral intelligence and, 7
of "not-so-good" person, 21, 26

psychodynamics and, 33
reciprocity of, 94
standards of, 170, 190, 191
witnesses to, 5–6, 7, 31
see also conduct
beliefs:
adolescents and, 140, 141, 156–57
courage and, 117–20
moral, 120, 141–42
necessity for, 178, 193
standing up for, 19, 119–20
Benedictine monks, 186–87
Bennett, William J., 197
Betsy (introspective speller), 107–11,
112–13
bonding, mother-infant, 67, 79
Bonhoeffer, Dietrich, 183
Book of Virtues, The (Bennett, ed.), 197
Books That Build Character (Kilpatrick,
George and George, eds.), 197
Booth, John Wilkes, 123
brain, development of, 69
Brill, A. A., 191
Bronx Tale, A (film), 18–20, 197

Call of Stories, The (Coles), 198
callousness, of young people, 11
Call to Character, A (Kohl), 197
care, moral guidance and, 79
career choices, 130–33
caregivers:
grandparents as, 52–53, 55, 56
needs of, 85
Carver, Raymond, 179
cats, as teachers, 81–85
character:
assessment of, 34
behavior and, 16
defined, 7
development of, 9, 65, 69, 70, 86–87,
89, 131–32, 133, 140, 194
different views of, 28–29
intellect vs., 179, 182, 184

Charlie:
 and the Crowd, 41–51, 57, 58
 as ringleader, 42, 47
cheating, as moral matter, 34–41, 57
Childhood and Society (Erikson), 182,
  192–94
children, 98–134
 of absent parents, 44, 58, 59
 beliefs needed by, 193
 character development in, 89, 194
 civilization of, 95–97, 158
 cultural anthropology and, 69
 developmental stages of, 86
 disobedience of, 78, 80
 ethics of, 8, 9, 105, 113–14, 128,
  175–77
 good-hearted, 4–5
 ill, 175–77, 178
 learning from, 8–10
 love of, 7, 90, 121
 moral commitments needed by, 193
 moral experiences of, 115
 moral intelligence of, 9, 105
 as moral listeners, 85–88
 nature of, 93
 nursing homes visited by, 198
 pets and, 81–85
 preschool, *see* preschool children
 preverbal, 63–73; *see also* infants
 protection of, 59
 response to environment of, 64
 rewards to, 184–85
 as scolds, 115–16
 sexual abuse of, 51, 52, 58
 sexuality of, 89–90
 spoiled, 66–68, 70, 87, 90–91
 teaching "yes" and "no" to, 73–75,
  78–79, 85
 temperament of, 93
 "thank you" and "please" used by,
  184–85
 trouble and, 7–8
 young, *see* elementary school children

choices:
 of action, 57–59
 of adolescents, 157, 169
 of careers, 130–33
 at moral crossroads, 46, 164, 188, 193
 practicalities of, 164
 in youth culture, 164–65
civilization, child development as,
  95–97, 158
classroom:
 activities in, 106–7
 boredom in, 22–23, 108
 discussions in, 106–7, 174, 182–83
 ethical obligations within, 22
 history lessons in, 116–28, 174–75
 moral curriculum and, 199
 moral lessons in, 23–24, 50–51
 "not very good" person in, 22–24
 self-care as taught in, 54
 see also education
Coles, Bill, 189
Coles, Bobby, 84
Coles, Jane, 84
commitments, moral, 193, 196
communication:
 with adolescents, 139–40, 146,
  150–52, 165–66
 through language, 106
 tools of meanings and, 192
community:
 adolescents in, 143
 childhood and, 192–94
 citizenship in, 96–97, 101, 105
 delinquents and, 28
 elementary school children in, 99,
  101
 ethical obligations within, 22
 infants and, 94
 isolation from, 57
 service to, 183
 values of, 57
 withdrawal from, 95
companionship, moral, 162–64, 196

compassion:
  for pets, 83–84
  varying ideas about, 29
competitiveness, 66, 155
conduct:
  modesty in, 109–10
  and moral intelligence, 7
  reasoning vs., 181
  thinking vs., 3
  see also action; behavior
confrontation, avoidance of, 49–50, 85,
    138, 162
confusion, moral, 84
connectedness:
  adolescents and, 148–53, 159, 165–66
  mother-infant, 67, 79
conscience:
  of adolescents, 146–48, 156–57, 158,
    164
  ego vs. superego, 158
  of elementary school children, 98,
    105, 116
  flabby, 25
  parents and, 105
  protection of, 59
  training of, 58, 89, 116
consideration, 4
  in classroom, 106–7
control:
  over bodily functions, 86, 87, 99
  over impulse, 59, 158
cooperation, 75–76
corporal punishment, 76–77, 79
courage:
  action and, 119–20
  behavior and, 120–21
  beliefs and, 117–20
  defined, 118–20
  imagination and, 121
  lessons on, 116–23, 175
  sources of, 120
  stories of, 186
  tests of, 120

crossroads, see moral crossroads
Crowd, the, 41–51
  absent parents of, 44, 58
  afterthoughts on, 50–51
  confidentiality and, 44, 46–47
  confrontation and, 49, 50
  drinking and drugs and, 42–51, 57
  law and, 44, 45, 46, 48, 49
  peer observations of, 42
  school authorities and, 42, 43–44,
    47–51
cultural anthropology, 69
curiosity, see questions
curriculum, moral, 199
cynicism:
  of adolescents, 136, 156–57
  of young people, 11

David (leukemia victim), 175–77,
    178
death, by violence, 52, 55
decision points, see moral crossroads
Delia (teenage mother), 52–56
  aloneness of, 57, 58
  child-care classes and, 53, 54
  escape fantasies of, 55, 56
  on gangs, 53, 54
  hope of, 52, 53–54
  on motherhood, 53
delinquents, 28, 32–34
  in gangs, 53, 54
  parents of, 32
de Man, Paul, 180
destination, search for, 55, 56
diapers, freedom from, 86, 87, 88–89,
    91
direction:
  source of, 134
  spiritual life and, 177
  steering away from, 194
discipline, 79–81
  as education, 79
  fear instilled by, 82

discussions:
  in classroom, 106–7, 174, 182–83
  with mothers, 67–85, 138–43,
    165–66
  walking and, 187–89
disobedience:
  adolescents and, 142
  children and, 78, 80
  Tim's case, 123–29
doctors:
  as classroom speakers, 50–51
  observations of, 4–6
  training of, 6
dogs, as teachers, 81–85
Don (bottle-throwing baby), 70–73
drinking:
  by the Crowd, 42–51
  by pregnant women, 64
drugs:
  the Crowd as users of, 42–51, 57
  gangs and, 53, 54, 57
  as killers, 46
  moral/legal approach to discussion of,
    161–64
  Paul's use of, 160–62
  as self-medication, 45
  unborn child and, 64
dyads, 92

education:
  classroom activities in, 106–7
  discipline as, 79
  moral, 115–16, 199
  as panacea, 55–56
  sources of, 107
  see also classroom
ego:
  attention-getting and, 17
  defense mechanisms and, 157
  leadership and, 26
  of spoiled child, 70, 87, 89, 91
  superego vs., 158
  tension and, 22
  unreflecting, 21, 186

Ego and Mechanisms of Defense, The (A.
    Freud), 157
Elaine (cheater), 34–41, 49, 57
  caught in the act, 35–36, 37
  denial by, 38
  interests and skills of, 34–35, 41
  parents of, 38, 39–40, 58, 59
  peers and, 36–37
  psychotherapy and, 39, 40
  teacher and, 36–37, 38–41
elementary school children, 98–134
  accomplishments of, 106, 122
  behavior of, 122
  Betsy, 107–11, 112–13
  challenges of, 109, 114–15
  in the community, 99, 101
  consciences of, 98, 105, 116
  on courage, 116–23
  David, 175–77, 178
  empathy of, 99
  explorations by, 133
  Golden Rule and, 169
  history lessons of, 116–29
  imagination of, 133
  independence of, 133
  language of, 99, 101, 106–7, 114
  latency period of, 114
  magic years of, 133–34
  mixed messages to, 129–34
  moral analysis by, 120
  moral imagination of, 98–99
  moral introspection and, 183
  moral vision of, 102–5
  neediness of, 133
  "not very good," 22–24
  parents of, 102, 106, 115
  Pascal and, 111–14
  peers of, 106, 107
  projects of, 198–99
  qualities of, 133–34
  questions of, 99–102, 114, 133
  on school bus, 99–101
  as scolds, 115–16
  stories and, 170–74

teachers of, 98, 99, 106, 107–10, 113, 115–16
Tim, 123–29
values of, 121
vulnerability of, 133
Eliot, George, 21, 29–30, 186, 190, 198
Ellison, Ralph, 182
Emerson, Ralph Waldo:
"American Scholar" by, 179, 181–82
on character and intellect, 178–79, 181–82, 184
classroom discussions on, 183
each day as god to, 17
emotions:
conscience and, 105
in developmental stages, 86, 102
emphasis on, 32
of infants, 72–73, 87
language and, 107
moral issues vs., 39–40
patterns of, 64–65
problems of, 33
reciprocity of, 94
sharing of, 154
stinginess of, 91
empathy:
daily practice of, 25
of elementary school children, 99
Golden Rule and, 10
learning of, 83–84
as moral mutuality, 94–97
pain and, 172, 173
self-absorption vs., 94
energy, moral, 56
envy, 108
Erikson, Erik H., 33, 182, 191–96
Anna Freud and, 194–95
on kindness, 195–96
ethics:
of adolescents, 153, 162, 164
of children, 8, 9, 105, 113–14, 128, 175–77
decisions and, 188, 193
guidance and, 59

in interview relationship, 46
moral undertow and, 22
psychology as, 92–93
rules and, 58
stories and, 122
universality of, 170
evasion:
lying and, 40
moral, 40
example:
learning by, 126
teaching by, 5, 31, 132
see also role models
existence, nature of, 105, 112
experiences:
character shaped by, 86–87, 140
lives changed by, 172
moral, 3, 115
questions answered in, 114, 193–94
reflection turned into, 184
sharing of, 11, 24–25
experts:
advice to parents from, 16, 33, 77, 89, 91, 143
afterthoughts of, 50–51, 58–59
authoritative, 163
on child development, 86, 89
as classroom speakers, 50–51
competence of, 148
conferences with, 33
discussion steered by, 172
human development lessons from, 55
labeling by, 113
listening and learning by, 148–49
in loco parentis, 59
moral crossroads of, 43–45
psychological, 33
responsibilities of, 73
on spanking, 76–77, 79
superego and, 162
theory vs. practice of, 77, 150–51, 154, 182, 184

experts *(cont'd)*:
understanding by, 149
unequivocal solutions and, 78
expression, in classroom, 106–7

fads, 165
families:
authority in, 125, 127–28, 140,
141–43
customs of, 158
as dyads, 92
ethical obligations within, 22
generation gaps in, 138–40
genetics and, 93
ideals in, 93
infants as members of, 94
influences of, 69
kinship in, 143
loyalty to, 121
material success of, 156
moral constraints imposed by, 162
at moral crossroads, 39, 48
moral education in, 115–16
pets in, 81–85
power in, 125
psychology and, 32
tensions in, 137
traditions of, 122
values in, 93, 127–29, 137
fantasies:
in child development, 89
of escape, 55, 56
imagination and, 121
parents in, 131
of showdowns, 148
telescopes and, 104–5
fathers:
ambivalence of, 166
authority of, 127–28
influence of, 189
limitations of, 188–89, 190
literal-minded, 195
memories of, 186–91
pregnancy and, 63–64

stories told by, 186–87
values of, 188
violent behavior of, 82
walks taken by, 187–90
withdrawn, 90
see also parents
fear:
courage and, 118
of estrangement, 136
memories of, 81–82
stories of, 186
feeding:
attention and, 88
oral development and, 86
feelings, *see* emotions
fetus, influences on, 63–64
fighting, need for, 27
films:
Bronx Tale, A, 18–20, 197
Man Without a Face, The, 198
Freud, Anna, 191
on adolescents, 32, 33, 50, 146–48,
157–60, 162, 163–64, 165
on connectedness, 148–53
on ego and defense mechanisms,
157
on elementary school years, 98
Erikson and, 194–95
on infant's feelings, 72–73
on introspection, 50
parenthood and, 150
on "yes" and "no," 88–94
Freud, Sigmund, 90, 114, 158, 190–91
frustration, 87, 90, 91

gangs, 53, 54, 57
generation gaps, 138–40
generosity, in "Starry Time," 14–15
genetics, temperament and, 93
genital stage of developments
(attachments to parents), 86
Golden Rule:
as biblical ideal, 25
in daily life, 29

elementary school children and, 169
fetus and, 63
"good" person and, 10, 17
goodness:
    affirmation of, 17
    challenges to, 20
    and cheap talk, 17
    consequences of, 15, 16
    desirability of, 17
    Golden Rule and, 17
    of "good enough" mothers, 91–93, 97
    knowing vs. doing, 181
    modesty and, 110
    reminders of need for, 20
    self-discovery of, 104, 106
    stories about, 13–15
    survival of, 57
    teaching about, 5, 181
    varying ideas about, 29
"good" person, 13–20, 188
    behavior of, 4, 6, 29
    Bronx Tale and, 20
    daily struggles of, 20, 122
    descriptions of, 27
    development of, 9, 10–12
    Golden Rule and, 10, 17
    "goody-goody" person vs., 18
    heart of, 10
    infant as, 65, 67
    law and, 29
    "Starry Time" and, 13–15, 16
    virtues of, 29
grandparents, as caregivers, 52–53, 55, 56
Greer, Colin, 197
grown-ups, see adults; parents; teachers

head-shaking behavior, 143–45
Heidegger, Martin, 180
heroism, learning about, 175
history:
    assassinations in, 122–23, 125–26,
        127, 129
    lessons from, 116–29, 174–75
Holocaust, 180

Hopper, Edward, 179
Horney, Karen, 191
"How Much Land Does a Man Need"
    (Tolstoy), 197
humanity, struggle with, 24–25
humility, modesty, 109–11, 112,
    113–14
hypocrisy, 42–43

ideals:
    enactment of, 178
    in families, 93
    necessity for, 178
imagination:
    conscience and, 105
    courage and, 121
    of elementary school children, 133
    moral, see moral imagination
    vices of, 191
impulse, control over, 59, 158
independence:
    adolescents and, 135–36, 142, 153–55,
        160–62
    authority and, 107–8
    of elementary school children, 133
    loss of, 27, 28
indifference, and teaching limits, 84
indignation, 192–93
infants, 63–97
    as "bad" persons, 65, 67
    behavior of, 64–65, 66, 72–73, 79, 93,
        94–95
    bonding with mothers by, 67, 79
    bottle-throwing, 70–73
    breast-fed, bottle-fed vs., 69
    character development of, 69
    community and, 94
    confidence developed in, 93
    family influence on, 69
    as family members, 94
    "good-natured," 93
    as "good" persons, 65, 67
    love and, 90
    moral crossroads of, 67

infants (cont'd):
  moral development of, 73, 78–79
  naturalness of, 94
  and needs of others, 68–69, 70, 84–85, 94
  neglected, 64, 87
  possessiveness of, 72, 90, 91
  psychological attitudes and feelings of, 72–73, 87
  reciprocity and, 94
  signals sent to, 70–73, 88
  spanking of, 76–77, 79
  spoiled, 66–68, 87, 90–91
  teaching "yes" and "no" to, 73–75, 78–79, 85, 169
  unborn, 63–64
  values and, 63–64, 94
Insight and Responsibility (Erikson), 191–92
inspiration, 56
integrity:
  cheating and, 41
  lying and, 40, 45, 57
intellect vs. character, 179, 182, 184
intelligence:
  and academic achievement, 47
  classroom boredom and, 22–23
  cognitive trouble and, 33
  general vs. moral, 4
  moral, see moral intelligence
  motherhood as waste of, 52
introspection:
  through language, 106
  moral, 50, 73–75, 162, 177, 183
  values grounded in, 177
Invisible Man (Ellison), 182
inwardness:
  examined, 192
  spiritual, 175–77, 178
isolation:
  of adolescents, 136, 146, 148, 159
  from community, 57

James, Henry, nephew of, 195–96
James, William, 108–9, 195
judgments, moral, 28, 57, 163–64, 192
Jung, Carl, 180

Kaiser Foundation, 51
Kennedy, John F., 122–23, 124–26
Kilpatrick, William, 197
kindness, 4, 195–96
kinship, 143
Klein, Melanie, 72
Kohl, Herbert, 197
Kubie, Lawrence, 191

language:
  acquisition of, 66, 74, 93–94, 133
  in classroom activities, 106–7
  communication through, 106
  of elementary school children, 99, 101, 106–7, 114
  introspection through, 106
  listening and, 85–88
  moral introspection and, 73–75
  opinion and, 107
  of psychiatry and psychoanalysis, 67, 96
  reading and, 106
  stories and, 106
  teacher of, 175
law:
  "bad" person and, 27, 28
  the Crowd and, 44, 45, 46, 48, 49
  "good" person and, 29
  innocence and, 49
  moral, 191
leadership:
  adolescent ringleaders, 42, 47
  of "not-so-good" person, 26, 28, 41
  of school authorities, 50–51, 58
legal rights of adolescents, 143
letter to parents and teachers, 169–96
liberation, personal, 161
Liebow, Elliot, 182

life:
  gift of, 177
  nature of, 105
  purpose in, 112, 153, 155, 157,
    177–78, 190, 196
  quality of, 73
  spiritual, 177
limits:
  self-control and, 87, 89, 90
  setting of, 51, 58, 74, 79–81, 84
  testing of, 80
Lincoln, Abraham, 122–23, 174–75
listeners, moral, 85–88
"live and let live," 19
loneliness:
  of adolescents, 136, 143–46, 149, 153,
    155, 159
  of Americans, 179
love:
  of children, 7, 90, 121
  of country, 121
  lack of, 91
  and moral guidance, 79, 90
  of parents, 121
  possessiveness and, 90, 91
  preschoolers and, 90–94
  reciprocity of, 92–93, 94–97
  with reservations, 91
loyalty, 121
lying:
  evasion and, 40
  as moral matter, 40, 57
  self-deception and, 45

McIntosh, Rustin, 4–6
Maisie, and bottle-throwing baby, 70–73
Man Without a Face, The (film), 198
Margie (adolescent), 150–52
Marian (college student), 178–84
Marie:
  on adult hypocrisy, 42–43
  and the Crowd, 41–51, 57, 58
  as ringleader, 42, 47

"Master and Man" (Tolstoy), 197
memories:
  of author's father, 186–91
  of author's mother, 184–86, 189, 190
  of classroom discussions, 174, 175
  examination of, 172
  of fear, 81–82
  lives changed by, 174–75
  management of, 56
  questions answered in, 114
  redemptive use of, 172
  stories of, 5, 12, 186–87
  of teachers, 188, 189–90, 191
  teaching by use of, 144–45, 148
Menninger, Karl, 191
mentors:
  adolescents' search for, 159–60,
    162–64
  and moral intelligence, 4–8
  necessity for, 194
  see also role models
Middlemarch (Eliot), 21, 29–30, 198
Miller, Perry, 112
minds:
  and behavior, 7, 10, 17
  escape fantasies of, 55, 56
  heart and soul vs., 23
  of infants, 72–73
mixed messages, 129–34
modesty, 109–11, 112, 113–14
moods, of adolescents, 136, 143
moral alienation, 136–37
moral aloneness, 57
moral analysis, 120
moral anxiety, 147–48, 169–70, 193
moral archaeology, 59, 61–166
  in adolescence, 135–66; see also
    adolescents
  in early years, 63–97; see also infants
  in elementary school years, 98–134;
    see also elementary school
    children
moral arousal, 193

moral assumptions, 34
moral attitudes, 34
moral authority, *see* authority
moral behavior, *see* behavior
moral commitments, 193, 196
moral companionship, 162–64, 196
Moral Compass, The (Bennett, ed.),
    197
moral conduct, *see* conduct
moral conflict, 45–46
    Tim's case, 123–29
moral confusion, 84
moral crossroads, 30, 31–59
    adolescent sexual activity, 51–56
    of adult authority, 43–45
    cheating and, 34–41
    choices in, 46, 164, 188, 193
    courage and, 117–20
    drinking and drugs and, 41–51
    families at, 39, 48
    heading for trouble at, 32–34,
        47–50
    of infants, 67
    what ought to be done?, 56–59
moral curriculum, 115–16, 199
moral development:
    of infants, 73, 78–79
    mutual teaching of, 9
moral drift, 136
moral energy, 56
moral evasion, 40
moral experiences:
    of children, 115
    daily, 3
moral guidance, 170
    care and, 79
    ethics and, 59
    love and, 79, 90
    mutuality of, 8–10
moral imagination, 3–12
    conscience and, 105
    defined, 3
    growth of, 98–99
    stories and, 5, 7, 10–12

moral intelligence:
    acquisition of, 5, 6
    of children, 9, 105
    conduct and, 7
    mentors and, 4–8
    moral imagination and, 3
    use of term, 4–5
    witnesses to, 5
moral introspection, 50, 73–75, 162,
    177, 183
morality, basis of, 5, 81
moral judgments, 28, 57, 163–64, 192
moral laws, 191
Moral Life of Children, The (Coles), 3
moral moments:
    film as, 18–20
    learning in, 122
moral mutuality, 8–10, 94–97
moral outrage, 192
moral passion, 189
moral perspective, 57, 191
moral psychology, 190
moral questions, 50, 193
moral reasoning vs. moral conduct, 181
moral reflection, 121, 184
moral sensibility, origins of, 81
moral seriousness, 153–55
moral thinking, shaping of, 3
moral undertow, falling victim to, 22
moral vision, 102–5
moral work, 194
motherhood:
    adolescent desire for, 52
    classes in, 53, 54, 55
    joys of, 53
    moral conviction of, 64
    pain and, 173
    sex and, 59
    as waste of intellect, 52
mothers:
    adolescents as, 51–56
    balance sought by, 74–75
    bonding with infants, 67, 79
    cold, 90

controlling, 166
cooperation sought by, 75–76
crying, 78
discussions with, 67–85, 138–43,
    165–66
"good enough," 91–93, 97
helping nature of, 127–28
learning from mistakes of, 68–69
lessons from, 184–86
limitations of, 189
limits set by, 79–81, 84
memories of, 184–86, 189, 190
possessive infants and, 72
pregnancy and, 63
as servants, 71, 90
signals to infants from, 70–73
spanking by, 76–77, 79
stories told by, 186
time lacked by, 76, 77–79
"yes" and "no" taught by, 73–75,
    78–79
see also parents
motives, examination of, 190
mutuality, moral, 8–10, 94–97

narcissism, 89, 91
narratives, see stories
needs:
    of adolescents, 162
    of others, 68–69, 70, 84–85, 94
    of parents, 85, 149
    of young children, 133
"not very good" person, 21–30
    behavior of, 21, 26
    bully, 25–27
    con artist, 25–27
    development of, 10
    as intelligent, 22–24
    as leaders, 26, 28, 41
    qualities of, 21, 22, 23, 25, 26
    survival and, 28
    values of, 21, 28, 34
nouns, translation into verbs of, 16–17
nursing homes, visits to, 198

obligations, see responsibilities
O'Connor, Flannery, 109
"Old Grandfather and the Grandson,
    The" (Tolstoy), 10–11, 12, 170–74,
    197–98
opinion, development of, 107
oral stage of development (feeding), 86
Orwell, George, 189, 190
Oswald, Lee Harvey, 123, 125–26, 127,
    129
outrage, moral, 192

pain:
    bodily vs. psychological, 173
    empathy and, 172, 173
    forgetting of, 171–74
    necessity of, 172–73
parents:
    absent, 44, 58, 59
    accomplishments of, 130–31, 132
    of adolescents, 137, 138–43, 147,
        150–52, 153–57, 165–66, 188
    attachment to, 86
    of author, 184–91
    as authority figures, 140, 141–43
    behavior of, 5, 58–59, 127
    child's misdeeds and, 38, 39–40, 58,
        59
    coaching by, 92
    cold, 91
    common sense of, 67, 88
    competitiveness of, 155
    confrontation of, 49
    conscience and, 105
    credibility of, 77–78
    critical observation of, 124
    of delinquents, 32
    demands of, 130–31
    dissent with, 126–28
    dyads and, 92
    of elementary school children, 102,
        106, 115
    expert advice for, 16, 33, 77, 89, 91,
        143

parents *(cont'd)*:
  fantasies about, 131
  general tendencies of, 87, 88
  goals set by, 191
  guidance sought by, 149
  history lessons and, 175
  independence from, 135–36, 142,
    153–55, 160–62
  infants and, 63–65, 70–73, 88
  letter to, 169–96
  lives changed by, 174–75
  love of, 121
  moral guidance from, 170
  morality of, 5
  needs of, 85, 149
  outrage of, 49, 59
  of preschool children, 85–88, 91
  problems of, 154–55
  psychiatrists seen by, 44, 155
  psychology and, 40, 162
  questions answered by, 114
  reciprocity and, 94
  responsibilities of, 25, 85
  rewards from, 184–85
  as role models, 93, 116, 131, 132
  as rushed, 8, 9, 132–33
  school authorities and, 44, 49, 50
  spanking by, 76–77, 79
  toilet training and, 87
  unsure, 91
  values of, 63–64, 188
  working, 78
  see also adults; caregivers; fathers;
    mothers
Pascal, Blaise, 111–14, 183
passion, moral, 189
Paul (alienated teen), 160–64
peers:
  adolescents influenced by, 142, 143
  of the Crowd, 42
  on Elaine's cheating, 36–37
  of elementary school children, 106, 107
Pensées and the Provincial of Letters
    (Pascal), 112

perspective, moral, 57, 191
pets, learning from, 81–85
philosophy:
  of Pascal, 112
  study of, 182
  theory vs. practice of, 182
phobias, development of, 82
political power, 180
possessiveness, 72, 90, 91
Pound, Ezra, 180
power:
  in families, 125
  political, 180
prayer, 176–77
preschool children, 85–97, 158
  accomplishments of, 95–97, 105
  character development of, 105
  love and, 90–94
  as moral listeners, 85–88
  "yes" and "no" for, 88–90
privacy, adolescent need for, 160–62
psychoanalysis:
  child development and, 86, 89
  child sexuality and, 89–90
  language of, 67, 96
  parents in, 44, 155
psychodynamics, behavior explained by,
    33
psychological vulnerability, of unborn
    child, 64
psychology:
  adolescents and, 32, 139–40
  author's father and, 190–91
  emphasis on, 32, 40, 192–93
  as ethics, 92–93
  interviews and, 33
  language of, 67, 96
  memory and, 172
  moral, 190
  moral crossroads and, 48
  moral/legal approach vs., 161–64
  parents and, 40, 162
  of survival, 56
  testing and, 33

theory vs. practice in, 154, 182
therapeutic recommendations of, 50,
    163–64
of toilet training, 88
unconscious in, 190
vocabulary sought by, 136
punishment, corporal, 76–77, 79
purpose, sense of, 112
purposelessness, 59

quality of life, 73
quality time, 78
questions:
    of adolescents, 159
    of elementary school children,
        99–102, 114, 133
    exclamations and, 193–94
    of existence, 112
    about history, 117–20
    moral, 50, 193
    tackling of, 195
    about values, 130

reasoning, moral, moral conduct vs., 181
rebelliousness, of adolescents, 136–37,
    138, 147, 165
reciprocity, 92–93, 94–97
reflection, moral, 121, 184
regulation, foundation of, 85
relationships, interviewer-interviewee,
    46, 126, 144–46, 180–81
religion:
    freedom of, 117–20
    illness and, 175–77
    of Kennedy, 124–26
    moral beliefs in, 120, 141–42
    moral energy in, 56
    moral teaching in, 31
    practice of, 120
    prayer and, 176–77
    stories of, 55
responsibilities:
    of adolescents, 150, 161
    of adult authority, 43

of experts, 73
insight and, 191–92
losing sight of, 22
toward others, 192
of parents, 25, 85
of teachers, 25
rewards, 184–85
right and wrong:
    easy achievements and, 109, 118
    film and, 19, 198
    in history lesson, 117–22
    knowledge of, 80
    reconcilement of, 130
    self-discovery of, 104, 105
    teaching of, 58, 71–72, 79, 81–85
righteousness, 17, 115–16, 193
rights:
    of others, 22
    of teenagers, 143
risk, courage and, 119–20
role models, 6, 7
    of adolescents, 165, 169
    parents as, 93, 116, 131, 132
    teachers as, 132
    see also mentors
routines, foundation of, 85
rules:
    breaking of, 123–29
    in daily context, 58
    enforcement of, 142
    setting of, 85, 128
    of spelling, 108–9
    of sports, 166

Sally (Delia's baby), 52, 53
schedule, foundation of, 85
school authorities:
    afterthoughts and, 50–51
    the Crowd and, 42, 43–44, 47–51
    leadership of, 50–51, 58
    see also teachers
school bus, first time on, 99–101
schools, see classroom; education
scolds, children as, 115–16

self, caring for, 54, 86
self-absorption:
   of adolescents, 135
   early roots of, 85
   empathy vs., 94
   of "not-so-good" person, 22, 28
   of spoiled child, 70, 87, 89, 91
   of young people, 11
self-accusation, 11, 146
self-control, 59, 69, 83, 87, 89, 90, 92
self-deception, 45
self-effacing modesty, 109–11
selfishness, 28, 65, 85
self-respect, 19, 57, 159
self-righteousness, 17, 115–16
self-satisfaction, 18, 114
Senn, Milton J. E., 66–67
sensibility, moral, 81
seriousness, moral, 153–55
sex:
   abstinence and, 141, 142
   adolescents and, 51–56, 59, 114, 141,
      143, 153–55, 161
   child abuse and, 51, 52, 58
   childhood and, 89–90
   and motherhood, 59
sharing:
   our own stories, 24
   in "Starry Time," 14–15, 16
Shaw, George Bernard, 108–9
Sisyphus, myth of, 16–17, 18
"smart" people, see intelligence
society:
   childhood and, 192–94
   choices presented by, 164–65
   confrontation avoided in, 50
   loneliness and, 179
   relativistic, 162
sociology, delinquents and, 33
space and time, 112
spanking, 76–77, 79
spiritual inwardness, 175–77, 178
spoiled children, 66–69
   egos of, 70, 87, 89, 91

love and, 90–91
   use of term, 68–69
Stalin, Joseph, 180
standards, contempt for, 146
"Starry Time" (Axelrod), 13–15, 16
stories:
   bottle-throwing baby, 70–73
   case studies as, 33, 34, 184
   cheating, 34–41
   of courage, 186
   the Crowd, 41–51
   disillusionment with Harvard,
      178–84
   ethical issues in, 122
   from father, 186–87
   of fear, 186
   of grandparents, 55
   "How Much Land Does a Man
      Need," 197
   imagination and, 121
   language and, 106
   leukemia, 175–77, 178
   "Master and Man," 197
   meaning and purpose in, 178
   of memories, 5, 12, 186–87
   moral conflict, 123–29
   moral imagination and, 5, 7, 10–12
   from mother, 186
   myth of Sisyphus, 16–17, 18
   "Old Grandfather," 10–11, 12,
      170–74, 197–98
   personal, 11, 24–25
   questions answered in, 114
   reading to the blind, 198
   religious, 55
   a second chance, 160–64
   spelling, 107–11, 112–13
   "sprouting," 150–52
   "Starry Time," 13–15, 16
   teaching by, 5, 7, 31, 50, 58, 132
   teenage mother, 52–56
   of withdrawn boy, 95
   youth culture conflict, 164–66
structure, foundation of, 85

superego:
  ego vs., 158
  psychological experts and, 162

talking it up, 17
Tally's Corner (Liebow), 182
teachers:
  of apathy, 84
  authority of, 96, 126, 128–29
  behavior of, 5
  doctors as, 4–6
  dogs and cats as, 81–85
  of elementary school children, 98, 99,
    106, 107–10, 113, 115–16
  of history, 174–75
  of language, 175
  as learners, 8–10
  letter to, 169–96
  in loco parentis, 59
  memories of, 188, 189–90, 191
  moral authority of, 24–25, 43, 44, 58
  moral lessons of, 23–24, 170
  and not-so-good children, 22–24
  in nursery school, 65, 66
  optimistic, 96
  parents as, 84, 85–88
  responsibilities of, 25
  responsiveness of, 191
  as role models, 132
  school authorities and, 50–51
  unwillingness to act, 38, 43–44
teaching:
  as civilization, 96
  in classrooms, 50–51
  climate of opinion and, 51
  by example, 5, 31, 132
  to go beyond *why*, 194
  about goodness, 5, 181
  memories used in, 144–45, 148
  of needs of others, 68–69, 70
  peculiarities of, 32
  of right and wrong, 58, 71–72, 79,
    81–85
  in stories, 5, 7, 31, 50, 58, 132

of values, 25, 59, 96–97, 169
of "yes" and "no," 73–75, 78–79, 85, 92
teenagers, *see* adolescents
telescope, and moral vision, 102–5
Tennyson, Alfred, Lord, 193
tension:
  in families, 137
  and not-so-good person, 21, 22
"thank you" and "please," use of, 184–85
Thompson, Clara, 191
Tim (Catholic kid), moral conflict of,
    123–29
time:
  consciousness of, 133
  lack of, 8, 9, 76, 77–79, 132–33
  moral possibilities in, 17
  quality, 78
  space and, 112
toilet training, 86, 87, 88–89, 91
Tolstoy, Leo, 186
  on moral introspection, 183
  stories by, 10–11, 12, 170–74, 197–98
trouble:
  adolescents in, 147
  avoidance of, 26, 48–50
  blame and, 27
  children and, 7–8
  drawing others into, 22–24
  gangs and, 53, 54
  heading for, 32–34, 47–50
  moral vs. psychological, 33
  no end to, 54
truculence, 59
trust:
  adolescents and, 146, 160, 161
  of adults, 58
  cold parents and, 91
  interviewer-interviewee, 46
  lack of, 94
  "live and let live" and, 19

unconscious, 190
understanding:
  efforts at, 149

understanding (cont'd):
    judgment vs., 163–64
    meaning of, 84

value, as verb, 64
values:
    of adolescents, 45, 140, 162, 164
    of adults, 58, 127–29
    of author's father, 188
    career choices and, 130–33
    of civilization, 96–97
    clarification of, 9, 25
    clashes of, 127
    of community, 57
    courage and, 117–20
    development of, 9, 59, 131, 133
    differences in, 27, 29, 127–29, 137
    of elementary school children, 121
    in families, 93, 127–29, 137
    infants and, 63–64, 94
    in moral archaeology, 59
    moral introspection and, 177
    moral judgment and, 28, 57
    of "not-so-good" person, 21, 28,
        34
    as noun, 64
    of parents, 63–64, 188
    questions about, 130
    teaching of, 25, 59, 96–97, 169
verbs, from nouns, 16–17
Vienna Psychoanalytic Institute,
    195

virtues:
    of Benedictine monks, 187
    in character building, 131–32
    interpretations of, 29
vision, moral, 102–5
Vivaldi, Antonio, 23, 24

whiners, 65
Winnicott, D. W., 91–93, 97
wisdom, accumulated, 195
witnesses:
    to behavior, 5–6, 7, 31
    imitation by, 7
    moral imagination and, 3–12
    to moral intelligence, 5
    to our lives, 136
Wolfe, Gregory, 197
Wolfe, Suzanne, 197
wonder, sense of, 107
words, translating into action of, 16–17,
    182–84, 190
work, moral, 194
working parents, 78

Yale Child Study Center, 66
yearnings, dealing with, 90
"yes" and "no":
    as absolutes, 126
    Anna Freud on, 88–94
    teaching of, 73–75, 78–79, 85, 88–90,
        92, 169
youth, see adolescents; children

About the Author

ROBERT COLES is a Pulitzer Prize–winning author as well as a child psychiatrist, research psychiatrist for the Harvard University Health Services, and professor of psychiatry and medical humanities at the Harvard Medical School. He is also the James Agee Professor of Social Ethics at Harvard. He has published more than a thousand articles, reviews, and essays and over fifty books, including *The Spiritual Life of Children*, *The Moral Life of Children*, and *The Call of Service*.